McCORMICK ON EVIDENCE

Seventh Edition
2016 Pocket Part

By

Robert P. Mosteller,
General Editor
J. Dickson Phillips Distinguished Professor of Law,
University of North Carolina

Contributing Authors

Kenneth S. Broun
Henry Brandis Professor of Law Emeritus, University of North Carolina

George E. Dix
George R. Killam, Jr. Chair of Criminal Law, The University of Texas

Edward J. Imwinkelried
Edward L. Barrett, Jr. Professor of Law
University of California, Davis

David H. Kaye
Distinguished Professor of Law and Weiss Family Scholar, The
Pennsylvania State University, Penn State Law

E. F. Roberts
Edwin H. Woodruff Professor of Law Emeritus, The Cornell Law School

Eleanor Swift
Professor of Law Emerita,
University of California at Berkeley School of Law

Volume 1

Chapters 1–20

PRACTITIONER TREATISE SERIES®

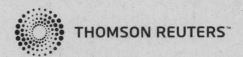

THOMSON REUTERS™

For Customer Assistance Call 1-800-328-4880

Mat #41851724

D0235755

Authors' Introduction to the 2016 Supplement to McCormick on Evidence 7th Edition

The strength of the effort to update McCormick on Evidence is the addition of new major cases and articles throughout the entire treatise. Hundreds of new authorities are added, which are not discussed here. Highlighted below are some of the notable developments discussed in the new material.

Chapter 3 revisits two of the most troublesome issues in the Opinion area. Section 11 discusses the distinction between lay and expert opinion testimony. The expert discovery provisions in Federal Rule of Civil Procedure 26 and the differing admissibility standards under Federal Rule of Evidence 701-02 have magnified the importance of the distinction at common law. Section 11 also sets out a proposal for drawing the line between the two types of opinion. Section 13 addresses one of the thorniest problems under Rule 702, namely, differentiating the foundation for validating a general theory or technique from the foundation for an opinion applying the theory or technique to specific facts–the so-called G2i (general to the individual) problem. Section 13 cites to an insightful 2014 University of Chicago Law Review article in point.

Chapter 4 updates the treatise on the evolving law governing the procedures for Cross-Examination. The wide array of procedures includes CC-TV, two-way teleconferencing, shields, support persons, support animals, and the use of pseudonyms and disguises. Section 19 of the supplement includes numerous citations to recent cases and law review articles analyzing the various procedures.

In Chapter 5, Section 41 presents an extended discussion of the new developments under Federal Rule of Evidence 608(b). On the one hand, Section 19 notes the Supreme Court's 2013 decision in *Nevada v. Jackson* asserting that "[t]he constitutionality of this" ban on extrinsic evidence "cannot be seriously disputed." On the other hand, the section points to the mounting evidence that there are serious misgivings about singling out 608(b) as the only impeachment technique subject to a complete ban on extrinsic evidence. Section 19 observes that a growing number of decisions admit extrinsic evidence of judicial and jury findings, and that some jurisdictions have carved out an exception for extrinsic evidence of false accusations in sexual assault prosecutions.

Chapter 7 takes up Competency rules. Section 68 of the supplement discusses the Supreme Court's 2014 decision in *Warger v. Shauers*. Prior to *Warger*, despite the sweeping language of Rule 606(b), several lower courts had allowed litigants to offer jurors' statements about occurrences during deliberation to show that panelists had lied during voir dire as the basis for a new trial. The *Warger* Court construed 606(b) as barring such evidence. However, the supplement notes that in dictum the Court added that there could be a showing of "juror bias so extreme that . . . the [constitutional] jury trial right has been abridged."

Chapter 14, on Confessions, notes some changes in state treatment of confessions, with one state eliminating the corroboration requirement and another finding merit in the trustworthiness approach to avoid errors based on false confessions. It also discusses the split between the Justices in the Supreme Court's 2013 decision in *Salinas v. Texas* regarding the constitutional limits on the use of pre-custody and pre-warning silence by a criminal suspect.

Chapter 17, on Character and Habit Evidence, and Chapter 18, on Similar Happenings, contain additional illustrations from both classic and recent cases.

Chapter 19, on Insurance Against Liability, includes some elaboration on the purposes for which proof of insurance is admissible and further analysis of when the connection of expert witnesses to insurers may be proved to impeach these witnesses.

Chapter 20, on Experimental and Scientific Evidence, is updated with:

- Description of general developments following *Daubert v. Merrill Dow Pharmaceuticals*
- Cases on special problems of interpreting mixed DNA samples and low-template DNA
- Recent literature on the accuracy of eyewitness identifications
- Cases on expert testimony about false confessions

- Notes on advances in fingerprint identification and concerns about hair comparisons.

In Chapter 22 on Authentication, cases involving the use of electronic messages and documents have substantially increased in recent years, due primarily to the increased use of text messages, social media and cell phone records in criminal prosecutions. Section 227 has been completely revised and updated to include separate analysis of the authentication of emails, text messages, website data and postings, chatroom communications, social media postings and messaging, as well as computer-generated documents.

In Chapter 23, recent cases involving the application of the "Best Evidence" rules to such messages and documents have also been incorporated throughout.

Chapter 24, which examines the definition of hearsay, discusses the change in Federal Rule of Evidence 802(d)(1)(B) to expand admission of prior inconsistent statements for their truth when they are properly admissible to rehabilitate credibility. Such rehabilitating statements are now admissible beyond those rebutting charges of recent fabrication or improper influence or motive examined in *Tome v. United States*. In Section 252 on Confrontation, the 2015 Supreme Court decision in *Ohio v. Clark*, which revisits the "ongoing emergency" situation in the context of child abuse, is examined. Its impact on Confrontation Clause analysis with regard to child abuse reporting laws, statements by children in general, and statements to private individuals is also noted.

Chapter 33, which examines the hearsay exception for Statements Against Interest, discusses statements that inculpate the declarant made to private individuals. The status of the "ear witness" generally liberates the statement from confrontation problems and has impact in multiple ways regarding admission under the hearsay exception.

Chapter 34, which includes the exception for Ancient Documents, discusses the Federal Rules Advisory Committee's recommendation that this exception be eliminated largely because of its potential to admit unreliable hearsay stored in digital form.

Chapter 35 on Judicial Notice, includes discussion of the rapidly expanding use of online sources in judicial notice of adjudicative facts.

THOMSON REUTERS PROVIEW™

This title is one of many now available on your tablet as an eBook.

Take your research mobile. Powered by the Thomson Reuters ProView™ app, our eBooks deliver the same trusted content as your print resources, but in a compact, on-the-go format.

ProView eBooks are designed for the way you work. You can add your own notes and highlights to the text, and all of your annotations will transfer electronically to every new edition of your eBook.

You can also instantly verify primary authority with built-in links to WestlawNext® and KeyCite®, so you can be confident that you're accessing the most current and accurate information.

To find out more about ProView eBooks and available discounts, call 1-800-344-5009.

Table of Contents

CHAPTER 4. CROSS-EXAMINATION AND SUBSEQUENT EXAMINATIONS

CHAPTER 5. IMPEACHMENT AND SUPPORT

CHAPTER 9. THE PRIVILEGE FOR MARITAL COMMUNICATIONS

CHAPTER 10. THE CLIENT'S PRIVILEGE: COMMUNICATIONS BETWEEN CLIENT & LAWYER

CHAPTER 11. THE PRIVILEGE FOR CONFIDENTIAL INFORMATION SECURED IN THE COURSE OF THE PHYSICIAN-PATIENT RELATIONSHIP

CHAPTER 12. PRIVILEGES FOR GOVERNMENTAL SECRETS

TITLE 6. PRIVILEGE: CONSTITUTIONAL

CHAPTER 13. THE PRIVILEGE AGAINST SELF-INCRIMINATION

CHAPTER 14. CONFESSIONS

CHAPTER 15. THE PRIVILEGE CONCERNING IMPROPERLY OBTAINED EVIDENCE

TITLE 7. RELEVANCY AND ITS COUNTERWEIGHTS

CHAPTER 16. RELEVANCE

CHAPTER 17. CHARACTER AND HABIT

CHAPTER 18. SIMILAR HAPPENINGS AND TRANSACTIONS

Title 1 INTRODUCTION

Chapter 1

Preparing and Presenting the Evidence

> **KeyCite®:** Cases and other legal materials listed in KeyCite Scope can be researched through the KeyCite service on Westlaw®. Use KeyCite to check citations for form, parallel references, prior and later history, and comprehensive citator information, including citations to other decisions and secondary materials.

§ 1 Planning and preparation of proof as important as the rules of evidence

Add at beginning of section:

The rules of evidence are arguably the most important doctrinal area in the law.[1] Evidentiary doctrines are critical to maintaining the legitimacy of any legal system because they help to ensure that the system's rules are applied properly. Actors in the market place cannot have confidence in the safety of their investments if their legal system's evidentiary rules do not assure the accurate determination of facts in commercial disputes. Likewise, citizens cannot have confidence that their most precious civil liberties are secure if the evidentiary rules do not provide a solid basis for believing that the facts relevant to the existence and exercise of those liberties will be adjudicated accurately.

---

[1] Allen, Opening Remarks, Proceedings, Fifth International Conference on Evidence Law and Forensic Science, Adelaide, Australia June 2015 (2016).

§ 2 Preparation for trial on the facts without resort to the court's aid

Replace "should" in second sentence of second paragraph with:

ought to

Add after first sentence of third paragraph:
Some have suggested that in the United States, trial by jury is becoming trial by expert.[4.50]

[4.50]Pizzi, Expert Testimony in the   US, 145 New L.J. 82 (Jan. 27, 1995).

Replace third sentence of fourth paragraph with:
In the computer age, it can also be vital to collect electronic files and e-mail messages, which are often voluminous.[7.50] The compilation of electronic files can be such a massive, complicated undertaking that attorneys frequently hire digital forensics experts to oversee the collection process.

[7.50]Dysart, The Trouble with Terabytes, 97 A.B.A. J. 33, 33 (Apr. 2011) ("Perhaps no case could be a more monumental example of the reality of modern . . . e-discovery than the ongoing Viacom copyright infringement lawsuit against YouTube filed back in 2008. In that dispute, the judge ordered that 12 terabytes of data be turned over, according to Matthew Knouff. 'People often say that one terabyte equals 50,000 trees, and 10 terabytes would be the equivalent of all the printed collections in the Library of Congress,' says Knouff, who is general counsel of Complete Discovery Source, a New York City-based . . . discovery services provider. For the Viacom/YouTube case, then, the demand was for the printed equivalent of the entire Library of Congress. And then some.").

Add in second sentence of fifth paragraph, after "planning":

demonstrative

n. 9.   tions § 4.09[5] (9th ed. 2015).
Imwinkelried, Evidentiary Founda-

Add new footnote in sixth sentence of seventh paragraph, after "necessary":
Finally, on the eve of trial before the witnesses take the stand, the counsel calling a witness may need to reinterview the witness to confirm what he is prepared to swear to, to refresh his memory if necessary,[9.30] and to ready him for the probable cross-examination.

Add after sixth sentence of seventh paragraph, replacing "The" in the next sentence, with:
The counsel must be aware that if the witness resorts to his or

her pretrial statement during the interview to revive their memory, that may waive any evidentiary privilege that would otherwise attach to the statement at trial.[9.50] Again, the

---

[9.30]At the interview, the counsel can reassure the witness that it will not be fatal to his or her credibility if they initially forget a detail at trail. Quite to the contrary, during closing argument the counsel can turn the witness's honest forgetfulness into useful proof of the witness's truthfulness. When the witness could not remember a particular detail, he or she honestly told the jury that.

[9.50]See § 9 infra.

Replace "indicated" in sentence including footnote 14 with:

ruled

Add in sentence following sentence containing footnote 14, after "additional":

informal

n. 15.
Cavanagh, Twombly's Seismic Disturbances, 38 Litig. 6, 7 (Winter 2012).

---

§ 3 Invoking the court's aid in preparing for trial: Right to interview witnesses; discovery and depositions; requests for admission; pretrial conferences

Add in sentence following footnote 2, after "such a right":

to interview

n. 3.
Sonde & Gettman, Ex Parte Communication and Inadvertent Disclosures, Prac. Litig. 61, 65-69 (May 1996);

n. 4.
Imwinkelried & Garland, Exculpatory Evidence: The Accused's Constitutional Right to Introduce Favorable Evidence § 4-2a(2), at 179-80 nn.58-59 (4th ed. 2015)

n. 5.
Add in second sentence of third paragraph in note, preceding "subpoena":
a defense
Add at end of note:
However, in U.S. v. Valenzuela-Bernal, 458 U.S. 858, 102 S. Ct. 3440, 73 L. Ed. 2d 1193, 11 Fed. R. Evid. Serv. 1 (1982), the Supreme Court ruled that there is no constitutional violation unless the defendant can advance a plausible explanation of the assistance that the defense would have received from the testimony of the deported witness.

n. 9.
Add at end of note:
State legislation can also be relevant. Under the Arizona Victims' Right law, victims have a right to refuse to be interviewed before trial. In addition, the statute provides that if the victim is under 18 years of ago, their representative has a right to deny permission for an interview. In J.D. v. Hegyi, 236 Ariz. 39, 335 P.3d 1118 (2014), the Arizona Supreme Court held that the representative retains that right even after the victim attains the age of 18.

Replace sentence ending in footnote 12:
To furnish the necessary detail, the civil rules provide for fairly thorough post-pleading discovery processes by which each party can learn the possible evidence in the case and identify the specific fact issues that will be genuinely disputed at trial.[12]

Replace "is" in first sentence of third paragraph following the heading "Formal Discovery Devices" with:

can be

Replace "for this" in sentence ending in footnote 14 with:

on deposition

Add in sentence following footnote 14, after "in some states, the":

more popular,

n. 17.   Question Ch. 18 (2014);
Capra & Greenberg, The Form of the

Add after footnote 20:
Especially in commercial litigation, production often involves such vast amounts of information that production is the most crucial phase of pretrial discovery.

Add after footnote 21:
The issue arose so frequently and pretrial privilege reviews to preclude waiver became so costly that in 2008, Congress took the extraordinary step of passing legislation governing the waiver of the attorney-client privilege in this setting.[21.50]

_____

[21.50]See § 93.

Add in fourth sentence of fifth paragraph following the heading "Formal Discovery Devices" with:

text of the

Add in sentence ending in footnote 27, preceding "conditions":

restrictions or

Replace sentence ending in footnote 33 with:
Federal Rule of Criminal Procedure 16 is a broad discovery provision concerning defense discovery of reports, scientific tests, grand jury testimony, books, documents, tangible objects, and places.[33]

Add in sentence ending in footnote 36, after "disposed of by trial":

, and the percentage was even lower in many states

n. 36.
Refo, The Vanishing Trial, 30 Litig. 1, 2 (Winter 2004) (in addition to reviewing the data on federal trials, the article discusses the trends in state court; the National Center for State Courts reported on trends in state courts from 1976 to 2002; "In the 22 states for which data was available, civil jury trials are down by 28% and, in 2002, represented 0.6% of the total civil dispositions").

§ 4   The order of presenting evidence at the trial

Add after footnote 1:
Even if the panelist's attitude is not unfavorable enough to necessitate striking him, the attorney might engage in factual indoctrination and attempt to obtain the panelist's promise that the panelist will not vote against the attorney's client "solely" or "merely" because of that item of evidence.[1.30]

[1.30]Carlson & Imwinkelried, Dynamics of Trial Practice: Problems and Materials § 4.8(A), at 84-86 (4th ed. 2010).

Add after second sentence of third paragraph:
The attorney will typically discuss both the anticipated evidence in the case and the ultimate burden of proof that the jury will eventually have to apply to evaluate the sufficiency of the evidence.[1.50]

[1.50]See Ch. 36 infra.

In fifth and sixth sentences of fourth paragraph, replace two instances of "documents" with:

exhibits

Replace third and fourth sentences of fifth paragraph, beginning with "Suppose, for example,. . ." of fifth paragraph, with:
Suppose, for example, that a civil defendant contemplates calling a doctor as a witness but that the physician is scheduled to conduct a life-or-death surgery on a day that will probably fall within the defense case-in-chief. The defense would seek the judge's leave to present the physician's testimony "out of order." In these circumstances, the trial judge might grant the defense permission to interrupt the plaintiff's case in order to present the surgeon's testimony.

n. 10.
U.S. v. Murray, 736 F.3d 652 (2d Cir. 2013) (the defense has the right to sur-rebuttal when (1) the government's rebuttal testimony raises a new issue and (2) the proffered defense evidence is not merely tangential but rather capable of discrediting the essence of the government's rebuttal evidence; in the instant case, the trial judge erred in excluding defense surrebuttal evidence that the defendant had innocent reasons for being in the area of the cell phone tower);

n. 11.
U.S. v. Smith, 751 F.3d 107, 114 (3d Cir. 2014), cert. denied, 135 S. Ct. 497, 190 L. Ed. 2d 374 (2014) and cert. denied, 135 S. Ct. 383, 190 L. Ed. 2d 270 (2014) ("If [reopening] comes at a stage in the proceeding where the opposing party will have an opportunity to respond and attempt to rebut the

evidence introduced, the possibility of prejudice is greatly lessened. [However,] a party that seeks to reopen must provide a reasonable explanation for its failure to initially present the evidence.");
U.S. v. Gray, 405 F.3d 227, 67 Fed. R. Evid. Serv. 130 (4th Cir. 2005) (the prosecution may move to reopen even after the defendant has moved for a judgment of acquittal);
; People v. Whipple, 97 N.Y.2d 1, 734 N.Y.S.2d 549, 760 N.E.2d 337 (2001) (the intermediate appellate court held that the trial judge erred in allowing the prosecution to reopen its case in order to present evidence essential to establishing a prima facie case of guilt; however, on further appeal, the intermediate appellate court's holding was reversed; reopening did not unduly prejudice the defendant, since the missing element was simple to prove and not seriously contested).

Add after footnote 12:
Indeed, on his or her own motion or at a party's request a judge may call a witness.[12.50]

[12.50]See § 8 infra.

Replace sentence ending in footnote 14 with:
The judge has discretion to exercise the power to interrogate witnesses in order to clarify the witness's testimony and fill in key gaps in the record.

n. 14.
U.S. v. Cruz-Feliciano, 786 F.3d 78 (1st Cir. 2015), cert. denied, 136 S. Ct. 274, 193 L. Ed. 2d 200 (2015);
State v. Gardner, 286 Ga. 633, 690 S.E.2d 164 (2010);

n. 15.
Add after first paragraph:
The analysis differs when the judge intervenes in a bench proceeding without a jury. U.S. v. Modjewski, 783 F.3d 645, 97 Fed. R. Evid. Serv. 225 (7th Cir. 2015), cert. denied, 136 S. Ct. 183, 193 L. Ed. 2d 146 (2015) (in the instant case, the judge actively questioned a defense expert during the sentencing phase of a criminal trial; there was no jury to prejudice; in contrast, in bench proceedings, the judge's questions warrant a reversal

only if they "show 'such a high degree of favoritism or antagonism as to make fair judgment impossible.' Liteky v. United States, 510 U.S. 540, 555, 114 S. Ct. 1147, 127 L. Ed. 2d 474 (1994)").

n. 16.
; King, When Jurors Ask Questions, 41 Litig. 9 (Spr. 2015) ("Two years ago, Illinois joined the ranks of nearly 40 other states that permit the use of juror questions directed to witnesses. As in most states, the use of juror questions in Illinois is based on the judge's discretion or the agreement of the parties").

n. 19.
Replace contents of footnote with:
Taylor v. U.S., 792 F.3d 865, 868 n.2, 92 Fed. R. Serv. 3d 310 (8th Cir.

2015) (a cautionary instructions alerts the jury "to view testimony from" certain types of witnesses with "'greater care and caution than the testimony of an ordinary witness'"); U.S. v. Worthing, 434 F.3d 1046, 1049 (8th Cir. 2006) (cooperating witnesses); U.S. v. Telfaire, 469 F.2d 552 (D.C. Cir. 1972); U.S. v. Starzecpyzel, 880 F. Supp. 1027, 42 Fed. R. Evid. Serv. 247 (S.D.N.Y. 1995) (the appendix sets out a cautionary instruction on questioned document examination testimony); People v. Guzman, 47 Cal. App. 3d 380, 121 Cal. Rptr. 69 (2d Dist. 1975) (disapproved of on other grounds by,

People v. McDonald, 37 Cal. 3d 351, 208 Cal. Rptr. 236, 690 P.2d 709, 46 A.L.R.4th 1011 (1984)) (eyewitness testimony). In People v. McDonald, 37 Cal. 3d 351, 208 Cal. Rptr. 236, 690 P.2d 709, 46 A.L.R.4th 1011 (1984) (overruled on other grounds by, People v. Mendoza, 23 Cal. 4th 896, 98 Cal. Rptr. 2d 431, 4 P.3d 265 (2000)) the court discussed expert testimony about the weaknesses of eyewitness testimony as well as cautionary instructions on the subject. See Imwinkelried, Expert Witness: Cautionary Instructions, Nat' L.J., July 31, 2006, at 12.

Add preceding sentence ending in footnote 23:
In the common law order, the witnesses testify one after another. Exercising their discretion, though, some American courts are now experimenting with concurrent expert testimony at bench trials; in this procedure, in order to identify and narrow the real points of disagreement between opposing experts, the experts take the stand at the same time, are subject to questioning by the judge, and can respond to testimony by the opposing expert.[22.50]

[22.50]Sonenshein & Fitzpatrick, The Problem of Partisan Experts and the Potential for Reform Through Concurrent Evidence, 32 Rev. Litig. 1 (Wint.

2013) (this practice, sometimes termed "hot-tubbing," has been used extensively in Australia).

Add after "practical matter" in sentence ending in footnote 23:
though,

n. 24.
4 Weinstein's Federal Evidence

§ 611.02 (rev. 2014)

Title 2 EXAMINATION OF WITNESSES

Chapter 2

The Form of Questions on Direct; The Judge's Witnesses; Refreshing Memory

---

KeyCite®: Cases and other legal materials listed in KeyCite Scope can be researched through the KeyCite service on Westlaw®. Use KeyCite to check citations for form, parallel references, prior and later history, and comprehensive citator information, including citations to other decisions and secondary materials.

---

§ 5 The form of questions: (a) Questions calling for a free narrative versus specific questions

Add new note to first sentence of section:
Any experienced litigator knows that at trial, the vast majority of objections relate to the issue of the form of the question rather than substantive evidence doctrines such as hearsay.[0.50]

[0.50]*See generally* Capra & Greenberg, The Form of the Question: Text, Materials and Exercises on the Evidentiary Rules of Form (2014).

Replace sentence ending in footnote 4 with:
Moreover, specific interrogation can be preferable because it can make it easier to present complicated testimony in proper order, help a nervous witness, or prevent boring testimony by a dull witness.

n. 4.
Replace last sentence and cite at end of note with:
A more recent edition of Weinstein is generally to the same effect. 4

Weinstein's Federal Evidence § 6.11. 06[b] (rev. 2012).

n. 5.
State v. McDowell, 2003 WI App 168,

266 Wis. 2d 599, 669 N.W.2d 204 (Ct. App. 2003), judgment aff'd, 2004 WI 70, 272 Wis. 2d 488, 681 N.W.2d 500 (2004);

In sentence including footnote 9, replace "former" with:

restyled

§ 6   The form of questions: (b) Leading questions

n. 1.
Gardner, The Perception and Memory of Witnesses, 18 Cornell L.Q. 391, 405 (1933).

n. 4.
Delete first sentence, including quote at beginning of footnote.

n. 5.
See U.S. v. Miller, 782 F.3d 793, 799-800 (7th Cir. 2015) ("A question is leading if 'phrased in such a way as to hint at the answer the witness should give' "; however, in the instant case, "the question was ambiguous enough that we cannot say that trial judge abused her discretion in allowing it.").

n. 6.
Add at end of third bulleted para-

graph in footnote:
This last style is sometimes referred to as "conversational" cross-examination. The cross-examiner makes an on-spot-judgment that the witness is so compliant that it is safe to use this approach.
Rutberg, Conversational Cross-Examination, 29 Am. J. Trial Advoc. 353, 365-66 (2005).

n. 7.
; Jones v. State, 982 N.E.2d 417 (Ind. Ct. App. 2013) ("a leading question is one which, embodying a material fact, admits of a conclusive answer in the form of a simple yes or no").

Add in sentence including footnotes 7 and 8, after parenthetical with "State whether or not . . .":
or " 'fig leaf' words" such as "if any"[7.50]

[7.50]Capra & Greenberg, The Form   of the Question 34 (2014).

Add after footnote 8:
For that matter, the questioner's nonverbal conduct can make an otherwise proper question objectionably leading.[8.50]

[8.50]U.S. v. Greene, 704 F.3d 298, 311 (4th Cir. 2013) ("a prosecutor cannot . . . physically point to a defendant and ask a witness if the defendant is the person who committed the crime. [I]t is clearly inadmissible and inappropriate to point to the defense table while asking a witness if the perpetrator . . . was in the courtroom"). A sim-

ilar problem can arise if the questioner points while asking a witness to identify certain locations on a map, chart, or diagram.

n. 9.
Capra & Greenberg, The Form of the Question 42 (2014) (one option is " 'loaded' with factual detail");

Replace "an" in fifth sentence of first paragraph following heading "The Propriety of Leading Questions" with:

a friendly

n. 11.

Replace contents of footnote with:
U.S. v. Smith, 378 F.3d 754, 755-56, 65 Fed. R. Evid. Serv. 102 (8th Cir. 2004), cert. granted, judgment vacated, 543 U.S. 1136, 125 S. Ct. 1330, 161 L. Ed. 2d 94 (2005) and opinion vacated, (Apr. 27, 2005) and judgment vacated, (Apr. 27, 2005). In an extreme case, People v. Murillo, 231 Cal. App. 4th 448, 179 Cal. Rptr. 3d 891 (2d Dist. 2014), as modified, (Dec. 9, 2014), although the victim refused to answer, the trial judge allowed the prosecutor to keep the witness on the stand and ask 110 leading questions about the victim's out-of-court statements identifying the defendant as the shooter. The appellate court held that this line of questioning

was " 'tantamount to devastating direct testimony' " and violative of the Confrontation Clause.

n. 13.
Miller v. Fairchild Industries, Inc., 885 F.2d 498, 514 (9th Cir. 1989), as amended on denial of reh'g and reh'g en banc, (Sept. 19, 1989)

Add at end of first paragraph of footnote:
According to Rosa-Rivera v. Dorado Health, Inc., 787 F.3d 614, 617 (1st Cir. 2015), an appellate court should not find an abuse of discretion by the trial judge unless the appellant identifies "some specific information that [his or her] counsel might have elicited if permitted the use of leading questions."

Add new footnote after "opponent, appears hostile" in paragraph containing footnote 14:
Thus, if the witness on direct is legally identified with the opponent, appears hostile[13.50] to the examiner, or is reluctant or uncooperative, the danger of suggestion disappears.

[13.50]People v. Seumanu, 61 Cal. 4th 1293, 192 Cal. Rptr. 3d 195, 220-21, 355 P.3d 384 (2015) ("an obviously hostile witness"); Capra & Greenberg, The Form of the Question 67, 69, 72 (2014) (the witness's actual hostility can be manifested in several ways; before trial, the witness might refuse to meet with the attorney; at trial, the witness's "surly" demeanor in the form of gestures, "facial expressions, and

voice inflection" can evidence hostility; likewise, evasive and argumentative answers can provide a basis for the judge finding that the witness is hostile).

n. 15.

Replace cite to Advisory Committee Note with:
Fed. R. Evid. 611(c) advisory committee note.

Replace "In" at beginning of sentence following footnote 15 with:
By way of example, in

n. 17.

Replace cite at end of second paragraph with:
See Fed. R. Evid. 611(c) advisory committee note.

n. 18.
; Capra & Greenberg, The Form of the

Question 35, 48 (2014) (the questioner may use "framing" or "introductory" questions to suggest the general topic but not the specific tenor of the answer to the question about the topic).

n. 19.
See Idaho Code § 9-202.

Add in sentence including footnotes 19-20, after "ignorant,":
hesitant,[19.50]

[19.50]U.S. v. Farlee, 757 F.3d 810, 822, 94 Fed. R. Evid. Serv. 1289 (8th Cir. 2014), cert. denied, 135 S. Ct. 504, 190 L. Ed. 2d 379 (2014) (the trial judge noted that "Oakie was hesitant in responding and lengthy delays preceded the answers").

n. 20.
U.S. v. Callahan, 801 F.3d 606, 623, 98 Fed. R. Evid. Serv. 568 (6th Cir.

2015) ("S.E. was cognitively impaired, suffered a traumatic brain injury . . ., had 'learning issues,' and was receiving disability benefits due to 'mental retardation.' ");

n. 21.
Blasi v. Attorney General of Com. of Pennsylvania, 120 F. Supp. 2d 451, 472 (M.D. Pa. 2000), decision aff'd, 275 F.3d 33 (3d Cir. 2001)

Add in sentence ending in footnote 22, after "simultaneously":

to some degree

n. 22.
  Replace cite to "Advisory Committee Note" in first paragraph with:
Fed. R. Evid. 611(c) advisory committee note.

n. 23.
Dunn v. Owens-Corning Fiberglass,

774 F. Supp. 929 (D.V.I. 1991), aff'd in part, vacated in part on other grounds, 1 F.3d 1362, 1371 (3d Cir. 1993)

n. 25.
  Delete cross-reference to footnote.

§ 7   The form of questions: (c) Argumentative, misleading, and indefinite questions

Add after second sentence of the first paragraph:
The first problem is that of the argumentative question. This problem can conceivably arise during direct examination, particularly when the direct examiner calls an adverse party or hostile witness to the stand. However, the objection is lodged far more frequently on cross-examination.

Replace third sentence of first paragraph sentence with:
The examiner may not ask a question that merely pressures the witness to assent to the questioner's inferences from or interpretations of the testimony already admitted.[0.50]

[0.50]People v. Shazier, 60 Cal. 4th 109, 175 Cal. Rptr. 3d 774, 331 P.3d 147 (2014) (rather than attempting in good faith to glean new information from the witness, the questioner resorts to the tactic of posing queries that are not actually addressed to the witness; the questioner may not really expect an answer to the question; indeed, the query may be unanswer-

able; in reality, the questioner is attempting to insinuate an inference or make a speech to the jury); People v. Chatman, 38 Cal. 4th 344, 42 Cal. Rptr. 3d 621, 656, 133 P.3d 534 (2006).
n. 1.
Smith v. Estelle, 602 F.2d 694, 700 n. 7 (5th Cir. 1979), judgment aff'd, 451 U.S. 454, 101 S. Ct. 1866, 68 L. Ed. 2d 359 (1981)

Add new footnote at the end of sentence containing footnote 1:
or "badgering the witness."[1.30]

[1.30]Capra & Greenberg, The Form of the Question 193 (2014) ("badgering" can take many forms; for example, the questioner's tone and manner may be objectionable; the questioner might adopt an insulting or mocking demeanor, shout at the witness, attempt to intimidate the witness by drawing too close, point a finger at the witness's face, or employ facial expressions such as rolling his or her eyes to convey disbelief; the authors cite McDonald v. State, 340 So. 2d 103, 106 (Ala. Crim. App. 1976), State v. Daye, 281 N.C. 592, 189 S.E.2d 481, 483 (1972), and Clark v. State, 365 S.W.3d 333, 336-38 (Tex. Crim. App. 2012) as examples).

Replace "the rule" in sentence following sentence with footnote 1 with:

this form of question,

Add new footnote at the end of first paragraph:

When the cross-examiner becomes argumentative, he is in effect previewing his summation; and he will later have an ample opportunity to argue the inferences during his summation to the jury.[1.50]

[1.50]Saltzburg, Rhetorical Questioning, 17 Crim. Just. 38 (Spr. 2000) (the questioning poses special risks when the phrasing of the question uses legal terms and pressures the witness to draw a legal conclusion).

Add at end of third paragraph:

Likewise, indefinite wording is dangerous when the wording includes a legalism.[3.50] The meaning of the legalistic term may differ from the general, popular meaning of the expression.

[3.50]Capra & Greenberg, The Form   of the Question 114-15 (2014).

§ 8   The judge may call witnesses; the judge and jurors may question witnesses

Replace "questions" in first sentence of paragraph following heading "Judges" with:

issues

n. 5.
U.S. v. Cisneros, 203 F.3d 333, 349 (5th Cir. 2000), reh'g en banc granted, opinion vacated, 206 F.3d 448 (5th Cir. 2000) and on reh'g en banc, 238 F.3d 310 (5th Cir. 2001)

n. 6.
Replace contents of footnote:
    U.S. v. Cruz-Feliciano, 786 F.3d 78 (1st Cir. 2015), cert. denied, 136 S. Ct. 274, 193 L. Ed. 2d 200 (2015); U.S. v. Vallone, 698 F.3d 416, 468 (7th Cir. 2012), cert. granted, judgment vacated on other grounds, 133 S. Ct. 2825, 186 L. Ed. 2d 881 (2013) and opinion modified and reinstated, 752 F.3d 690 (7th Cir. 2014) (a trial judge is not a "wallflower[ ] or . . . potted plant[]"); U.S. v. Catalan-Roman, 585 F.3d 453 (1st Cir. 2009), as amended, (Dec. 23, 2009) (a trial judge is not a mere umpire; rather, he or she is the governor of the trial and has a perfect right to participate actively); U.S. v. Smith, 452 F.3d 323, 332-33, 70 Fed. R. Evid.

Serv. 625 (4th Cir. 2006) ("even a stern and short-tempered judge's ordinary efforts at courtroom administration . . . do not establish bias or partiality"; "A tart remark or two might be what is needed to keep a lengthy trial on track."); Stevenson v. District of Columbia Metropolitan Police Dept., 248 F.3d 1187, 1190, 56 Fed. R. Evid. Serv. 1335 (D.C. Cir. 2001) ("Judges may do so repeatedly and aggressively to clear up confusion and manage trials . . . . moreover, '[t]he precepts of fair trial and judicial objectivity do not require a judge to be inert' "); U.S. v. Montas, 41 F.3d 775, 41 Fed. R. Evid. Serv. 701 (1st Cir. 1994); U.S. v. Rodriguez-Rodriguez, 685 F. Supp. 2d 293, 297 (D.P.R. 2010) (the judge is not a "bloodless automaton"). In one of the celebrated Watergate prosecutions, Judge John Sirica resorted to judicial questioning to elicit the true facts about the break-in. U.S. v. Liddy, 509 F.2d 428, 438, 28 A.L.R. Fed. 1 (D.C. Cir. 1974).

Add in sentence ending in footnote 7, after "rhetorical":

dicta

n. 7.
U.S. v. Smith, 857 F. Supp. 1466, 1471 (D. Kan. 1994), aff'd, 63 F.3d 956, 42 Fed. R. Evid. Serv. 1296 (10th Cir. 1995), cert. granted, judgment vacated on other grounds, 516 U.S. 1105, 116 S. Ct. 900, 133 L. Ed. 2d 834 (1996) (the Tenth Circuit has "encouraged" trial judges to exercise their power to question witnesses; when the record in a criminal case needs clarification on facts determinative "of guilt or innocence"; the "trial judge has an obligation, on his own initiative," to clarify the facts.).

Add in sentence ending in footnote 10, preceding "comment":

forbidden

n. 14.
Berry v. U.S., 884 F. Supp. 2d 453, 458-59 (E.D. Va. 2012) (the court discusses U.S. v. Godwin, 272 F.3d 659 (4th Cir. 2001); there the Fourth Circuit remarked that "[t]ime and again, the [trial] court engaged in active questioning unfavorable to the defense"); People v. Sorrels, 208 Cal. App. 4th 1155, 1164-66, 146 Cal. Rptr. 3d 204, 211-12 (2d Dist. 2012), as modified on denial of reh'g, (Sept. 18, 2012) (the court discusses People v. Campbell, 162 Cal. App. 2d 776, 329 P.2d 82 (2d Dist. 1958); in that case, the trial judge's "questions . . . were calculated to and did elicit testimony seriously adverse to the defendant");

Add new footnote at the end of third sentence of fourth paragraph:
In a judge-tried case, the judge's question might betray a premature judgment.[14.50]

[14.50]There is a different standard in a bench proceeding than in a jury trial. In U.S. v. Modjewski, 783 F.3d 645, 97 Fed. R. Evid. Serv. 225 (7th Cir. 2015), cert. denied, 136 S. Ct. 183, 193 L. Ed. 2d 146 (2015), the judge actively questioned a defense expert in a sentencing hearing without a jury. In a bench proceeding, to obtain a reversal, the defendant must show that the judge's questions manifested " 'such a high degree of favoritism or antagonism as to make fair judgment impossible.' Liteky v. United States, 510 U.S. 540, 555, 114 S. Ct. 1147, 127 L. Ed. 2d 474 (1994)."

n. 19.
State v. Slaughter, 2014-Ohio-862,

2014 WL 895425 (Ohio Ct. App. 2d
Dist. Montgomery County 2014) (the
trial judge called the defendant's girl-
friend as a witness; although she possessed important information that the
jury should hear, she had already
indicated that she was aligned with
the defendant);

n. 21.
   Replace beginning of note with:
Unif. R. Evid. 614 provides:

n. 26.
See also Breyer, Introduction, in Reference Manual on Scientific Evidence (3d
ed. 2011).

Add in sentence ending in footnote 28, after "as we have seen,":

under Rule 614(a)

n. 34.
   Add at beginning of footnote:
King, When Jurors Ask Questions, 41
Litig., Spr. 2015, at 9 ("Two years ago,
Illinois joined the ranks of the nearly
40 other states that permit the use of
written juror questions directed to
witnesses. As in most states, the use
of juror questions in Illinois is based
on the judge's discretion or the agreement of the parties"); Frank, The Jury
Wants to Take the Podium—But Even
with the Authority to Do So, Can It?
An Interdisciplinary Examination of
Jurors' Questions of Witnesses at
Trial, 38 Am. J. Trial Advoc. 1, 6,
51-60 (2014) ("Save only a small minority of jurisdictions, juror questioning is today authorized . . . . [T]he
Supreme Court has never ruled on this
procedure, having denied certiorari
four times on cases where juror questioning was an issue on appeal . . .";
Appendix 1 in the article is a useful
circuit-by-circuit and state-by-state
survey of the state of the law in both
criminal and civil cases);

§ 9   Refreshing recollection

   Add at end of second paragraph:
The use of the statement or map to refresh the witness's memory
is more likely to be successful if the witness has physically
handled and discussed the document during the pretrial
interview.

   *Replace "a record" in second sentence of second paragraph fol-
lowing heading "Confusion with the Past RecollectionRecorded
Hearsay Exception" with:*

an accurate *record*

   *Add after second sentence of third paragraph following heading
"Confusion with the Past RecollectionRecorded Hearsay
Exception":*
The memorandum need not be accurate or independently
admissible.

n. 11.
   Delete U.S. v. Carey cite.

   *Add new footnote to first sentence of second paragraph follow-
ing heading "The Case for Distinguishing Between the Two Prac-*

tices," after "stimulus,":
Any kind of stimulus,[11.50]

[11.50]U.S. v. Weller, 238 F.3d 1215, 1221 (10th Cir. 2001) ("anything may be used to refresh a witness's recollection, even inadmissible evidence").

Replace "restriction" in sentence ending in footnote 16 with:

regard

n. 16.
Replace cite in first paragraph:
People v. Betts, 272 A.D. 737, 74 N.Y.S.2d 791 (1st Dep't 1947), judgment aff'd, 297 N.Y. 1000, 80 N.E.2d 456 (1948);

Replace cite in second paragraph:
U.S. v. McKeever, 169 F. Supp. 426 (S.D. N.Y. 1958), rev'd on other grounds, 271 F.2d 669 (2d Cir. 1959);

Replace "this" in sentence following footnote 16 with:
On balance,

n. 19.
Delete second paragraph & quote of former Fed. R. Evid. 612.

Add after footnote 22:
If there is no seeming nexus between the content of the memorandum and the fact the witness purported to remember, the jurors may disbelieve the witness's testimony that reviewing the memorandum revived the witness's memory of the fact.

Replace "qualifies as independent evidence" with:

is independently

n. 26.
Delete cross-reference to footnote in second paragraph.

Replace "of" in sentence including footnote 27 with:

without viewing

Replace "Rule 612" in sentence ending in footnote 32 with:
Rule 612(a)(2)

Add after footnote 35:
The Advisory Committee Note to Rule 612 states that "access" should be granted "only to those writings which may fairly be said in fact to have an impact upon the testimony of the witness."[35.50]

[35.50]Fed. R. Evid. 612 advisory committee note.

n. 37.

U.S. v. Bertoli, 854 F. Supp. 975 (D.N.J.

1994), aff'd in part, vacated in part on
other grounds, 40 F.3d 1384 (3d Cir.
1994)

Chapter 3

The Requirement of Firsthand Knowledge: The Opinion Rule & Expert Testimony

> **KeyCite®:** Cases and other legal materials listed in KeyCite Scope can be researched through the KeyCite service on Westlaw®. Use KeyCite to check citations for form, parallel references, prior and later history, and comprehensive citator information, including citations to other decisions and secondary materials.

§ 10   The requirement of knowledge from observation

n. 1.
2 Wigmore, Evidence §§ 650-70 (Chadbourn rev. 1979); 3 Weinstein's Federal Evidence Ch. 602 (rev. 2014);

n. 3.
   Delete *"and former Fed. R. Evid. 602" from second paragraph.*

Add after footnote 3:
More broadly, the requirement is that the witness have gained knowledge of the fact through his or her sensory experience. Thus, a lay witness may testify not only about events he or she observed but also about sensations such as pain that they experienced.[3.50]

[3.50]Andrews v. Seales, 881 F. Supp. 2d 671, 673 (E.D. Pa. 2012); Ramirez v. Colonial Freight Warehouse Co., Inc., 434 S.W.3d 244 (Tex. App. Houston 1st Dist. 2014) (the witness recalled that he suffered pain in his back, neck, and shoulder immediately after being struck by a truck). *See* White v. City of Birmingham, Ala., 96 F. Supp. 3d 1260, 1273-74 (N.D. Ala.

2015), as amended, (May 27, 2015)   that "the crash knocked him out").
(the witness had personal knowledge

Start new paragraph after footnote 4.

n. 7.
Elizarraras, 631 F.2d at 374

Add to sentence ending in footnote 9, after "the fact,":

on motion

Replace "then makes" in sentence ending in footnote 11 with:

later make

Add in sentence ending in footnote 18, preceding "overall reliability":

judge's assessment of the

n. 20.
; Merritt Hawkins & Associates, LLC v. Gresham, 79 F. Supp. 3d 625, 631-32, 96 Fed. R. Evid. Serv. 439 (N.D. Tex. 2015) (the president of a company had sufficient personal knowledge to testify about the damages caused by two former employees who took confidential information with them when they transferred to a competing company)
Add to precede Seltzer v. I.C. Optics Ltd. cite:
U.S. v. Stabl, Inc., 800 F.3d 476, 486, 92 Fed. R. Serv. 3d 797 (8th Cir. 2015) ("industry experience"); U.S. v. Kerley, 784 F.3d 327, 337-38, 97 Fed. R. Evid. Serv. 357 (6th Cir. 2015) (employees' testimony about their employer's underwriting guidelines, policies, and procedures); Siebert v. Gene Security Network, Inc., 75 F. Supp. 3d 1108, 1113-14, 96 Fed. R. Evid. Serv. 76 (N.D. Cal. 2014) (institutional operations and practices);

Add at end of footnote:
But see Metro Hospitality Partners, Ltd. v. Lexington Ins. Co., 84 F. Supp. 3d 553, 563-68 (S.D. Tex. 2015) (" '[A]n officer or employee of a corporation may testify to industry practices and pricing . . . without qualifying as an expert . . . .' "; Rule 702 does " 'not place any restrictions on the . . . practice of allowing business owners or officers to testify based on personal knowledge obtained from their position and experience.' A corporate owner or officer is competent to testify about lost profits . . . 'if the witness has direct knowledge of the business accounts underlying the profit calculation' "; however, the hotel's human resources director was not qualified to testify about matters involving the hotel's relevant internal costs, profits, or losses; the director lacked knowledge of the hotel's finances and accounting.).

§ 11   The evolution of the rule against opinions: opinions of laymen

n. 2.   in Illinois 8 (1942)
King and Pillinger, Opinion Evidence

Add in sentence ending in footnote 7, preceding "more restrictive":

broader,

n. 7.   in Illinois at 7
King and Pillinger, Opinion Evidence

Replace end of sentence ending in footnote 11, after comma, with:

but instead a difference in degree on a spectrum with no bright line boundaries

n. 11.   in Illinois 1-6, 21-23 (1942)
King and Pillinger, Opinion Evidence

Add new footnotes in sentence including footnotes 16-18:
The so-called "collective fact" or "short-hand rendition"[15.50] rule, permitting opinions on such subjects as a person's age,[16] a car's speed,[16.50]

[15.50]U.S. v. Reda, 787 F.3d 625, 629-30, 97 Fed. R. Evid. Serv. 923 (1st Cir. 2015) (an undercover agent could use the term, "kickback," in his testimony because it was employed as a factual short-hand rather than a legal term of art).

[16.50]*But see* Zorn v. State, 315 S.W.3d 616 (Tex. App. Tyler 2010) (the appellate court indicated that it was not error for a trial judge to bar a specific speed estimate by a 14-year-old who did not have a driver's license).

n. 18.
People v. Vigil, 2015 COA 88M, 2015 WL 4042473 (Colo. App. 2015), as modified on denial of reh'g, (Aug. 13, 2015) (a sergeant who had examined the defendant's shoes could testify to a lay opinion that the shoes "visually appeared to be a match" to shoeprints found at a burglary scene); People v. Acosta, 2014 COA 82, 338 P.3d 472 (Colo. App. 2014) (a witness could testify that the defendant was "very guilty looking" after an incident; the opinion summarized the witness's perception of how the defendant looked and acted immediately after the incident);

Add at end of footnote:
There are also liberal federal decisions. Ghee v. Marten Transport, Ltd., 570 Fed. Appx. 228 (3d Cir. 2014) (a lay witness could testify that his injuries would prevent him from operating a tractor-trailer in the future).

Add in sentence ending in footnote 19, preceding "person's handwriting style":

person[18.50] or of a

[18.50]U.S. v. Albino-Loe, 747 F.3d 1206, 94 Fed. R. Evid. Serv. 160 (9th Cir. 2014), cert. denied, 135 S. Ct. 499, 190 L. Ed. 2d 375 (2014) (the witness's prior contact with the defendant gave the witness a sufficient level of familiarity with the defendant to identify the defendant); State v. Robinson, 2015 ME 77, 118 A.3d 242 (Me. 2015) (the witness identified the defendant as the person shown in an unavailable surveilliance video; the witness was familiar with the defendant's physical attributes and body movements because the witness had known the defendant for two years).

n. 19.
U.S. v. Harris, 786 F.3d 443, 97 Fed. R. Evid. Serv. 673 (6th Cir. 2015) (The witnesses were sufficiently familiar with the defendant's handwriting style; in one case the defendant had hand-delivered his letters to her; "courts have permitted handwriting identification based on ever-looser degrees of familiarity. The witness does not have to observe the defendant writing; other categories of experience . . . can demonstrate familiarity, such as seeing . . . writings purporting to be those of the alleged author when the circumstances would indicate that they were genuine. The Eighth Circuit . . . [has] previously held that a witness' single exposure to an uncontested signature and single exposure to a contested one constituted ade-

quate familiarity.");

n. 21.
Add after first two sentences of footnote:
Brown & Davis, Eight Gates for Expert Witnesses: Fifteen Years Later, 52 Hous. L. Rev. 1, 10 (2014) ("the Property Owner Rule—like an individual, an entity's officers, if they have adequate knowledge of a property, may now testify regarding the value of the entity's property").

n. 23.
Delete "and former Fed. R. Evid. 701" from first paragraph.

Replace beginning of fourth paragraph with:
The Advisory Committee Note to Rule 701 observes:

Add in sentence containing footnote 24, deleting the comma after "supporting an inference":

—when the "poor, poor power of speech" fails—

Add after sentence following footnote 26:
Many veteran litigators have an instinctive sense that jurors find more concrete testimony more persuasive.

Replace "Under these" in sentence including footnotes 32-33 with:
Given these liberal

n. 33.
U.S. v. Churchwell, 807 F.3d 107, 118-19, 98 Fed. R. Evid. Serv. 1378 (5th Cir. 2015) (a lay witness was permitted to testify to his belief that the defendant knew that certain passport applications were fraudulent); U.S. v. Gyamfi, 805 F.3d 668, 672-74 (6th Cir. 2015) (The officer described the defendant as "nervous"; "testimony about the appearance of a person '[is] a typical example of Rule 701 evidence.' Additionally, testimony related to a person's manner of conduct

is also categorized as a prototypical example of Rule 701 evidence."); ; People v. Smith, 61 Cal. 4th 18, 186 Cal. Rptr. 3d 550, 574-75, 347 P.3d 530 (2015) (the witness "merely recounted his observations of the defendant's action and appearance. '[A] witness may testify about objective behavior and describe behavior as being consistent with a state of mind' ")

n. 36.
4 Weinstein's Federal Evidence §§ 701.02 and 701.05 (rev. 2014)

Add new footnote to end of fifth sentence of paragraph following footnote 37:
One was "to eliminate the risk that the reliability requirements of Rule 702 will be evaded through the simple expedient of proffering an expert in lay witness clothing."[37.30]

[37.30]Daubert v. Merrell Dow Pharmaceuticals, Inc., 509 U.S. 579,   113 S. Ct. 2786, 125 L. Ed. 2d 469, 37 Fed. R. Evid. Serv. 1 (1993).

Add new footnote to end of first sentence of paragraph including 38-44:

Of course, the difficulty in administering the 2000 amendment is drawing the line between lay and expert testimony.[37.50]

[37.50]Young v. McDonald, 766 F.3d 1348, 1353 (Fed. Cir. 2014) (a layperson could not opine that a person suffered from PTSD; " 'Because of the complexity of PTSD, the application of careful clinical judgment is necessary to identify and describe the relationship between past events and current symptoms . . . . PTSD can occur hours, months, or years, after a military stressor' "); Columbia Gas Transmission, LLC v. Vlahos, 94 F. Supp. 3d 728, 739-40 n.4 (E.D. Va. 2015) ("the operation and maintenance of a high-pressure natural gas pipeline is beyond the scope of permissible lay testimony and expert testimony is required"); People v. Froehler, 2015 COA 102, 2015 WL 4571431 (Colo. App. 2015) (on the one hand, a police officer could testify to the "date created" and "date modified" displayed when he plugged a flash drive into a computer and right-clicked on the images; on the other hand, the officer lacked the specialized expert knowledge required to testify about a software program used to search the defendant's home computer; the judge erred in admitting the officer's testimony about the program's capabilities and limitations).

Add at end of section:

One commentator has attempted to elaborate on the differences in reasoning processes underlying lay and expert opinions.[45]

- The essential insight is that whenever any witness—lay or expert—forms an opinion about the significance of the facts in the case, she is making a comparative judgment. One term of the comparison is a generalization such as one about the normal appearance of a particular person's handwriting style or the symptomatology of a certain disease. Lay and expert witnesses differ in how they derive their generalization. In the case of lay opinion, the witness must develop the generalization exclusively or primarily through firsthand experience such as personal observation of other examples of the author's handwriting.[46] In contrast, in the case of expert opinion, the witness can rely on prior empirical studies and discoveries. To paraphrase Sir Isaac Newton, modern experts stand on the shoulders of the giants who preceded them.[47] A contemporary physicist need not duplicate the research conducted by Fermi or Oppenheimer before utilizing a generalization derived from their research.[48]

- The second term of the comparison is a case-specific fact such as questioned document or a set of case-specific facts such as a patient's case history. Lay and expert witnesses differ in how they acquire their information about the case-specific fact. In the case of lay opinion about the speed of an automobile, the witness must have personally observed the auto in question.[49] In the case of expert opinion, the expert can gain the information from a variety of sources: personal knowledge, the contents of a hypothetical question, admissible hearsay, and even inadmissible secondhand reports if it is the customary, reasonable practice of experts in the witness's field to consider reports from such sources.[50]

Thus, in order to justify the admission of a layperson's opinion, the proponent must demonstrate that: (1) the witness is relying on a generalization developed through personal experience, and (2) the witness has personal knowledge of the case-specific fact. If either element is missing, the conclusion may not be admitted as a lay opinion. When either element is missing, if the evidence is to be admitted at all, it must satisfy the requirements for expert testimony.[51]

---

[45]Imwinkelried, Distinguishing Lay from Expert Opinion: The Need to Focus on the Epistemological Differences Between the Reasoning Processes Used by Lay and Expert Witnesses, 68 SMU L. Rev. 73 (2015).

[46]U.S. v. Amador-Huggins, 799 F.3d 124, 130 (1st Cir. 2015), cert. denied, 136 S. Ct. 345, 193 L. Ed. 2d 247 (2015) (the trial judge properly allowed an FBI agent to testify that a bumper might not have exhibited severe damage even if it had been struck at a relatively high rate of speed; the defense contended that the judge should have analyzed the testimony as expert evidence; "Marchand was not offering a research-backed opinion . . . ."; rather, the basis of his opinion was that his personal experience using the bumping technique in carjacking cases; "in his experience, he had seen bumpers that had been hit under circumstances similar to those [in the instant case] that were not 'badly damaged' "); U.S. v. Lloyd, 807 F.3d 1128, 1154, 99 Fed. R. Evid. Serv. 39 (9th Cir. 2015) (lay witnesses may not base opinions on hearsay sources); U.S. v.

Torralba-Mendia, 784 F.3d 652, 660, 97 Fed. R. Evid. Serv. 414 (9th Cir. 2015) (a layperson may not base an opinion on hearsay); Riley v. University of Alabama Health Services Foundation, P.C., 990 F. Supp. 2d 1177, 1187-88 (N.D. Ala. 2014) (a lay witness must derive the basis for an opinion from his or her own senses, not from the reports of others).

[47]Quoted in Synder, History of the Physical Sciences 28 (1969).

[48]Imwinkelried, The "Bases" of Expert Testimony: The Syllogistic Structure of Scientific Testimony, 67 N.C. L. Rev. 1, 9 (1988). See also Maguire, Evidence: Common Sense and Common Law 29 (1947) (experts draw their generalizations from a wide range of sources, including "much hearsay—lectures by teachers, statements in textbooks, reports of experiments and experiences of others in the same field").

[49]See § 10 supra.

[50]See §§ 14-16 infra.

[51]U.S. v. Kilpatrick, 798 F.3d 365, 381, 98 Fed. R. Evid. Serv. 197 (6th Cir. 2015).

§ 12   The relativity of the opinion rule: Opinions on the ultimate issue

Add in sentence ending in footnote 2, preceding "more insistent":

understandably

n. 3.
U.S. v. Richter, 796 F.3d 1173, 1195-96, 98 Fed. R. Evid. Serv. 36 (10th Cir. 2015), cert. dismissed in part by, 2016 WL 1251448 (U.S. 2016) ("'an expert may not simply tell the jury what result it should reach without providing any explanation of the criteria on which that opinion is based or any means by which the jury can exercise independent judgment'"); U.S. v. Grzybowicz, 747 F.3d 1296, 1310 (11th

Cir. 2014); Camacho v. Nationwide Mut. Ins. Co., 13 F. Supp. 3d 1343, 1365-66 (N.D. Ga. 2014); Elat v. Ngoubene, 993 F. Supp. 2d 497, 512, 93 Fed. R. Evid. Serv. 550 (D. Md. 2014); Adams v. City of New York, 993 F. Supp. 2d 306, 326, 93 Fed. R. Evid. Serv. 700 (E.D. N.Y. 2014); Sharkey v. J.P. Morgan Chase & Co., 978 F. Supp. 2d 250, 252, 92 Fed. R. Evid. Serv. 798 (S.D. N.Y. 2013);

Replace "announced" in sentence ending in footnote 4 with:

went to the length of announcing

Add after footnote 11:
After all, as previously stated, the courts routinely admit skilled lay observer opinions about identity, and identity is often an ultimate question in a lawsuit.

Replace sentence ending in footnote 13 with:
Even under the most liberal rules, those opinions are excludable under Rule 403 on the ground that their value is outweighed by "a danger of one or more of the following: unfair prejudice, confusing the issues, misleading the jury, undue delay, wasting time, or needlessly presenting cumulative evidence."[13]

Add in first sentence of paragraph including footnotes 14-16, after "many close":

, technical

Add after sentence that follows footnote 23:
An expert opinion is not automatically inadmissible because it refers to the law.[23.10] If the expert's opinion tracks the language of the legal rule[23.30] but the technical meaning of the legal term happens to coincide with the term's colloquial meaning, there is little danger that the opinion will mislead the jury.[23.50] Alternatively, suppose that the meanings differ. Even then the danger is minimal if the expert enables the jury to exercise independent judgment by specifying the criteria on which the opinion is based[23.70] so long as the criteria themselves are expert in nature. (If the criteria are common sense, lay norms, there is no need for expert testimony on the topic.)[23.90]

[23.10]U.S. v. Richter, 796 F.3d 1173, 1195, 98 Fed. R. Evid. Serv. 36 (10th Cir. 2015), cert. dismissed in part by, 2016 WL 1251448 (U.S. 2016). *See also* Camacho v. Nationwide Mut. Ins. Co., 13 F. Supp. 3d 1343, 1365-66 (N.D. Ga.

2014) (it is true that "the court must be the jury's only source of law"; however, "[a]n expert does not invade the court's authority by discoursing broadly over the entire range of the applicable law where the opinion is focused on a specific question of fact"; an insurance expert could testify about the duties owed by an insurer during the claims handling process; an expert's " 'passing reference to a legal principle or assumption in an effort to place his opinion in some sort of context will not justify the outright exclusion of the expert's [testimony] in its entirety' ").

[23.30]Elat v. Ngoubene, 993 F. Supp. 2d 497, 512-13, 93 Fed. R. Evid. Serv. 550 (D. Md. 2014) ("human trafficking").

[23.50]U.S. v. Volkman, 797 F.3d 377, 388 (6th Cir. 2015), cert. denied, 136 S. Ct. 348, 193 L. Ed. 2d 250 (2015) ("A witness's testimony contains a legal conclusion only if 'the terms used by the witness have a separate, distinct and specialized meaning in the law different from that present in the ver-nacular' "); U.S. v. Reda, 787 F.3d 625, 629-30, 97 Fed. R. Evid. Serv. 923 (1st Cir. 2015) ("kickback"). See Longlois v. Stratasys, Inc., 88 F. Supp. 3d 1058, 1063, 90 Fed. R. Serv. 3d 1545 (D. Minn. 2015) (" 'legal conclusions with no analytical reasoning' ").

[23.70]U.S. v. Richter, 796 F.3d 1173, 1195-96, 98 Fed. R. Evid. Serv. 36 (10th Cir. 2015), cert. dismissed in part by, 2016 WL 1251448 (U.S. 2016).

[23.90]See the discussion of appropriate subject-matter for expert testimony in § 13 infra.

n. 28.
Cordoves v. Miami-Dade County, 104 F. Supp. 3d 1350, 1365 (S.D. Fla. 2015) ("If testimony 'track[s] the language of the applicable statute' or uses a term that 'has specialized legal meaning that is more precise than the lay understanding of the term,' the testimony is an impermissible legal conclusion.");

n. 31.
State v. Larsen, 828 P.2d 487 (Utah Ct. App. 1992), aff'd, 865 P.2d 1355 (Utah 1993)

Add preceding sentence including footnotes 32-33:
By its terms, Federal Rule of Evidence 704(b) applies only to expert testimony.

n. 32.
Delete first paragraph and quote of former Fed. R. Evid. 704(b).

Replace first two questions in sentence ending in footnote 34 with:

"Was the accused suffering from a specific mental disease or defect?"; "Explain the characteristics of that mental disease and defect";

Add at end of section:
In short, these judges permit the expert to go to the very brink of 704(b)'s prohibition but do not allow the expert to violate the explicit prohibition.

§ 13   Expert witnesses: Subjects of expert testimony, qualifications, and cross-examination

n. 2.
4 Weinstein's Federal Evidence Ch. 702 (rev. 2012)

n. 9.
Brown & Davis, Eight Gates for Expert Witnesses: Fifteen Years Later, 52 Hous. L. Rev. 1, 35 (2014) ("The help-

fulness gate does not mean that an expert can only testify about something that the jury knows nothing about. While the expert 'must possess some additional [insight] beyond that possessed by the average person, the gap need not necessarily be monumental.' An expert may aid the jury in understanding even familiar matters if the expert's experience or training provides a more thorough or refined understanding than ordinary experience provides. Evidence is helpful when it provides a further depth or precision of understanding about subjects which lie well within common experience");

n. 10.
Delete first paragraph and quote of former Fed. R. Evid. 702.

n. 11.
4 Weinstein's Federal Evidence § 702.03[2] (rev. 2014);

n. 14.
U.S. v. Vastola, 899 F.2d 211, 234, 29 Fed. R. Evid. Serv. 1366 (3d Cir. 1990), cert. granted, judgment vacated, 497 U.S. 1001, 110 S. Ct. 3233, 111 L. Ed.

2d 744 (1990) ("the usual trial practice of moving for the admission of expert testimony")

n. 15.
Add to end of first paragraph of footnote:
; Padilla v. Hunter Douglas Window Coverings, Inc., 14 F. Supp. 3d 1127, 1132, 93 Fed. R. Evid. Serv. 858 (N.D. Ill. 2014) (" 'Whether a witness is qualified as an expert can only be determined by comparing the area in which the witness has superior knowledge, skill, experience, or education with the subject matter of the witness's testimony' ").
Add to end of fourth paragraph of footnote:
But see State v. D'Ambrosio, 67 Ohio St. 3d 185, 1993-Ohio-170, 616 N.E.2d 909 (1993) ("the better practice . . . is to let experts testify in terms of possibility"). Of course, even if the expert's testimony is admissible, without more testimony phrased in terms of mere possibility may be legally insufficient to defeat a pretrial summary judgment motion or a directed verdict motion at trial.

Add in sentence including footnotes 16-17, after "commonly the case from":

a combination of

n. 17.
Fed. R. Evid. 702 advisory committee note.

n. 20.
Waldorf v. Shuta, 916 F. Supp. 423, 429 (D.N.J. 1996), aff'd, 142 F.3d 601, 40 Fed. R. Serv. 3d 910 (3d Cir. 1998);

n. 23.
Add to end of first paragraph of footnote:
See also Padilla v. Hunter Douglas Window Coverings, Inc., 14 F. Supp. 3d 1127, 1131-35, 93 Fed. R. Evid. Serv. 858 (N.D. Ill. 2014) (a former Commissioner of the U.S. Consumer Product Safety Commission was un-

qualified to testify as an expert on window blind design and safety; the witness was not an engineer, had no training on the subject, and lacked practical experience in window blind design); Elat v. Ngoubene, 993 F. Supp. 2d 497, 515, 93 Fed. R. Evid. Serv. 550 (D. Md. 2014) (the witness was unqualified to opine about the plaintiff's alleged emotional distress; although the witness had a master's degree in psychology, she was not a licensed psychologist or licensed therapist and had not conducted a psychological examination of the plaintiff; her opinion was based solely on her lay observations as an interviewer).

Add to end of first paragraph following heading "The Validity of the Expert's Underlying Technique or Theory":
As we shall see in § 203, the clear majority of states now apply

some version of the *Daubert* validation standard. Indeed, in recent years some of the states which had been the staunchest advocates of the *Frye* standard have incorporated the reliability/validation standard into their jurisprudence.[29.50]

[29.50]California did so by case law in Sargon Enterprises, Inc. v. University of Southern Cal., 55 Cal. 4th 747, 149 Cal. Rptr. 3d 614, 288 P.3d 1237, 286 Ed. Law Rep. 1191 (2012). The following year Florida amended Fla. Stat. Ann. § 90.702 of its evidence code to codify the *Daubert* standard.

Replace "The" at the beginning of second paragraph following heading "The Validity of the Expert's Underlying Technique or Theory":
After the rendition of the *Daubert* decision, the

n. 37.
Smith v. Haden, 872 F. Supp. 1040, 1045 (D.D.C. 1994), judgment aff'd, 69 F.3d 606 (D.C. Cir. 1995);

Add in fifth sentence of sixth paragraph following heading "The Validity of the Expert's Underlying Technique or Theory", preceding "epistemological":

validation and

Add in eighth sentence of seventh paragraph following heading "The Validity of the Expert's Underlying Technique or Theory", preceding "the judge":

at a more fundamental level

Add in tenth sentence of seventh paragraph following heading "The Validity of the Expert's Underlying Technique or Theory", preceding "recent developments":

relatively

Add new footnote at end of fourth sentence in paragraph beginning with "What is the specific technique or theory that the expert will testify about?":
It is also clear that it is not enough for the witness to assert in conclusory fashion that she is relying on her general "expertise," "knowledge," or "education."[40.50]

[40.50]Padilla v. Hunter Douglas Window Coverings, Inc., 14 F. Supp. 3d 1127, 1137, 93 Fed. R. Evid. Serv. 858 (N.D. Ill. 2014) (" 'a witness who invokes "my expertise" rather than an- alytical strategies widely used by specialists is not an expert as Rule 702 defines that term' "); Sharkey v. J.P. Morgan Chase & Co., 978 F. Supp. 2d 250, 252, 92 Fed. R. Evid. Serv. 798

(S.D. N.Y. 2013) (an expert witness may not "[s]imply rehash [the] evidence" and assert that his or her analysis of the evidence leads to a particular conclusion).

n. 42.
Kumho Tire Co., Ltd., 526 U.S. at 151.

n. 43.
Daubert, 509 U.S. at 597.

Start new paragraph after footnote 43.

n. 44.
Joiner, 522 U.S. at 144

Add new paragraph following the paragraph including footnotes 49-50:

The *Fujii* approach is the soundest. At any given time in a scientific discipline, the theories circulating in the discipline will vary in the extent of their empirical validation. Some may rest on extensive validation, others might have barely enough supporting data to pass muster under *Daubert,* and still others will fall far short. Rather than generalizing about the validity of the whole discipline, it makes much more sense to focus on the specific theory or technique that the expert is relying on and test the degree to which that theory or technique has been validated.

n. 54.
Kumho Tire Co., Ltd., 526 U.S. at 150

Replace portion of sentence including footnotes 54-55 after footnote 54 with:
and the Advisory Committee Note to the 2000 amendment to Federal Rule 702

n. 55.
Fed. R. Evid. 702 advisory committee note to 2000 amendment

n. 57.
Daubert, 509 U.S. at 590.

Add in paragraph beginning with "How can the proponent validate that type of use of the expert's specific technique or theory?" preceding last sentence:
The bottom line is the validation of that claim.

n. 60.
Fed. R. Evid. 901 advisory committee note.

n. 61.
Kumho Tire Co., Ltd., 526 U.S. at 151.

Replace "does not" in third sentence of paragraph beginning with "Opinion #2":

is inadequate to

Add after first sentence in paragraph beginning with "Opinion #3":

This is sometimes termed the G2i problem—the challenge of justifying an inference from the general to the individual.[64.50]

[64.50]Faigman, Monahan & Slobogin, Group to Individual (G2i) Inference in Scientific Expert Testimony, 81 U. Chi. L. Rev. 417, 419, 430, 432, 451-52 (2014). Of course, if the expert cannot validate the general theory—a proposition such as opinion #1 or #2—the expert cannot leap to any conclusion about the particular instance. If the expert cannot marshal sufficient warrant to justify opinion #1 or #2, the court should certainly not allow the expert to venture opinion #3. However, even if the expert can validate the general theory, the expert may lack an adequate basis for expressing opinion #3. According to the authors, "scientists almost invariably inquire into phenomena at the group level . . . ." If that is the extent of the expert's testing data, the expert should be limited to testifying about "general group-level phenomena." "Testing the basis of diagnostic testimony" such as opinion #3 requires a different type of research that is often difficult to design and conduct. There might be a large number of variables to control in any experiment. However, regardless of

how difficult the task is, after General Elec. Co. v. Joiner, 522 U.S. 136, 118 S. Ct. 512, 139 L. Ed. 2d 508, 48 Fed. R. Evid. Serv. 1, 177 A.L.R. Fed. 667 (1997), the trial judge may not allow the expert to connect the general theory to the individual case solely by the expert's subjective ipse dixit. It is ideal when the expert can show that the standard for making the connection is empirically supported. Failing that, the expert may be able to point to the results of proficiency tests or a feedback loop. In principle, even when the expert can lay an adequate foundation for a general conclusion such as opinion #1 or #2, the judge ought to demand a further, additional foundation for G2i conclusions such as opinion #3. See also Faigman, Where Law and Science (and Religion?) Meet, 93 Tex. L. Rev. 1659, 1675-76 (2015).

n. 66.
Kumho Tire Co., Ltd., 526 U.S. at 152.

n. 70.
Fed. R. Evid. 702 advisory committee note.

Add new footnote to third sentence of paragraph including footnotes 71-73:

At trial, the opponent may certainly point to the factor of the expert's failure to use a superior, scientific methodology to validate his or her premises as a basis for attacking the weight of the expert's testimony.[71.50]

[71.50]Imwinkelried, The Methods of Attacking Scientific Evidence § 10-8   (5th ed. 2014).

Add after footnote 73:

As previously stated, the bottom line should be the question of whether the expert has presented sufficient empirical data and reasoning to validate the hypothesis that by applying the specific theory or technique he or she proposes relying on, the expert can accurately draw the particular inference he or she contemplates testifying to.

n. 74.
Daubert, 509 U.S. at 588.

Add after "in 2000," in paragraph including footnotes 74-76:

reflecting on the *Daubert* line of precedent, the Supreme Court itself remarked that that line of authority prescribes "exacting" standards of reliability.[75.50]

Add to beginning of sentence ending in footnote 76:
In the same year,

[75.50]Weisgram v. Marley Co., 528 U.S. 440, 120 S. Ct. 1011, 145 L. Ed. 2d 958, 53 Fed. R. Evid. Serv. 406, 45 Fed. R. Serv. 3d 735 (2000).

Replace last two sentences of paragraph under heading "The Trustworthiness of the Expert's Minor Premise":
As we shall see, there are three basic methods in which the expert can gain the minor premise information: She could acquire personal knowledge of the facts; other witnesses could provide admissible evidence of the facts, and the expert could be asked to hypothetically assume those facts; or the expert can rely on certain types of secondhand out-of-court reports about the facts.

n. 79.   27.
Imwinkelried, 69 Wash. U. L.Q. at 25-

Add new footnote to fourth sentence of paragraph including footnotes 80-83:
Rule 402 generally provided that relevant evidence is admissible unless it can be excluded under the Constitution, statute, a provision of the Federal Rules themselves, or other court rules adopted pursuant to statutory authority such as the Federal Rules of Civil and Criminal Procedure.[81.50]

[81.50]*See* Fed. R. Evid. 101(b)(5), 402.

n. 86.
Delete first paragraph of footnote.

n. 87.
Add at end of footnote:
The upshot is that if the expert has answered a hypothetical question on direct, during cross-examination even without supporting evidence the ques-

tioner may modify the hypothesis by adding facts, deleting facts, or varying the facts. Imwinkelried, The Methods of Attacking Scientific Evidence § 11-2[c][i]-[iv] (5th ed. 2014).

n. 88.
Delete first paragraph of footnote.

n. 92.
Delete contents of footnote following citation sentence.

Add to end of paragraph including footnotes 88-93:
In the instruction, the judge should identify the theory on which

the passage in the publication is logically relevant to impeach the expert's reasoning process.[93.50]

[93.50]Since this practice permits resort to the text for the limited purpose of impeachment rather than as substantive evidence, the text must be used for a purpose other than showing the truth of the assertions in the text. For example, the cross-examiner might utilize the test to show that: The expert carelessly misapplied the text he or she supposedly relied on; the expert prematurely rejected without good reason a contrary passage in a text he or she recognizes as authoritative; or the expert conducted incomplete research and neglected to find a contrary passage in an authoritative text. Imwinkelried, Rationalization and Limitation: The Use of Learned Treatises to Impeach Opposing Expert Witnesses, 36 Vt. L. Rev. 63, 70-77 (2011).

Add in sentence ending in footnote 94, preceding "such inquiries":

in the judge's discretion,

§ 14   Grounds for expert opinion: Hypothetical questions

n. 1.
4 Weinstein's Federal Evidence Ch. 703 (rev. 2012);

n. 2.
Add at end of footnote.

Of course, the admissible evidence could take the form of a hearsay statement that qualifies under an exemption from or exception to the hearsay prohibition.

Add after hypothetical questions at end of first paragraph:

This phrasing is sometimes referred to as the "long form" of a hypothetical question.

Add new footnote to fourth sentence of second paragraph:

First, on direct examination an expert may state an opinion and the theoretical "reasons" for the opinion without prior disclosure of the underlying data or facts.[4.50]

[4.50]Fed. R. Evid. 705.

n. 5.
Add in third sentence of footnote, after "content":
to former Rule 705

n. 6.
Add in first sentence of second paragraph of footnote, after "content":

to the former Rule

n. 8.
Fed. R. Evid. 703 advisory committee note.

Add at end of sentence ending in footnote 11, after "part of it":

—the so-called "short form" of a hypothetical question

Add in sentence ending in footnote 17, preceding "present admissible":

ordinarily

Delete sentence ending in footnote 18 and footnote.

Renumber footnote 19 to 18.

n. 18.   411 F.2d 533 (3d Cir. 1969);
Friedman v. General Motors Corp.,

Add after renumbered footnote 18:
However, that requirement for hypothetical questions is no longer in effect in jurisdictions following the Federal Rules of Evidence.[19]

---

[19]It could be argued that material which may be relied on by the expert under Fed. R. Evid. 703 should be includable in a hypothetical question if such material may be relied on in an opinion without the use of a hypothetical question under Rule 705. Neither Rule 703 nor Rule 705 expressly requires that an hypothesis be based on admissible evidence. Furthermore, it has been urged that an expert may state his opinion without specifying the elements of the hypothesis that the opinion rests on. Some judges think that these notions are impractical; they rule that so long as a hypothetical question is used, the proponent must indicate that such a question must be based on admissible evidence in the record. Logsdon v. Baker, 517 F.2d 174 (D.C. Cir. 1975); Iconco v. Jensen Const. Co., 622 F.2d 1291 (8th Cir. 1980). This position finds support in the California Law Revision Commission comment to California Evidence Code § 802:

[I]n some cases, a witness is required to [state the basis for his opinion on direct examination] in order to show that his opinion is applicable to the action before the court. Under existing law, where a witness testifies in the form of an opinion not based upon his personal observation, the assumed facts upon which his opinion is based must be stated . . . in order to permit the trier of fact to determine the applicability of the opinion in light of the existence or nonexistence of such facts. Evidence Code Section 802 will not affect the rule set forth in these cases, for it based essentially on the requirement that all evidence must be shown to be applicable—or relevant—to the action.

§ 15   Expert's opinion based on reports of others and inadmissible or unadmitted data and facts

Replace "reports" at end of third sentence of first paragraph with:

statements, sometimes referred to as secondhand reports

n. 4.
Add at end of second paragraph of footnote:
However, judicial support for this restrictive view appears to be waning. George v. Ericson, 250 Conn. 312, 736 A.2d 889 (1999).

Replace end of sentence ending in footnote 6, after "if":

"experts in the particular field would reasonably rely on those kinds of facts or data in forming an opinion on the subject."

n. 6.
Delete paragraph and quote at beginning of footnote.

Add to sentence ending in footnote 7, preceding "reports":

secondhand

n. 8.
Add to end of footnote:
Of course, if the secondhand report is admitted for that narrow purpose, on request the trial judge would give the jury a limiting instruction under Fed. R. Evid. 105.

n. 9.
[Rheingold, The Basis of Medical Testimony, 15 Vand. L. Rev. 473, 531 (1962)];

Replace "relied upon" in second sentence of first paragraph under heading "The Substantive Question Under Rule 703" with:

rely on

n. 10.
In re Japanese Electronic Products Antitrust Litigation, 723 F.2d 238, 277 (3d Cir. 1983), decision rev'd on other grounds, 475 U.S. 574, 106 S. Ct. 1348, 89 L. Ed. 2d 538 (1986) and (abrogated on other grounds by, Pfeiffer by Pfeiffer v. Marion Center Area School Dist., Bd. of School Directors for Marion Center Area School Dist., 917 F.2d 779 (3d Cir. 1990))

Replace "problem" in second sentence of third paragraph under heading "The Substantive Question Under Rule 703" with:

question

Replace "an" in second sentence of first paragraph under heading "The Procedure for Administering Rule 703" with:

a secondhand

Add new footnote at the end of sentence ending with "and even submit it to the jurors for their inspection?":
If the report is in writing, may the proponent formally introduce the report, have the expert quote it, and even submit it to the jurors for their inspection?[22.50]

[22.50]Of course, if the judge admitted the report only for the limited purpose of showing the basis of the expert's opinion, on request the trial judge would give the jury a limiting instruc-tion under Federal Rule 105.

n. 25.
Add at end of footnote:
But see Sklansky, Evidentiary Instructions and the Jury as Other, 65 Stan.

L. Rev. 407, 410, 414-19, 424-30, 451 (2013) (the author surveys 33 published studies of the efficacy of instructions; in his view, the assertions about the ineffectiveness of instructions are "at best greatly exaggerated. Eviden- tiary instructions probably do work although imperfectly and better under some circumstances than others"; "The conventional wisdom about evidentiary instructions—'of course they don't work'" is "unduly pessimistic").

Replace "Several" in sentence including footnotes 27-28 with:
A number of

Add to beginning of first paragraph under heading "The Impact of Williams v. Illinois on the Future of Rule 703":
As previously stated, the conventional wisdom is that secondhand reports admitted under Rule 703 are used for a legitimate, noneharsay purpose. However, in 2012, five Supreme Court justices challenged the orthodoxy.

n. 31.
Add at end of footnote:
See Imwinkelried, The Gordian Knot of the Treatment of Secondhand Facts Under Federal Rule of Evidence 703 Governing the Admissibility of Expert Opinions: Another Conflict Between Logic and Law, 3 U. Denv. Crim. L. Rev. 1 (2013).

Add to first sentence of fifth paragraph under heading "The Impact of Williams v. Illinois on the Future of Rule 703", preceding "report":

secondhand

n. 33.
Fed. R. Evid. 703 advisory committee note.

Add to last paragraph in section, preceding "report":

secondhand

§ 16 Should the hypothetical question be retained?

Replace "seem to" in sentence ending in footnote 3 with:

generally

n. 5.
Delete first two sentences of first paragraph of footnote.

n. 6.
Delete cross-reference to footnotes.

§ 17 Proposals for improvement of the practice relating to expert testimony

n. 12.
Replace first paragraph in footnote and quote with:
Effective December 1, 2011, restyled Fed. R. Evid. 706 provides:
(a) Appointment Process. On a party's motion or on its own, the

court may order the parties to show cause why expert witnesses should not be appointed and may ask the parties to submit nominations. The court may appoint any expert that the parties agree on and any of its own choosing. But the court may only appoint someone who consents to act.

(b) Expert's Role. The court must inform the court of the expert's duties. The court may do so in writing and have a copy filed with the clerk or may do so orally at a conference in which the parties have an opportunity to participate. The expert: (1) must advise the parties of any findings the expert makes; (2) may be deposed by any party; (3) may be called to testify by the court or any part; and (4) may be cross-examined by any part, including the party that called the expert.

(c) Compensation. The expert is entitled to reasonable compensation, as set by the court. The compensation is payable as follows: (1) in a criminal case or in a civil case involving just compensation under the Fifth Amendment, from any funds that are provided by law; and (2) in any other civil case, by the parties in the proportion and at the time the court directs—and the compensation is then charged like other costs.

(d) Disclosing the Appointment to the Jury. The court may authorize disclosure to the jury that the court appointed the expert.

(e) Parties' Choice of Their Own Experts. This rule does not limit a party calling its own experts.

Delete first two sentences of second paragraph of footnote.

Add after next to last sentence of paragraph beginning with "Limited court appointments of experts to provide the judge and jury with a primer on the relevant expertise":
Moreover, the use of limited appointments might make courtroom appearance more attractive to some experts. Outstanding scientists often express the sentiment that they dislike serving as expert witnesses because they find adversary litigation too combative. That sentiment is understandable because, in the typical case, they are asked to opine on an ultimate issue in the case and oppose another expert who has formed a contrary opinion on that issue. If they were offered the opportunity to play a more limited role and merely teach the judge and jury about the general theories and techniques in their field, these scientists might be more willing to participate in litigation.

Replace "it" in seventh sentence of paragraph beginning with "The use of pretrial conferences to narrow the disagreements between the opposing experts.

the conference

Add after quote ending in footnote 23:
Concurrent testimony by experts.[23.50] The next proposal represents a step beyond merely holding a pretrial conference with the experts. Some other common law jurisdictions, notably Australia, have gone farther and developed the practice of concurrent expert testimony—sometimes referred to as "hot-tubbing." In this practice, the opposing experts are required to meet before trial. At trial, the opposing witnesses take the stand at the same time. After preliminary statements, the witnesses are questioned by

the judge and can respond to statements by each other. In one survey of Australian judges, 94.9% responded that they were satisfied with the procedure and thought that the practice had improved the presentation of expert testimony in that jurisdiction. There are several advantages to the procedure. One is that the procedure helps the trier of fact identify the points of agreement and disagreement between the experts. Narrowing the scope of the controversy is especially helpful. Another advantage is that the procedure creates a disincentive to overstated testimony; the expert realizes that the opposing expert is immediately available to point out any exaggeration and explain why the overstatement is fallacious. Some American administrative agencies have used the procedure at their hearings, and a few American trial judges have employed the procedure during bench trials. It may prove difficult to adapt the procedure to jury trials. A free-flowing exchange between the opposing experts could expose the jury to inadmissible evidence. Further, it might be awkward to employ the procedure at a trial during which all the jurors are permitted to pose questions. However, it certainly seems worthwhile to explore the use of this innovative practice at American bench trials.

[23.50]Sonenshein & Fitzpatrick, The Problem of Partisan Experts and the Potential for Reform Through Concurrent Evidence, 62 Defense L.J. 60 (Nov. 2013). The article originally appeared at 32 Rev. Litig. 1 (Wint. 2013). More broadly, procedures designed to facilitate the development of consensus among experts may improve the quality of expert testimony. Wong, Aharoni, Aliyev & De Bois, The Potential of Blind Collaborative Justice: Testing the Impact of Expert Blinding and Consensus Building on the Validity of Forensic Testimony (Rand Corp. 2015).

n. 39.
See Breyer, Introduction, in Reference Manual on Scientific Evidence (3d ed. 2011).

Replace "are signs" in sentence ending in footnote 40 with:

is some evidence

§ 18   Application of the opinion rule to out-of-court statements

Replace first two sentences of second paragraph with:
However, the emerging view is that the opinion doctrine should not be viewed as an absolute rule of exclusion. Rather, the doctrine ought to be conceived a relative norm for the examination of witnesses, preferring when it is feasible the more concrete testimony to the more general and inferential.[3]

Replace "premise" in third sentence with:

conception

Add after footnote 6:

As previously stated, the personal knowledge requirement applies to hearsay declarants as well as trial witnesses.[7]

---

[7]See § 10 supra.

Chapter 4

Cross-Examination and Subsequent Examinations

> **KeyCite®:** Cases and other legal materials listed in KeyCite Scope can be researched through the KeyCite service on Westlaw®. Use KeyCite to check citations for form, parallel references, prior and later history, and comprehensive citator information, including citations to other decisions and secondary materials.

§ 19   The right of cross-examination: Effect of deprivation of opportunity to cross-examine

n. 3.
U.S. v. Mills, 138 F.3d 928, 938, 49 Fed. R. Evid. Serv. 237, 50 Fed. R. Evid. Serv. 59 (11th Cir. 1998), opinion modified on reh'g, 152 F.3d 1324 (11th Cir. 1998)

n. 10.
State v. Bray, 335 S.C. 514, 517 S.E.2d 714 (Ct. App. 1999), aff'd but criticized

on other grounds, 342 S.C. 23, 535 S.E.2d 636 (2000).

Add to first paragraph of footnote, after State v. Bray cite:
The general trauma a child suffers from the defendant's alleged actions and trial is insufficient. State ex rel. Montgomery v. Padilla, 237 Ariz. 263, 349 P.3d 1100 (Ct. App. Div. 1 2015),

as amended, (May 28, 2015) and petition for certiorari filed, 84 U.S.L.W. 3484 (U.S. Feb. 11, 2016).

Add new heading preceding second paragraph of footnote:

Closed-Circuit Television
Ault v. Waid, 654 F. Supp. 2d 465, 486-90 (N.D. W. Va. 2009), aff'd, 414 Fed. Appx. 546 (4th Cir. 2011);

Add to end of second paragraph:
If the defendant is in another room during the witness's testimony, the defendant must have a means of immediately communicating with his or her counsel in the courtroom. U.S. v. Partin, 990 F. Supp. 2d 1219, 1223-26 (M.D. Ala. 2013), subsequent determination, 2014 WL 2831665 (M.D. Ala. 2014). *See* White v. State, 223 Md. App. 353, 116 A.3d 520 (2015) (a forensic serologist's testimony was admitted via a two-way live video conference; the use of the technology did not violate the defendant's confrontation right; the use of the technology promoted the policy of protecting the physical well-being of a significant witness, and the trial judge made adequate, case-specific findings of necessity); Comment, Complying with the Confrontation Clause in the Twenty-First Century: Guidance for Courts and Legislatures Considering Videoconference Testimony Provisions, 86 Temple L. Rev. 150, 151, 155-56 (2013) (" 'At least three circuit courts and three state supreme courts have sustained videoconference testimony for infirm witnesses whose health would not allow them to travel to trial. Another circuit found that the United States' interest in its national security excused a witness's physical presence. Additionally, some courts have permitted the use of such testimony for foreign witnesses, particularly those who live in locations beyond the United States' subpoena power, though others reject this practice").

Some have argued more broadly that as a general proposition, the use of two-way videoconferencing or closed circuit television satisfies the right to personally confront adverse witnesses. Fuster-Escalona v. Florida Dept. of Corrections, 170 Fed. Appx. 627, 629-30 (11th Cir. 2006); U.S. v. Gigante, 166 F.3d 75, 79-83, 51 Fed. R. Evid. Serv.

1 (2d Cir. 1999) (two-way videoconferencing preserves rather than infringes face-to-face confrontation); Harmon, Child Testimony via Two-Way Closed Circuit Television: A New Perspective on Maryland v. Craig in United States v. Turning Bear and United States v. Bordeaux, 7 N.C. J. L. & Tech. 157 (2005) ("The Supreme Court's case-specific holding in Maryland v. Craig was directed at one-way closed circuit testimony"); Comment, Confronting Confrontation in a FaceTime Generation: A Substantial Public Policy Standard to Determine the Constitutionality of Two-Way Live Video Testimony in Criminal Trials, 75 La. L. Rev. 175, 177, 211 (2014) (since two-way video is a "better approximation of true physical confrontation," rather than applying the *Craig* standard, the courts should use a substantial public policy standard to determine the constitutionality of using such technology); Comment, Virtually Face-to-Face: The Confrontation Clause and the Use of Two-Way Video Testimony, 13 Roger Williams U. L. Rev. 565 (2008); Comment, Accusations from Abroad: Testimony of Unavailable Witnesses Via Live Two-Way Videoconferencing Does Not Violate the Confrontation Clause of the Sixth Amendment, 41 U.C. Davis L. Rev. 1671 (2008). *But see* Comment, Complying with the Confrontation Clause in the Twenty-First Century: Guidance for Courts and Legislatures Considering Videoconference Testimony Provisions, 86 Temple L. Rev. 150, 151, 155-56 (2013); Comment, Avoiding Virtual Justice: Video-Teleconference Testimony in Federal Criminal Trials, 56 Cath. U. L. Rev. 683, 684-86 (2007) (the courts have accepted this technology in civil trials; however, in "federal criminal trials . . . there is no clear evidentiary rule . . .. [T]here is dissonance among federal criminal decisions"); Comment, Virtual Confrontation: Is Videoconferencing Testimony by an Unavailable Witness Unconstitutional, 74 U. Chi. L. Rev. 1581, 1582-84 (2007).

Add new heading to precede third paragraph of footnote:

Screens and Shields
Add new heading to precede fourth paragraph of footnote:

Support Persons and Animals
Lucas, 505 F. Supp. at 354
People v. Andrade, 238 Cal. App. 4th
1274, 190 Cal. Rptr. 3d 442, 459-61
(1st Dist. 2015) (the trial judge's failure to sua sponte hold a hearing on the
necessity for a support person did not
violate the defendant's right to confrontation); People v. Spence, 212 Cal.
App. 4th 478, 511-19, 151 Cal. Rptr.
3d 374, 400-06 (4th Dist. 2012) (a support person and a therapy dog); People
v. Myles, 53 Cal. 4th 1181, 139 Cal.
Rptr. 3d 786, 274 P.3d 413 (2012) (a
support person); People v. Stevens, 67
Cal. Rptr. 3d 567, 572-73 (Cal. App.
1st Dist. 2007), review granted and
opinion superseded, 72 Cal. Rptr. 3d
623, 177 P.3d 232 (Cal. 2008) and
judgment aff'd, 47 Cal. 4th 625, 101
Cal. Rptr. 3d 14, 218 P.3d 272 (2009)
(a support person for a 16-year-old
victim); People v. Ybarra, 57 Cal. Rptr.
3d 732, 739 (Cal. App. 5th Dist. 2007),
as modified, (May 9, 2007) and review
granted and opinion superseded, 65
Cal. Rptr. 3d 143, 166 P.3d 2 (Cal. 2007)
Bowers, The Use of "Therapy Dogs" in
Indiana Courtrooms: Why a Dog Might

Not Be a Defendant's Best Friend, 46
Ind. L. Rev. 1289, 1298, 1311-13 (2013)
(discussing the use of support dogs,
teddy bears, and dolls);
*Add new heading to precede fifth
paragraph of footnote:*

Pseudonyms and Disguises
U.S. v. Ramos-Cruz, 667 F.3d 487,
500-01 (4th Cir. 2012) (Salvadoran
citizens permitted to testify under
pseudonyms); U.S. v. El-Mezain, 664
F.3d 467 (5th Cir. 2011), as revised,
(Dec. 27, 2011) (the witnesses were a
legal advisor to the Israel Security and
an employee of the Israeli Defense
Forces; the government presented evidence that terrorist organizations had
sought out the witnesses' true identities);
People v. Brandon, 52 Cal. Rptr. 3d
427, 442 (Cal. App. 2d Dist. 2006), as
modified, (Dec. 20, 2006) and review
granted and opinion superseded, 56
Cal. Rptr. 3d 475, 154 P.3d 1001 (Cal.
2007) and review dismissed, cause
remanded, 67 Cal. Rptr. 3d 172, 169
P.3d 96 (Cal. 2007)
Delete sixth paragraph of footnote.

Add after first sentence of third paragraph:
Of course, the threshold question is whether the witness's re-
sponses amount to a refusal to testify. If the witness suffers a
genuine memory loss, many courts refuse to characterize the
witness's response as a refusal necessitating the striking of the
testimony.[14.30] However, it can be argued that if the witness
untruthfully claims a memory loss, the witness is impliedly refusing to testify. Yet, there is authority that even if the witness is
feigning memory loss, the witness is still deemed available for
cross-examination; " '[t]he witness . . . is in fact subject to cross-
examination, providing a jury with the opportunity to see the demeanor and assess the credibility of the witness . . . .' "[14.50] Assume, though, that the witness expressly refuses to answer
questions.

[14.30]People v. Noriega, 237 Cal. App.
4th 991, 188 Cal. Rptr. 3d 527, 535-36
(4th Dist. 2015), review denied, (Sept.
16, 2015).
[14.50]Noriega, 188 Cal. Rptr. 3d at
535-46.
n. 15.
Whitley v. Ercole, 725 F. Supp. 2d 398
(S.D. N.Y. 2010), rev'd on other grounds

and remanded, 642 F.3d 278 (2d Cir.
2011); Avincola v. Stinson, 60 F. Supp.
2d 133, 154–56 (S.D.N.Y. 1999);
Mercado v. Stinson, 37 F. Supp. 2d 267
(S.D.N.Y. 1999)
Combs v. Com., 74 S.W.3d 738 (Ky.
2002), as amended, (May 24, 2002) and
as amended, (June 10, 2002) (the
defense witness selectively invoked

her Fifth Amendment privilege);

n. 16.
Moormeister v. Golding, 84 Utah 324, 27 P.2d 447 (1933), aff'd, 84 Utah 345, 35 P.2d 307 (1934)

Delete cross-reference.

n. 17.
Delete cross-reference.

n. 18.
Add after "See also":
U.S. v. Wilkens, 742 F.3d 354, 93 Fed. R. Evid. Serv. 888 (8th Cir. 2014), cert. denied, 134 S. Ct. 2744, 189 L. Ed. 2d 778 (2014) ("Direct testimony may remain on the record, even though the witness asserts the privilege against self-incrimination on cross-examination, if the Fifth Amendment is invoked on cross-examination as to collateral matters rather than the details of the direct testimony"); al-though here the witness invoked the privilege during the direct, the court applied the same standard; however, the court found that "[t]his testimony is not collateral matter . . . ."); U.S. v. Davis, 690 F.3d 912, 923-24, 89 Fed. R. Evid. Serv. 232 (8th Cir. 2012), cert. granted, judgment vacated, 133 S. Ct. 2852, 186 L. Ed. 2d 903 (2013) (since the defense witness's refusal related to the substance of his direct testimony rather than a collateral matter, the trial judge did not abuse discretion in striking the entirety of the witness's testimony);

n. 21.
Delete cross-reference.

n. 29.
Curtice v. West, 2 N.Y.S. 507 (Sup 1888), aff'd, 121 N.Y. 696, 24 N.E. 1099 (1890);

Add new footnote to end of second sentence in paragraph including footnotes 30-34:

Although the preceding paragraphs deal with the conduct of parties and witnesses, the infringement of the right of cross-examination may result from the judge's action. The judge has wide discretionary control over the *extent* of cross-examination upon particular topics.[29.50]

[29.50]U.S. v. Landron-Class, 696 F.3d 62, 72, 89 Fed. R. Evid. Serv. 339 (1st Cir. 2012) ("Where the defense is permitted to cross-examine a witness regarding a cooperation agreement, the details of the other charges may not be necessary to establish the potential for bias.").

n. 31.
Alford, 282 U.S. at 694
Van Arsdall, 475 U.S. at 679

n. 32.
See the discussion of *Davis* in Imwinkelried & Garland, Exculpatory Evidence: The Accused's Constitutional Right to Introduce Favorable Evidence § 8-7 (4th ed. 2015).

n. 33.
Imwinkelried & Garland, Exculpatory Evidence: The Accused's Constitutional Right to Introduce Favorable Evidence § 8-7 (4th ed. 2015).

Add in sentence ending in footnote 34, preceding "forecloses":

completely

n. 34.
Sasson, 62 F.3d at 883

Add new paragraph after footnote 34:

A related issue is whether the trial judge may impose a time limit on the duration of the cross-examination. Again, it is well-settled that the judge has discretion to reasonably limit the extent of the cross-examination. However, an unduly severe time limitation might preclude the questioner from exploring an important topic during the cross-examination. Consequently, before announcing a firm time limit, the judge should engage in a particularized assessment to ensure that the allotted time is adequate.[35]

---

[35]In re Peters, 642 F.3d 381, 389   (2d Cir. 2011).

§ 20   Form of interrogation

n. 1.

Replace first sentence of second paragraph of footnote with:
Rev. Unif. R. Evid. (1974) 611(c) provides: "Ordinarily leading questions should be permitted on cross-examination."

n. 4.

Delete "former Fed. R. Evid. 611 and" from first sentence of second paragraph of footnote.

§ 21   Scope of cross-examination: Restriction to matters opened up on direct: the various rules

n. 5.

Delete "and former Fed. R. Evid. 611(b)" from first sentence of second paragraph of footnote.
Construction and Application of Provision of Rule 611(b) of Federal Rules of Evidence that Cross-Examination Should be Limited to Subject Matter of Direct Examination, 93 A.L.R. Fed. 2d 243.

n. 15.

Add after "E.g.,"

U.S. v. Bozovich, 782 F.3d 814, 815-17, 97 Fed. R. Evid. Serv. 167 (7th Cir. 2015) (the defendant's pre-arrest statements to agents about who supplied him with heroin were reasonably related to the subject matter of the defendant's direct examination; the defendant's direct testimony " 'opened him[ ] up for cross-examination' " about the pre-arrest statements);

Delete cross-reference at end of footnote.

Add new footnote to seventh sentence of paragraph including footnotes 15-16:
These instructions list the essential legal elements which the burdened party must prove to prevail on that theory.[16.30]

[16.30]The most popular instruction set in federal practice is O'Malley, Grenig & Lee, Federal Jury Practice and Instructions (6th ed. 2006) (9 vols.).

Add new footnote to end of tenth sentence of paragraph including footnotes 15-16:
Under the legal test, on cross-examination the prosecutor could

inquire about distinct acts by the accused so long as the other acts were logically relevant to the element of *mens rea*; the prosecution would not be limited to the historical events mentioned during the witness's direct examination.[16.50]

[16.50]Fed. R. Evid. 404(b)(2) expressly states that evidence of a person's other misconduct can be admitted on a non-character theory of logical relevance to prove "intent." This may be "the most common use of uncharged misconduct evidence." Leonard, The New Wigmore:

Evidence of Other Misconduct and Similar Events § 7.1, at 426 (2009).

n. 20.

Delete cross-reference to note from second paragraph of footnote.

Add at end of section:

The Questioner's Ability to Introduce Exhibits During Cross

Suppose that the cross-examiner would like to introduce an exhibit relevant to a fact that is within the scope of cross-examination under whatever view the jurisdiction takes. The question is whether the trial judge may enforce a rule that a questioner may not introduce exhibits during cross-examination. The better view is that if the cross-examiner can lay the foundation for an exhibit, the cross-examiner may proffer the exhibit at that time.[24] Nevertheless, in their courtroom some trial judges do not permit cross-examiners to introduce exhibits. Appellate courts have generally upheld the practice for the stated reason that the practice affects only the timing of the introduction of the exhibit.[25]

---

[24]Tanford, The Trial Process: Law, Tactics and Ethics 387 (2d ed. 1993). *See also* Tanford, The Trial Process: Law, Tactics and Ethics 292 (4th ed. 2009).

[25]U.S. v. Vallone, 698 F.3d 416,

454-57 (7th Cir. 2012), cert. granted, judgment vacated, 133 S. Ct. 2825, 186 L. Ed. 2d 881 (2013) and opinion modified and reinstated, 752 F.3d 690 (7th Cir. 2014).

§ 23   Formal and practical consequences of the restrictive rules: effect on order of proof: Side-effects

Add new footnote to eighth sentence in second paragraph:
Admittedly, to a degree the restrictive rules promote the orderly presentation of proof.[4.50]

[4.50]The Supreme Court itself has acknowledged the litigant's felt need to tell a coherent, compelling story at trial. Old Chief v. U.S., 519 U.S. 172, 117 S. Ct. 644, 136 L. Ed. 2d 574, 45

Fed. R. Evid. Serv. 835 (1997); *see* Lempert, Narrative Relevance, Imagined Juries, and a Supreme Court Inspired Agenda for Jury Research, 21 St. Louis U. Pub. L. Rev. 15 (2002).

§ 24 The scope of the judge's discretion under the wide-open and restrictive rules

n. 6.
Fed. R. Evid. 611(b) advisory commit-

tee note, Preliminary Draft, 46 F.R.D. 161, 304.

Add to sentence ending in footnote 12, after "discretion":

to require recall

§ 25 Application of wide-open and restrictive rules to the cross-examination of parties: (a) Civil parties

n. 4.
Delete cross-reference to footnote.

n. 8.
Delete cross-reference to footnote.

§ 26 Application of wide-open and restrictive rules to the cross-examination of parties: (b) The accused in a criminal case

n. 1.
4 Weinstein's Federal Evidence § 611.04 (rev. 2014);

S.E.2d 874 (1968), judgment vacated on other grounds, 392 U.S. 665, 88 S. Ct. 2310, 20 L. Ed. 2d 1359 (1968).

n. 3.
State v. McDaniel, 272 N.C. 556, 158

Replace sentence ending in footnote 8 with:
Eventually, constitutional doctrine may well determine the outer limits of cross-examination concerning the degree to which the accused waives his privilege of self-incrimination by taking the stand and testifying.[8]

§ 27 Merits of the systems of wide-open and restricted cross-examination

n. 1.
4 Weinstein's Federal Evidence § 611. 03[1] (rev. 2012).

n. 7.
Delete cross-reference to footnote.

§ 28 Cross-examination about witness's inconsistent past writings: Must examiner show the writing to the witness before questioning about its contents?

n. 3.
Nizer, The Art of Jury Trial, 32 Cornell L.Q. 59, 68 (1946).

to the former Rule

n. 12.
Add in second paragraph of footnote, after "content":

Replace "essence" in last sentence of last paragraph of section with:

thrust

§ 29   The standard of relevancy as applied on cross-examination: Trial judge's discretion

Research References
West's Key Number Digest, Witnesses ⚮267, 270

n. 8.
Add after "See also" in second paragraph of footnote:
U.S. v. Ramos-Cruz, 667 F.3d 487, 500-01 (4th Cir. 2012) (two Salvadoran citizens were allowed to testify under pseudonyms; the government submitted in camera affidavits describing specific threats against the witnesses); U.S. v. El-Mezain, 664 F.3d 467 (5th Cir. 2011), as revised, (Dec. 27, 2011) (the witnesses were a legal advisor for the Israel Security Agency and an employee of the Israeli Defense Forces; the government presented evidence

that terrorist organizations had sought out the witnesses' true identities); People v. Ramirez, 55 Cal. App. 4th 47, 64 Cal. Rptr. 2d 9 (1st Dist. 1997) (it was permissible for a rape victim to testify as "Jane Doe");

Replace after "But see":
Wilson v. Vermont Castings, 977 F. Supp. 691, 48 Fed. R. Evid. Serv. 189 (M.D. Pa. 1997), aff'd, 170 F.3d 391, 51 Fed. R. Evid. Serv. 922 (3d Cir. 1999)

n. 10.
Alford, 282 U.S. at 692

Move sentence ending in footnote 12 to end of third paragraph.

Renumber footnote 13 to footnote 12.

The courts recognize that a rule strictly limiting cross questions to those relevant to the issues on the historical merits would cripple these kinds of examination.[13]

---

[13]Accordingly, some opinions point out that the rules of relevancy are not applied with the same strictness on cross-examination as on direct: State v. Smith, 140 Me. 255, 37 A.2d 246 (1944); O'Sullivan v. Simpson, 123 Mont. 314, 212 P.2d 435 (1949); Grocers Supply Co. v. Stuckey, 152 S.W.2d 911 (Tex. Civ. App. Galveston 1941), writ refused (during cross-examination,

any fact bearing on witness's credit is relevant). Fed. R. Evid. 611(b) and Unif. R. Evid. 611(b) permit cross-examination upon "matters affecting the witness's credibility." Rule 611(a) clearly emphasizes the trial judge's discretion in these matters.

n. 16.
Alford, 282 U.S. at 694

§ 30   The cross-examiner's art

n. 3.
Nizer, The Art of Jury Trial, 32 Cornell

L.Q. 59, 68 (1946)

Add in sentence following footnote 4, preceding "expense":

time and

Replace sentence ending with footnote 6 with:
Oral suggestions to the cross-examiner at the counsel table should be avoided.[6]

Add to end of first sentence following sub-heading "Know when to conclude the cross-examination and try to end on a high note", after "witness":

to embellish

Replace "combative" in last sentence of second paragraph following sub-heading "Cross-examine for the jury, not for your client" with:
aggressive

§ 31 Cross-examination revalued

n. 6.
Gardner, The Perception and Memory of Witnesses, 18 Cornell L.Q. 391, 404 (1933);

n. 7.
State v. Foster, 81 Wash. App. 444,

915 P.2d 520 (Div. 1 1996), aff'd, 135 Wash. 2d 441, 957 P.2d 712 (1998)

Delete cross-reference to footnote.

§ 32 Redirect and subsequent examinations

Replace "uniform practice" in sentence ending in footnote 3 with:

consensus

n. 5.
Delete second paragraph of footnote, including quote of Rule.
Add after "E.g.," in third paragraph of footnote:
U.S. v. Hansen, 563 Fed. Appx. 675

(11th Cir. 2014) (the judge has discretion to terminate the defendant's redirect examination of a witness in order to avoid wasting timing and protect the witness from harassment);

Add after footnote 8:
The most intelligent use of redirect is usually to give the witness an opportunity to deny or explain a seemingly impeaching fact mentioned during cross-examination.

Chapter 5

Impeachment and Support

KeyCite®: Cases and other legal materials listed in KeyCite Scope can be researched through the KeyCite service on Westlaw®. Use KeyCite to check citations for form, parallel references, prior and later history, and comprehensive citator information, including citations to other decisions and secondary materials.

---

§ 33   Introduction: Bolstering, impeachment, and rehabilitation

Add to sixth sentence of fourth paragraph, preceding "attack on the witness's character":

ad hominem

Add in last sentence of fourth paragraph, after "other facts":

such as bias

Add to third sentence of fifth paragraph, after "good faith basis":

in fact

§ 34   Prior inconsistent statement impeachment: Degree of inconsistency required

n. 1.
4 Weinstein's Federal Evidence Chs. 607, 613 (rev. 2012);

n. 2.
4 Weinstein's Federal Evidence Chs. 607, 613 (rev. 2012);

Add to seventh sentence of second paragraph, preceding "consider":

may

Replace "it" at end of sentence ending in footnote 10 with:

the statement

n. 12.
Add after "See":
U.S. v. Carter, 776 F.3d 1309, 1328 (11th Cir. 2015) ("a witness may not be impeached with a third party's characterization or interpretation of a prior oral statement unless the witness has subscribed to or otherwise adopted the statement as his own"); U.S. v. Cervantes, 646 F.3d 1054, 1060 (8th Cir. 2011) (the defendant "adopted" the statements "as his own");

Add in sentence following footnote 15, after "On request,":

under Federal Rule 105

n. 16.
Add at end of footnote:
In People v. Campbell, 2015 IL App (1st) 131196, 395 Ill. Dec. 55, 37 N.E.3d 891 (App. Ct. 1st Dist. 2015), appeal denied, 397 Ill. Dec. 457, 42 N.E.3d 372 (Ill. 2015), at trial the witness testified about a shooting. At a prior grand jury hearing, the witness had testified about neighborhood criminal gangs, unrelated shootings, and the death of the defendant's brother. Those statements at the grand jury hearing did not constitute prior inconsistent statements, since the witness did not give any trial testimony on those topics.

Add to sentence ending in footnote 18, following "Under the":

better and

n. 20.
U.S. v. Catalan-Roman, 585 F.3d 453 (1st Cir. 2009), as amended, (Dec. 23, 2009)

Add at end of footnote:
See also U.S. v. Meza, 701 F.3d 411, 426, 89 Fed. R. Evid. Serv. 1139 (5th Cir. 2012) ("The plain language of the Rule makes no exception for prior inconsistent statements that are explained instead of denied. [E]xplanations and denials run the gamut of human ingenuity, ranging from a flat denial, to an admitted excuse, to a slant, to a disputed explanation, or to a convincing explanation. Whether flatly denied or convincingly explained, the inconsistency can stay inconsistent").

Add after footnote 24:

The jury can later decide which sense of the term the witness had in mind at the time of the statement.

n. 25.

Replace second sentence and quote with:

See the comment by Davis, J. in Judson v. Fielding, 227 A.D. 430, 237 N.Y.S. 348 (3d Dep't 1929), aff'd, 253 N.Y. 596, 171 N.E. 798 (1930):

In considering the evidence so sharply in dispute, the jury was entitled to know the contrary views the witness had expressed when the incident was fresh in his mind, uninfluenced by sympathy or other cause. Very often by calm reflection a witness may correct inaccurate observations or erroneous impressions hastily formed. But the jury should have all the facts in making an appraisement of the value and weight to be given the testimony.

§ 35   Prior inconsistent statements: Opinion in form

n. 3.

Judson v. Fielding, 227 A.D. 430, 237 N.Y.S. 348 (3d Dep't 1929), aff'd, 253 N.Y. 596, 171 N.E. 798 (1930)

Replace "another" in first sentence of second paragraph with:

the logically antecedent

Replace sentence ending in footnote 6 with:

Wigmore contended that the rule ought to go no farther than excluding opinion as superfluous when the proponent can conveniently resort to more concrete statements.[6]

Add to sentence including footnotes 8-10, after "later opinions":

routinely

§ 36   Prior inconsistent statements: Extrinsic evidence and previous statements as substantive evidence of the facts stated

n. 6.

Miller v. Com., 241 Ky. 818, 45 S.W.2d 461 (1932) (overruled in part by, Jett v. Com., 436 S.W.2d 788 (Ky. 1969)) (while *Jett* bars the substantive use of the evidence in those circumstances, it overrules *Miller* to the extent that *Miller* barred the impeachment use of the evidence)

§ 37   Prior inconsistent statements: Requirement of preliminary questions on cross-examination as "foundation" for proof by extrinsic evidence

Add new heading at beginning of section:

The Common Law

n. 8.

Add after first sentence of second paragraph of footnote:

U.S. v. Brown, 788 F.3d 830, 834, 97 Fed. R. Evid. Serv. 1017 (8th Cir. 2015) (" 'A claimed inability to recall, when disbelieved by the trial judge, may be viewed as inconsistent with previous statements when the witness does not deny that the previous statements were in fact made.' . . . But '[t]he trial judge may be accorded reasonable discretion in determining whether a claim of faulty memory is inconsistent with statements previously given.' . . . 'Where a witness in good faith asserts that she cannot remember the relevant events, the trial court may, in its discretion, exclude the allegedly prior inconsistent statement.' ");

n. 9.
U.S. v. Cooper, 767 F.3d 721, 728, 95 Fed. R. Evid. Serv. 432 (7th Cir. 2014),

cert. denied, 135 S. Ct. 1015, 190 L. Ed. 2d 884 (2015) and cert. denied, 135 S. Ct. 1016, 190 L. Ed. 2d 884 (2015) (the witness claimed that she could not recall her prior statement to the grand jury); United States v. Corcoran, 2014 WL 7335548 (N.M.C.C.A. 2014), review denied, 74 M.J. 461 (C.A.A.F. 2015) ("Evasiveness or inability to recall may constitute an inconsistency");

n. 10.
The decision in U.S. v. Whalen, 578 Fed. Appx. 533 (6th Cir. 2014), discusses the split of authority.

Add new heading preceding fourth paragraph:

Federal Rule of Evidence 613

Add to sentence ending in footnote 13, preceding "requirements":

express

n. 13.
Add in second sentence of footnote, after "content":

to the former Rule

Add new heading preceding sixth paragraph:

The Case for Granting the Trial Judge Discretion to Require a Foundation

Replace first sentence of sixth paragraph with:
To understand the policy rationale for the common law limitations on extrinsic evidence of inconsistent statements, one must keep in mind that if prior inconsistent statements are admissible only for purposes of impeachment, the traditional foundation requirement serves the useful function of helping confine the use of such statements as to credibility and discouraging the trier of fact from misusing them as substantive evidence.

Replace "formally" in fifth sentence of sixth paragraph with:

theoretically

Add to last sentence of sixth paragraph, after "prior statement":

during cross-examination

Replace "sweeping" in second sentence of eighth paragraph with:

radical

Add to sixth sentence of eighth paragraph, after "trial testimony":

and there is a significant time lapse between the witness's testimony and the later introduction of the extrinsic evidence about the inconsistent statement

n. 16.
Whitley v. Ercole, 725 F. Supp. 2d 398, 413 (S.D. N.Y. 2010), rev'd on other grounds and remanded, 642 F.3d 278 (2d Cir. 2011)

Add new heading above ninth paragraph:

Miscellaneous Issues

Replace sentence ending in footnote 20 with:
Suppose that the person attacked is not on the stand but instead the testimony introduced was given at a deposition, prior trial, or some other hearing, and the person made an inconsistent statement before the hearing. At common law, most prior decisions applying the traditional requirements exclude the inconsistent statement unless the foundation question was asked at the prior hearing.[20]

n. 21.
  Delete cross-reference to footnote.
n. 22.
  Add to first sentence of third paragraph, after "content":

to the former Rule

n. 29.
  Delete "Former Fed. R. Evid. 613(b) and" from first paragraph of footnote.

Replace first sentence of last paragraph with:
Again in jurisdictions in which a foundational question is required but the cross-examiner overlooks it, the judge should have discretion to admit extrinsic evidence of the inconsistent statement based on such factors as the cross-examiner's ignorance of the inconsistent statement at the time when the witness was cross-examined, the importance of the testimony under attack, and the practicability of recalling the witness.

n. 31.
  Delete cross-reference to footnote from second paragraph.

§ 38   Prior inconsistent statements: Rule against impeaching one's own witness

Replace first heading in section:

The Common Law Voucher Rule

Add after footnote 4:
However, at common law the voucher rule is not limited to prior inconsistent statement impeachment.

Add in sentence including footnotes 5-6, after "largely":

intact

Add new heading after third paragraph:

The Early Reforms

Replace second sentence of fifth paragraph with:
However, whether the reform was effected by statute or decision, at this point in the evolution of the voucher rule some courts imposed two troublesome limitations.

n. 13.
Replace cite in second paragraph: Fed. R. Civ. P. 32 advisory committee note (1972).

Add to sentence ending in footnote 14, preceding "statements":

prior inconsistent

Add new heading above sixth paragraph:

Federal Rule of Evidence 607

Add to first sentence of sixth paragraph, preceding "abandoned":

gone farther and altogether

Replace "These rules" in sentence ending in footnote 17 with:
Rule 607

Add after footnote 17:
Under Rule 607, there is no requirement that the proponent show that the witness's testimony was either surprising or positively harmful.

Start new paragraph with sentence following footnote 17 and att at beginning:
Yet, in some situations, several courts have refused to give Rule 607 a literal construction.

Add to beginning of sentence ending in footnote 18:
In particular,

n. 20.
Replace quote in footnote:
The rule in this Circuit, however, is that "the prosecutor may not use such a statement under the guise of impeachment for the primary purpose of placing before the jury substantive evidence which is not otherwise admissible." Miller, 664 F.2d at 97; Whitehurst v. Wright, 592 F.2d 834, 839-40 (5th Cir. 1979); United States v. Dobbs, 448 F.2d 1262 (5th Cir. 1971). Every circuit to consider this question has ruled similarly. See, e.g., United States v. Webster, 734 F.2d 1191, 1192 (7th Cir. 1984); United States v. Fay, 668 F.2d 375, 379 (8th Cir. 1981); United States v. DeLillo, 620 F.2d 939, 946 (2d Cir. . . . 1980); United States v. Morlang, 531 F.2d 183, 190 (4th Cir. 1975); United States v. Coppola, 479 F.2d 1153, 1156-58 (10th Cir. 1973); United States v. Michener, 152 F.2d 880, 883 n.3 (3d Cir. 1945); Kuhn v. United States, 24 F.2d 910, 913 (9th Cir. . . . 1928).

n. 22.
Imwinkelried & Garland, Exculpatory
Evidence: The Accused's Constitutional

Right to Introduce Favorable Evidence
§ 8-2 (4th ed. 2015).

§ 39   Bias and partiality

n. 3.
Abel, 469 U.S. at 50
Imwinkelried & Garland, Exculpatory

Evidence: The Accused's Constitutional
Right to Introduce Favorable Evidence
§ 8-7[d], at 404-05 (4th ed. 2015).

Replace "article" in sentence ending in footnote 4 with:

rules

n. 4.
Abel, 469 U.S. at 51

n. 7.
    Add at end of footnote:
See Miller UK Ltd. v. Caterpillar, Inc.,
17 F. Supp. 3d 711, 723 (N.D. Ill. 2014)
("Financial interest in a case is always
relevant to the question of bias
. . . .").

n. 12.
U.S. v. Ozuna, 674 F.3d 677, 682 (7th
Cir. 2012) ("common membership in
an organization, even without proof
that the witness or party has personally adopted its tenets, is certainly
probative of bias");

Replace "toward" in sentence including footnotes 15-19 with:

against

n. 18.
    Add to end of footnote:
In State v. Hart, 239 N.C. 709, 80
S.E.2d 901, 41 A.L.R.2d 1199 (1954),
the court went beyond *Wray* and announced that as a general proposition,
a party has a right to impeach an opposing witness for bias.

n. 19.
U.S. v. Willis, 43 F. Supp. 2d 873,
880-81 (N.D. Ill. 1999), aff'd, 248 F.3d
1161 (7th Cir. 2000), as corrected, (Feb.

7, 2001)

n. 24.
    Add at end of footnote:
In 2002, the Kentucky Supreme Court
overruled *Current supra* to the extent
that it was contrary to the rule that
the amount of money a witness is paid
for testifying in a particular case is
disclosable on cross-examination.
Tuttle v. Perry, 82 S.W.3d 920 (Ky.
2002).

Add in sentence including footnotes 25-31, after "the witness"
following footnote 25:

could be but

n. 27.
Vogleson v. State, 250 Ga. App. 555,
552 S.E.2d 513 (2001), judgment aff'd,
275 Ga. 637, 571 S.E.2d 752 (2002)

n. 28.
Munchinski v. Wilson, 807 F. Supp.
2d 242, 287 (W.D. Pa. 2011), judgment
aff'd, 694 F.3d 308 (3d Cir. 2012)

Add after footnote 34:
As these cases indicate, the courts generally tend to permit the
impeachment so long as the underlying facts "support a reason-

able inference of bias that relates to a witness's credibility
. . . ."[34.50] However,

___

[34.50]U.S. v. Sigillito, 759 F.3d 913, 938 (8th Cir. 2014).

n. 35.

Add after "See":
U.S. v. Sanders, 708 F.3d 976 (7th Cir. 2013) (the trial judge did not abuse discretion in limiting the extent of the cross-examination of a government witness about her convictions and sentences; despite those limitations, the judge allowed the defense counsel to present the jury with his theory of the witness's motive to lie);

Add to first sentence following heading "Foundational Question on Cross-examination", after "foundational question":

on cross-examination

n. 42.
Delete "Former Fed. R. Evid. 611(a) and" from first sentence of footnote.

Add to paragraph including footnotes 41-43, adding to the beginning of sentence ending in footnote 43:
Assume that the judge exercises her discretion to require a foundation. On that assumption,

Add to sentence ending in footnote 48:

restyled

n. 48.
Replace cross-reference to footnote.
See this section, note 43

§ 40   Character: In general

n. 2.
Add at end of footnote:
A prediction of the person's conduct is especially suspect when it is based on only one instance of the person's conduct. Imwinkelried, Reshaping the "Grotesque" Doctrine of Character Evidence: The Reform Implications of the Most Recent Psychological Research, 36 Sw. U.L. Rev. 741, 761 (2008) ("in a 2001 survey of the literature, one psychologist points out that in the prior published studies attempting to predict behavior on the basis of inferences drawn from a single prior instance of conduct, the level of predictability was 'at best .30'—worse than flipping a coin").

§ 41   Character: Misconduct, for which there has been no criminal conviction

Add new heading above second paragraph:

The Split of Authority Over the Propriety of This Impeachment Technique

Add new footnote in first sentence of second paragraph, after "witness's":

Yet, the English common law tradition of "cross-examination to credit" permits counsel to broadly inquire about the witness's[2.50]

[2.50]Of course, it is assumed that the association or act is the witness's. *See* U.S. v. Abair, 746 F.3d 260, 93 Fed. R. Evid. Serv. 1204 (7th Cir. 2014) (the trial judge abused discretion in permitting the prosecutor to cross-examine the defendant about alleged false statements in a tax return; there was evidence that the defendant's husband had provided the allegedly false statements on the tax return, and there was no reason to doubt the defendant's testimony that she did not see the return before her husband filed it electronically).

Replace sentence ending in footnote 6 with:

By its terms, Federal Rule 608(b) permits the cross-examiner to inquire about acts which are relevant only to the witness's "character [trait] for . . . untruthfulness. . . ."

n. 6.

Delete paragraph with quote from Former Fed. R. Evid. 608(b).

Add in third paragraph of footnote, after after "E.g.,":

U.S. v. Parker, 790 F.3d 550, 559 (4th Cir. 2015) (fraudulent conduct); U.S. v. Bayard, 642 F.3d 59, 63 (1st Cir. 2011) (use of the victim's credit cards); U.S. v. Weekes, 611 F.3d 68 (1st Cir. 2010) (use of false social security numbers);

Add in third paragraph of footnote:
Redd v. New York State Div. of Parole, 923 F. Supp. 2d 393 (E.D. N.Y. 2013)

(the witness allegedly lied about her income in order to obtain the appointment of pro bono counsel);

n. 8.

Com. v. Ornato, 191 Pa. Super. 581, 159 A.2d 223 (1960), judgment aff'd, 400 Pa. 626, 163 A.2d 90 (1960);

n. 9.

Replace cross-reference to footnote in second sentence of footnote:
7

n. 11.

Remove reference to note from cite to Federal Rules of Eivdence.

Replace "sway" in sentence including footnotes 12-15 with:

should inform the exercise of the

Delete sentence ending in footnote 16.

Add at beginning of fifth paragraph:

Safeguards

Assume that the jurisdiction in question recognizes this impeachment technique. Nevertheless, there are important safeguards intended to prevent the abuse of the technique.

To begin with, the cross-examiner may not pose the question unless she has a good faith basis in fact for the inquiry.[16] There is no invariable requirement that the cross-examiner demonstrate the good faith basis at sidebar before posing the question; but if the direct examiner objects, the judge can require that the cross-examiner establish the basis before asking the question.

---

[16]See § 49 infra. See also U.S. v. McBride, 862 F.2d 1316, 1320, 27 Fed. R. Evid. Serv. 421 (8th Cir. 1988) ("[T]he prosecutor may not, by innuendo, attack a witness' credibility by asking about a witness' criminal conduct when the prosecutor has no basis for the question."). In the court's discretion counsel may be required to disclose his good faith basis outside the jury's presence prior to cross-examination. Michelson v. U.S., 335 U.S. 469, 472, 69 S. Ct. 213, 93 L. Ed. 168 (1948) ("The trial court asked counsel for the prosecution, out of the presence of the jury, 'Is it a fact according to the best information in your possession, that Michelson was arrested for receiving stolen goods?' Counsel replied that it was, and to support his good faith exhibited a paper record which defendant's counsel did not challenge."); U.S. v. Crippen, 570 F.2d 535, 538, 3 Fed. R. Evid. Serv. 671 (5th Cir. 1978) ("In a recorded colloquy with counsel, the trial judge made certain that there was a factual basis for the attempted impeachment, as there was in the defendant's own statements to the grand jury in the four pages of the transcript then admitted."); Graham, Evidence and Trial Advocacy Workshop, 21 Crim. L. Bull. 495, 510-11 (1985). But see U.S. v. Courtney, 439 Fed. Appx. 383 (5th Cir. 2011); U.S. v. Davis, 609 F.3d 663, 680-81 (5th Cir. 2010) (but "[t]hat does not mean that the basis in fact must be proved as a fact before a good faith inquiry can be made").

Replace fifth paragraph through footnote 26 with:

Next, while the witness's privilege discussed in the prior paragraph was non-constitutional in nature, in some cases the constitutional privilege against self-incrimination may give the witness the right to refuse to answer. A witness who without objecting partially discloses incriminating matter cannot later invoke the privilege when she is asked to complete the disclosure.[22] However, the mere act of testifying does not waive the privilege as to criminal activities relevant solely to attacking the witness's credibility.[23] While an accused, unlike an ordinary witness, has an option whether to testify at all, exacting a waiver as the price of taking the stand is somewhat inconsistent with the right to testify in one's own behalf. Therefore Federal Rule of Evidence and Revised Uniform Rule of Evidence 608(b) provides that the giving of testimony by any witness, including an accused, does not waive the privilege as to matters relating only to credibility.[24]

The final safeguard is the general prohibition of the use of extrinsic evidence to prove the witness's commission of the act of misconduct. The accepted rule limits proof to intrinsic impeachment, that is, cross-examination. Thus, if the witness stands his ground and denies the alleged misconduct, the examiner must ordinarily[25] "take his answer." That expression does not mean that the cross-examiner may not press further to extract an admission,[26] for instance, by reminding the witness of the penalties for perjury. Rather, it means that the cross-examiner may not later call other witnesses to prove the discrediting acts.[27] This limitation is incorporated in Federal Rule of Evidence 608(b).[28] On cross-examination, the questioner should ask the witness directly and bluntly whether he committed the untruthful act. It is improper to inquire whether the witness was "fired," "disciplined," or "demoted" for the alleged act—those terms smuggle into the record implied hearsay statements by third parties who may lack personal knowledge.[29]

---

[22]For more detailed discussion, see § 140 infra.

[23]Coil v. U.S., 343 F.2d 573 (8th Cir. 1965); Wiercinski v. Mangia 57, Inc., 33 F. Supp. 3d 118, 129-30 (E.D. N.Y. 2014), aff'd in part, rev'd in part on other grounds and remanded, 787 F.3d 106, 91 Fed. R. Serv. 3d 1595 (2d Cir. 2015).

Statements in such cases as People v. Sorge, 301 N.Y. 198, 93 N.E.2d 637 (1950), that a witness, including an accused, may be asked on cross-examination "about any vicious or criminal act in his life that has a bearing on his credibility" arguably overlook the constitutional limitation. When the question was raised in People v. Johnston, 228 N.Y. 332, 127 N.E. 186 (1920), the court conceded that the waiver resulting from an accused taking the stand did not extend to facts affecting only credibility.

[24]Fed. R. Evid. 608(b) & Unif. R. Evid. 608(b). See Griffin v. California, 380 U.S. 609, 85 S. Ct. 1229, 14 L. Ed. 2d 106 (1965); Ferguson v. State of Ga., 365 U.S. 570, 81 S. Ct. 756, 5 L. Ed. 2d 783 (1961). The accused's right to testify in his own behalf is of constitutional dimension. See Rock v. Arkansas, 483 U.S. 44, 107 S. Ct. 2704, 97 L. Ed. 2d 37, 22 Fed. R. Evid. Serv. 1128 (1987); Washington v. Texas, 388 U.S. 14, 87 S. Ct. 1920, 18 L. Ed. 2d 1019 (1967).

[25]Suppose that the "witness" being impeached is a hearsay declarant. The impeaching party has no opportunity to question the declarant about the impeaching act. In this situation, some courts hold that Fed. R. Evid. 806 overrides the restriction on extrinsic evidence. U.S. v. Washington, 263 F. Supp. 2d 413, 423 (D. Conn. 2003), adhered to on reconsideration, 294 F.

Supp. 2d 246 (D. Conn. 2003) (noting the split of authority); Hornstein, On the Horns of an Evidentiary Dilemma: The Intersection of Federal Rules of Evidence 806 and 608(b), 56 Ark. L. Rev. 543 (2003).

In Nevada v. Jackson, 133 S. Ct. 1990, 186 L. Ed. 2d 62 (2013), the Supreme Court asserted: "The[r]e are 'good reason[s]' for limiting the use of extrinsic evidence, and the [state] statute [upheld in this case] is akin to the widely accepted rule of evidence law that generally precludes the admission of evidence of specific instances of a witness' conduct to prove the witness' character for untruthfulness. See Fed. Rule. Evid. 608(b) . . . .. The constitutional propriety of this rule cannot be seriously disputed." But see Imwinkelried, Formalism Versus Pragmatism in Evidence: Reconsidering the Absolute Ban on the Use of Extrinsic Evidence to Prove Impeaching, Untruthful Acts That Have Not Resulted in a Conviction, 48 Creighton L. Rev. 213 (2015) (the article notes that this is the only impeachment technique subject to an absolute ban on extrinsic evidence; the article questions whether it is defensible to single out this impeachment technique for such a ban). Compare Rothstein, Just What Evidence of Witness Misdeeds Does Federal Rule of Evidence 608(b) Exclude?, 49 Creighton L.Rev. 121 (2015).

[26]Sorge, 301 N.Y. 198, 93 N.E.2d 637 (when witness denies, examiner in good faith may question further in hope of inducing witness to change answer). But the judge has discretion to limit further exploration of the matter. U.S. v. Bright, 630 F.2d 804, 6 Fed. R. Evid. Serv. 550 (5th Cir. 1980).

[27]U.S. v. Mahdi, 598 F.3d 883, 893 n.11 (D.C. Cir. 2010); State v.

Bowman, 232 N.C. 374, 61 S.E.2d 107 (1950) (improper for state to attack credibility of defendant's witness by calling other witnesses to testify to her acts of misconduct); 3A Wigmore, Evidence § 979 (Chadbourn rev. 1970). See also § 49 infra.

[28]U.S. v. Abel, 469 U.S. 45, 55, 105 S. Ct. 465, 83 L. Ed. 2d 450, 16 Fed. R. Evid. Serv. 838 (1984) (Rule 608(b) "limits the inquiry to cross-examination of the witness, however, and prohibits the cross-examiner from introducing extrinsic evidence of the witness' past conduct.").

As to preservation for appeal of alleged error with respect to a ruling on a motion in limine permitting use of a prior act of misconduct to impeach, see § 52 infra.

[29]U.S. v. Kielar, 791 F.3d 733, 742-43 (7th Cir. 2015) (the witness had been terminated from participating in Medicare and Medicaid); U.S. v. Teron, 478 Fed. Appx. 683 (2d Cir. 2012) (the cross-examination of a police officer about the findings of a Civilian Complaint Review Board); Young v. James Green Management, Inc., 327 F.3d 616, 626 n.7, 61 Fed. R. Evid. Serv. 688 (7th Cir. 2003); U.S. v. Davis, 183 F.3d 231, 257 n.12, 52 Fed. R. Evid. Serv. 732 (3d Cir. 1999), opinion amended, 197 F.3d 662 (3d Cir. 1999); State v. Mosley, 667 S.W.2d 767, 770-71 (Tenn. Crim. App. 1983); Saltzburg, Impeaching the Witness: Prior Bad Acts and Extrinsic Evidence, 7 Crim. Just. 28, 31 (Wint. 1993) ("counsel should not be permitted to circumvent the no-extrinsic-evidence provision by tucking a third person's opinion about prior acts into a question asked of the witness who has denied the act"). *But see* U.S. v. Dvorkin, 799 F.3d 867, 883, 98 Fed. R.

Evid. Serv. 360 (7th Cir. 2015) ("Rule 608(b) 'only prohibits the use of extrinsic evidence, not lines of questioning.' Consequently, the rule 'does not mandate the prohibition of questions regarding the punishment for a given course of conduct.' "; in footnote 38, the court concedes that there is contrary primary and secondary authority); U.S. v. DeSantis, 134 F.3d 760, 48 Fed. R. Evid. Serv. 807, 1998 FED App. 0018P (6th Cir. 1998) (administrative agency finding); Schmertz, Article VI, in Emerging Problems Under the Federal Rules of Evidence 115, 162 (3d ed. 1998) (there is a "disturbing" trend in the cases permitting "counsel to ask witnesses who have already denied the bad conduct whether third parties have expressed their belief that the witness has engaged in the bad acts"; U.S. v. Whitehead, 618 F.2d 523, 5 Fed. R. Evid. Serv. 1046 (4th Cir. 1980) ruled that the cross-examiner could question a defendant about his suspension from the practice of law).

The Advisory Committee Note accompanying the 2003 amendment to Rule 608 states:

It should be noted that the extrinsic evidence prohibition of Rule 608(b) bars any reference to the consequences that a witness might have suffered as a result of an alleged bad act. For example, Rule 608(b) prohibits counsel from mentioning that a witness was suspended or disciplined for the conduct that is the subject of impeachment, when that conduct is offered only to prove the character of the witness. See . . . Stephen A. Saltzburg, Impeaching the Witness: Prior Bad Acts and Extrinsic Evidence, 7 Crim. Just. 29, 31 (Winter 1993) ("counsel should not be permitted to circumvent the no-extrinsic-evidence prohibition by tucking a third person's opinion about prior acts into a question asked of the witness who has denied the act").

Start new paragraph and replace "On the other hand, if" in sentence ending in footnote 30 with:

However, there has been slippage from a broad, absolute prohibition of extrinsic evidence. For example, if

Add at end of fifth paragraph:

In these circumstances, some courts refuse to construe Rule 608(b) as forbidding the use of extrinsic documents during the witness's cross-examination.

Replace last paragraph with:

Some jurisdictions have gone father and allow extrinsic evidence of judicial and jury findings that the witness has given untruthful testimony.[31] These courts believe that those types of findings are so reliable that extrinsic evidence of the findings should be admissible despite the seemingly absolute prohibition codified in Rule 608(b).

---

[31]U.S. v. Cedeno, 644 F.3d 79, 81-82 (2d Cir. 2011), for additional opinion, see, 437 Fed. Appx. 8 (2d Cir. 2011) (a prior adverse credibility finding by a state court); U.S. v. Dawson, 434 F.3d 956, 957-58, 69 Fed. R. Evid. Serv. 292 (7th Cir. 2006) (a judicial determination); U.S. v. Nelson, 365 F. Supp. 2d 381, 387-91 (S.D. N.Y. 2005) (questions about adverse credibility findings against a witness in a previous hearing do not violate the ban on extrinsic evidence); Imwinkelried, Formalism Versus Pragmatism in Evidence: Reconsidering the Absolute Ban on the Use of Extrinsic Evidence to Prove Impeaching, Untruthful Acts That Have Not Resulted in a Conviction, 48 Creighton L. Rev. 213, 228-29 (2015) (collecting cases). In U.S. v. Holt, 486 F.3d 997, 1001-02, 73 Fed. R. Evid. Serv. 577 (7th Cir. 2007), the prosecution called a police officer as a

witness. While the trial judge permitted the defense to cross-examine the officer about underlying conduct, the judge forbade the defense from questioning the officer "about complaints, investigations or discipline." The court distinguished *Dawson*, supra. *But see* U.S. v. Richardson, 793 F.3d 612, 628-29, 97 Fed. R. Evid. Serv. 1512 (6th Cir. 2015), cert. granted, judgment vacated on other grounds, 2016 WL 763200 (U.S. 2016) ("a judicial opinion making a credibility determination does indeed appear to be the type of extrinsic evidence disallowed by Rule 608(b)"; the court also cited another, narrower basis for its decision, namely, that "the previous district judge's incredulity regarding Officer Herzog's testimony was not probative of his general character for truthfulness").

§ 42   Character: Conviction of crime

n. 1.
4 Weinstein's Federal Evidence Ch. 609 (rev. 2012);

n. 2.
Add to end of footnote:
See Comment, Using Prior Corporate Convictions to Impeach, 78 Calif. L. Rev. 1313 (1990) (the author argues that a corporate conviction should be usable to impeach a witness when he or she was directly or indirectly linked to the corporate crime; the person is directly linked when the person was the guilty agent who committed the act; the person is indirectly linked when the person was a corporate policymaker and the act reflected corporate policy).

n. 7.
Delete first paragraph and quote from footnote.

n. 8.
Add at the end of footnote:
See Foley v. Town of Lee, 863 F. Supp. 2d 130, 146, 88 Fed. R. Evid. Serv. 436, 2012 DNH 82 (D.N.H. 2012) ("A conviction for issuing bad checks under New Hampshire law requires proof that the defendant 'issued or passed the check knowing or believing that the check would not be paid by the drawee.' This amounts to proof of a 'dishonest act' for purposes of Rule 609(a)(2)"). *But see* U.S. v. Parker, 17 F. Supp. 3d 676, 678 (W.D. Ky. 2014) (a prior conviction for tampering with physical evidence did not qualify; "As defined by Kentucky law, tampering with physical evidence does not necessitate proving—or the witness admitting—a dishonest or false statement. Although some tampering offenses may indeed involve deceit or false

statements, some may not"); U.S. v.
Ollie, 996 F. Supp. 2d 351, 93 Fed. R.
Evid. Serv. 603 (W.D. Pa. 2014) (while

falsification of a firearms transaction
is crimen falsi, a burglary did not
qualify).

*Replace "settled that negatively" of sentence including footnotes
14-19 with:*

the prevailing view that

n. 20.
U.S. v. Agnew, 385 F.3d 288, 292, 65
Fed. R. Evid. Serv. 438 (3d Cir. 2004),
cert. granted, judgment vacated on
other grounds, 543 U.S. 1136, 125 S.
Ct. 1333, 161 L. Ed. 2d 94 (2005)

n. 23.
U.S. v. Alexander, 48 F.3d 1477, 1488,
41 Fed. R. Evid. Serv. 774 (9th Cir.
1995), as amended on denial of reh'g,
(Apr. 11, 1995);

n. 24.
; State v. Broadnax, 414 S.C. 468, 779
S.E.2d 789 (2015), reh'g granted, (Sept.
8, 2015) (In an earlier opinion, 401
S.C. 238, 736 S.E.2d 688 (App. 2013),
the intermediate appellate court found

error because the trial judge had
treated the robbery conviction as automatically admissible; the intermediate
court also held that the error was prejudicial; on appeal, the supreme court
majority agreed that the conviction
was not automatically admissible but
ruled the error harmless; although he
concurred, Supreme Court Justice
Hearn argued that the trial judge had
not erred; the justice noted that unlike the Advisory Committee Note to
Federal Rule 609, the commentary on
South Carolina Rule 609 does not
expressly refer to "crimen falsi.")

n. 28.
Mehrmanesh, 689 F.2d at 833 n.13

*Add in paragraph including footnotes 29-30, preceding sentence
ending with footnote 30:*
In its Note, the Committee indicated that it would be appropriate
to invoke the amendment when the proponent could "readily"
make the required showing by using "an indictment, a statement
of admitted facts, or jury instructions."

n. 31.
   *Add at end of second paragraph of
footnote:*
But see U.S. v. Arreola-Beltran, 827 F.
Supp. 2d 1188, 1196 (D. Idaho 2011)
("A plea of guilty—especially where
defendant has yet to be sentenced—is
not the same as a conviction for purposes of a Rule 609 impeachment
analysis. [U]ntil that sentencing oc-
curs, a defendant is entitled to with-

draw a guilty plea if they can show a
'just reason' for doing so . . . .").

n. 32.
; Starrs v. Com., 287 Va. 1, 752 S.E.2d
812 (2014) (the court overruled *Jewel,*
supra; the court reasoned that until
the court enters an order adjudicating
guilt, the court has not exercised its
judicial power to render judgment).

Add after first sentence of paragraph including footnotes 38-44
To begin with, the conviction must not only be final; it must also
be constitutionally valid. A conviction cannot be used if it was
obtained in violation of the defendant's right to counsel.[37.50]

[37.50]Loper v. Beto, 405 U.S. 473, 92   S. Ct. 1014, 31 L. Ed. 2d 374 (1972).

See also Roberts, Impeachment by Unreliable Convictions, 55 B.C. L. Rev. 563 (2014) (in U.S. v. Leviner, 31 F. Supp. 2d 23 (D. Mass. 1998), Judge Nancy Gertner "was required to sentence a man whose prior convictions and sentences carried a presumptive weight for sentencing purposes. Judge Gertner declined to accept the presumptive weight, and instead examined the circumstances of the convictions. They left her concerned that some of the convictions had been the result of racial profiling . . . and that she could be compounding injustice were she to 'give literal credit to the record.' Given these concerns, she sentenced Ms. Leviner as if these prior convictions did not exist").

n. 39.

Replace first paragraph of footnote, up to quote, with:
Unif. R. Evid. 609(c) distinguishes between pardons based upon findings of rehabilitation and subsequent good behavior or pardons based on findings of innocence, and other pardons. It provides:

n. 40.

Delete "Former Fed. R. Evid. 609(e)" from beginning of second paragraph of footnote.

n. 42.

Replace second paragraph of footnote, up to quote, with:
The Uniform Rule contains language similar to that of the former Rule. Effective December 1, 2011, restyled Fed. R. Evid. 609(b) reads:

Add after "See" in third paragraph of footnote:
U.S. v. Richardson, 597 Fed. Appx. 328, 338, 96 Fed. R. Evid. Serv. 850 (6th Cir. 2015) ("Richardson had been released from confinement more than ten years prior to the date of trial . . . ."); U.S. v. Stoltz, 683 F.3d 934,

939, 88 Fed. R. Evid. Serv. 1249 (8th Cir. 2012) (" 'confinement' for purposes of the ten-year time limit in Rule 609(b) does not include periods of probation"); United States v. Moore, 75 F. Supp. 3d 444, 454, 96 Fed. R. Evid. Serv. 217 (D.D.C. 2014) ("the clock starts running based on the 'witness's conviction [date] or [his] release from confinement, whichever is later' ");

n. 43.
Sharif v. Picone, 740 F.3d 263, 93 Fed. R. Evid. Serv. 576 (3d Cir. 2014) (noting the split of authority and ruling the conviction inadmissible);

Add after citation sentence in footnote, preceding "See":
However, Tilley v. Page, 181 Ga. App. 98, 351 S.E.2d 464 (1986) (overruled by, Pitmon v. State, 265 Ga. App. 655, 595 S.E.2d 360 (2004)), overruled *Clinkscales,* supra and held that a shoplifting conviction based on a *nolo contendere* plea was admissible for impeachment. In overruling *Tilley,* the *Pitmon* court indicated that there can be divided sentiments within the same jurisdiction.

n. 55.

Replace cross-reference:
§ 52 infra

n. 59.

Delete cross-reference to footnote.

n. 68.

Add at end of footnote:
But see Stanchi & Bowen, This Is Your Sword: How Damaging Are Prior Convictions to Plaintiffs in Civil Trials?, 89 Wash. L. Rev. 901 (2014) ("In our study, the prior conviction evidence did not have a direct impact on the outcome of the civil trial or the credibility of the witness with the conviction").

Replace sixth sentence of paragraph including footnote 68 with:
One horn of the dilemma is the realistic fear that if he stays off the stand, despite contrary judicial instructions his silence alone might prompt the jury to believe him guilty.

Add in sentence including footnote 72, before "proof":

subsequent

Add to beginning of paragraph after quote ending in footnote 75:
The "mere fact" method of proving the accused's prior conviction is intended to reduce the prejudice to an accused who wants to testify at trial. Some commentators have gone farther and argued that this impeachment is so highly prejudicial that conviction impeachment of an accused should be forbidden.

n. 76.
See Imwinkelried & Garland, Exculpatory Evidence: The Accused's Constitutional Right to Introduce Favorable Evidence § 4-2.a(1) (4th ed. 2015).

§ 43   Character: Impeachment by Proof of Opinion or Bad Reputation

n. 1.
4 Weinstein's Federal Evidence §§ 608. 10-.11 (rev. 2012);

n. 7.
Replace first sentence of footnote, up to quote with:
Unif. R. Evid. 608(a) provides:

n. 10.
Athridge v. Iglesias, 167 F. Supp. 2d 389, 398 (D.D.C. 2001), judgment rev'd on other grounds, 312 F.3d 474, 60 Fed. R. Evid. Serv. 214 (D.C. Cir. 2002)

Add at beginning of sentence ending with footnote 14:
In impeachment analysis, the

n. 16.
Shuster v. State, 62 N.J.L. 521, 41 A. 701 (N.J. Sup. Ct. 1898), aff'd, 63 N.J.L. 355, 46 A. 1101 (N.J. Ct. Err. & App. 1899)

n. 24.
State v. Swenson, 62 Wash. 2d 259, 382 P.2d 614 (1963) (overruled on other grounds by, State v. Land, 121 Wash. 2d 494, 851 P.2d 678 (1993))

Add at end of paragraph including footnotes 20-28:
Was the witness a member of the group long enough to have gained a reliable sense of the person's reputation within the group?

n. 29.
Add after first sentence of footnote:
U.S. v. Alcantara-Castillo, 788 F.3d 1186 (9th Cir. 2015) (the prosecutor asked the defendant whether a border patrol agent was "inventing stories" about the defendant); U.S. v. Rivera, 780 F.3d 1084, 1096, 96 Fed. R. Evid. Serv. 1280 (11th Cir. 2015) ("questions by a prosecutor that prod a defendant to accuse another witness of lying . . . are not proper"); Ruhl v. Hardy, 743 F.3d 1083, 1093 (7th Cir. 2014) (Illinois law); U.S. v. Truman, 688 F.3d 129, 143, 88 Fed. R. Evid. Serv. 1433 (2d Cir. 2012); Wilson v. Department of Corrections, 477 Fed. Appx. 715 (11th Cir. 2012) (Florida law);
Add after State v. Graves cite:
Ballard v. State, 408 S.W.3d 327, 332 (Mo. Ct. App. E.D. 2013) (it was objectionable for a prosecutor to ask the defendant whether "everyone has lied . . . except you");
Add after "But see":
U.S. v. DeSimone, 699 F.3d 113, 127, 89 Fed. R. Evid. Serv. 1133 (1st Cir. 2012) ("It is not improper to ask one witness whether another witness was 'wrong' or 'mistaken,' since such questions do not force a witness 'to choose between conceding the point and branding another witness a liar' ");

§ 44   Defects of capacity: Sensory or mental

n. 2.
Gardner, The Perception and Memory of Witnesses, 18 Cornell L.Q. 391 (1933);

n. 6.
Fed. R. Evid. 601 advisory committee note.

n. 8.
Browning v. Trammell, 717 F.3d 1092, 1105 (10th Cir. 2013) (" 'at the time of the event, as well as at the time of trial' ");
U.S. v. Dupree, 833 F. Supp. 2d 255,

264-65 (E.D. N.Y. 2011), vacated on other grounds and remanded, 706 F.3d 131, 90 Fed. R. Evid. Serv. 723 (2d Cir. 2013) ("the court will permit the defendants to cross-examine the witness regarding her use of anti-anxiety medication in 2009 for approximately six months. The period of time during which the witness used this medication occurred within the time period in issue in this case . . . .");

Delete cross-reference to footnote.

Add to sixth sentence of third paragraph, after "outweigh the time":

consumption

Add new heading above fourth paragraph:

Alcohol and Substance Abuse

n. 14.
Add in "Drink" paragraph of footnote:
Com. v. Williams, 2014 PA Super 88, 91 A.3d 240 (2014) ("[e]vidence of intoxication during the events that are the subject of the witness's testimony");
Add in "Drugs" paragraph of footnote:
Flythe v. District of Columbia, 4 F. Supp. 3d 222, 229-30 (D.D.C. 2014) (in U.S. v. Sellers, 906 F.2d 597, 602, 31

Fed. R. Evid. Serv. 459 (11th Cir. 1990), the court held that "such evidence may properly be limited to specific instances of drug use during relevant periods of trial and the transaction [at issue]");

n. 15.
Sabre International Security v. Torres Advanced Enterprise Solutions, LLC, 72 F. Supp. 3d 131, 89 Fed. R. Serv. 3d 1840 (D.D.C. 2014) (drinking habits);

Add to sentence ending in footnote 18, after "more":

contemporary

n. 18.
Kelly v. Maryland Casualty Co., 45 F.2d 782 (W.D. Va. 1929), aff'd, 45 F.2d 788 (C.C.A. 4th Cir. 1930)

n. 19.
U.S. v. Boyd, 833 F. Supp. 1277, 1359 (N.D. Ill. 1993), judgment aff'd, 55 F.3d 239 (7th Cir. 1995)

n. 20.
Kelly v. Maryland Casualty Co., 45 F.2d 782 (W.D. Va. 1929), aff'd, 45 F.2d 788 (C.C.A. 4th Cir. 1930),

n. 23.
State v. Wesler, 137 N.J.L. 311, 59 A.2d 834 (N.J. Sup. Ct. 1948), judgment aff'd, 1 N.J. 58, 61 A.2d 746 (1948)

n. 25.
Add at beginning of footnote:
U.S. v. Hill, 749 F.3d 1250, 1262, 94 Fed. R. Evid. Serv. 387 (10th Cir. 2014) (The court ruled it was error to admit expert opinion testimony about the defendant's credibility; the testimony did not involve specialized psychiatric knowledge; the opinion amounted to

an explanation that the jury was capable of understanding without expert testimony; the court distinguished U.S. v. Shay, 57 F.3d 126, 42 Fed. R. Evid. Serv. 341 (1st Cir. 1995); there "the court held that a psychiatrist should have been permitted to testify the defendant 'suffered from a recognized mental disorder known as pseudologia-fantastica' that caused him to tell false and self-aggrandizing stories. And in United States v. Hall, 93 F.3d 1337 (7th Cir. 1996), the court ordered a new trial following the exclusion of expert testimony suggesting that false confessions sometimes occur and that the defendant had a 'personality disorder that makes him susceptible to suggestion.' The court held that '[i]t was precisely because juries are unlikely to know that . . . psychologists have identified a personality disorder that will cause individuals to make false confessions that the testimony would have assisted the jury' . . . . Similarly, our decision in *Toledo* dealt with psychiatric testimony regarding the nature of delusions. 98 F.2d at 1469 . . . ." the court stated that these topics were "outside the ken of a normal juror");

Add at end of footnote:
; People v. Days, 131 A.D.3d 972, 15 N.Y.S.3d 823 (2d Dep't 2015), leave to appeal denied, 26 N.Y.3d 1108, 2016 WL 561767 (2016) (the defendant suffered from a diagnosable psychiatric disorder, and the techniques used during the interrogation made it more likely that he would make a false confession).

n. 26.
Delete cross-reference to footnote from parenthetical to Government of Virgin Islands v. Scuito cite.

n. 27.
Delete cross-reference to footnote at beginning of footnote.

n. 28.
Delete cross-reference to footnote.

n. 30.
Replace last sentence of footnote with:
In 2013, the A.P.A. released the fifth edition of the manual.

n. 32.
Add at end of footnote:
In Kumho Tire Co., Ltd. v. Carmichael, 526 U.S. 137, 119 S. Ct. 1167, 143 L. Ed. 2d 238, 50 Fed. R. Evid. Serv. 1373 (1999), the Supreme Court made it clear that *Daubert*'s requirement for a showing of reliability applies to all types of expert testimony, not merely hard, classically scientific testimony.

n. 34.
Replace Weihofen cross-reference with full cite:
Weihofen, Testimonial Competence and Credibility, 34 Geo. Wash. L. Rev. 53 (1965).

§ 45   Impeachment by "specific contradiction"

n. 1.
Add after first paragraph:
Since this is a separate impeachment technique, it sometimes can be used to circumvent limitations on other techniques. For example, some jurisdictions do not apply the conviction impeachment technique to convictions for violations of mere municipal ordinances. However, if a witness testifies that she has never before "had the experience of being stopped and interrogated by the police," evidence of a prior municipal ordinance violation may be admissible to contradict the testimony. State v. McCleary, 423 S.W.3d 888, 895 (Mo. Ct. App. E.D. 2014).

n. 5.
Delete cross-reference to footnote at end of footnote.

n. 10.
U.S. v. McDonnell, 64 F. Supp. 3d 783, 801 (E.D. Va. 2014), aff'd, 792 F.3d 478, 97 Fed. R. Evid. Serv. 1438 (4th Cir. 2015), certiorari granted in part, 136 S. Ct. 891, 193 L. Ed. 2d 784 (2016); Foley v. Town of Lee, 863 F. Supp. 2d 130, 137, 88 Fed. R. Evid. Serv. 436, 2012 DNH 82 (D.N.H. 2012);

Add after sixth sentence of last paragraph:
The drafters' decision to include Article VI in the Federal Rules reflects their realization that a witness's credibility is a fact of consequence under Rule 401.

Add after seventh sentence of last paragraph:
Although the Rules do not expressly limit specific contradiction on collateral matters, some federal courts continue to apply the common law restriction.[11.50]

Add at beginning of sentence including footnotes 12-13:
To be sure, the

[11.50]Jones ex rel. U.S. v. Massachusetts General Hosp., 780 F.3d 479, 495 (1st Cir. 2015).

n. 13.
See Montoya v. Shelden, 898 F. Supp. 2d 1279, 1293, 89 Fed. R. Evid. Serv. 894 (D.N.M. 2012) (on the one hand, Rule 608(b) codifies " 'an absolute prohibition on extrinsic evidence' "; on the other hand, that prohibition applies only under Rule 608(b); in particular, the prohibition does not apply " 'when extrinsic evidence is offered to show that a statement made by a defendant on direct examination is false, even if the statement is about a collateral issue' ").

§ 46   Beliefs concerning religion

n. 1.
4 Weinstein's Federal Evidence Ch. 610 (rev. 2012); Comment by Chadbourn on State v. Beal, 154 S.E. 604 (N.C. 1930), 9 N.C. L. Rev. 77 (1930)

n. 5.
Replace "Advisory Committee's Note" following "See" with:
Fed. R. Evid. 603 advisory committee note.

§ 47   Supporting the witness

Add in sentence ending in footnote 1, after "attack":
As we have seen, one general principle, recognized under both case law and the Federal Rules of Evidence, is that absent an attack[0.50] upon credibility, no bolstering evidence is allowed.[1]

[0.50]There is authority that an attack during opening statement suffices. See U.S. v. Grandison, 781 F.3d 987, 990-91, 96 Fed. R. Evid. Serv. 1493 (8th Cir. 2015); U.S. v. Chapman, 59 F. Supp. 3d 1194, 1213 (D.N.M. 2014) (the prohibition applies to expert as well as lay testimony).

n. 2.
Delete "quoted in part in note 366 supra" from citation following first sentence of footnote.

Delete cross-reference to footnotes 64, 67.

Add new footnote at end of first sentence of paragraph following heading "The General Ban on Bolstering":

As just stated, absent the introduction of impeaching facts, the witness's proponent ordinarily may not bolster the witness's credibility.[2.50]

[2.50]*But see* U.S. v. Davis, 779 F.3d 1305, 1308-11 (11th Cir. 2015), cert. denied, 136 S. Ct. 97, 193 L. Ed. 2d 81 (2015) (the prosecutor called a city police officer as a witness; it was permissible to elicit the witness's testimony that the officer was the police department's chaplain).

Replace "a" in fourth sentence of paragraph following heading "The General Ban on Bolstering" with:

an outcry or

n. 3.
   Add to end of footnote:
See also Graham, Admissibility of Children's Statements in Sexual Abuse Prosecutions: Prompt Complaint, Excited Utterance, Medical Diagnosis or Treatment, Child Sexual Abuse Hearsay Exception: Confrontation Clause, 50 Crim. L. Bull. 1260, 1268-69 (2014) ("Courts traditionally have employed three different theories to support admission of a prompt complaint: two of the theories are prior consistent statement and excited utterance; the third is the 'inherent inference' theory"—"the fact of a prompt complaint [is] admissible to rebut the natural inference that absence of evidence of a prompt complaint damaged the victim's credibility"; "Strict admissibility requirements have over time been relaxed in many jurisdictions. A complaint is now considered 'prompt' if the delay is explained. Some jurisdictions no longer require a showing of promptness. At the same time courts have expanded the scope of information admissible to rebut the inference. Originally only the fact that a complaint was made could be introduced; details of the complaint were not permitted. In many jurisdictions today, however, details are admissible and some jurisdictions admit the identity of the assailant"); Graham, Admissibility of Initial Complaint of Sexual Assault or Child Molestation, 48 Crim. L. Bull. 1075 (2012).

Replace sentence ending in footnote 5 with:
Likewise, prior consistent statements of identification can be admissible substantively or to bolster. If the declarant later appears as a witness and during direct examination identifies a person, it is permissible to elicit the witness's testimony that she previously identified the same person—even before cross-examination and any opportunity for impeachment. However, precisely because prior identifications may be introduced as substantive evidence and trigger constitutional requirements, that subject is also discussed elsewhere.[5]

Add at end of paragraph under heading "Corroboration":
At trial, many elements of a litigant's theory of the case are likely to be formally or virtually undisputed. On those elements, the litigant can be content to present enough evidence to barely satisfy the initial burden of going forward. However, on the key elements

that are sharply controverted, the litigant must present ample corroboration.

Add at end of sentence following footnote 7:
When may the party supporting the impeached witness offer evidence of the witness's good character for truth?[7.50]

[7.50]The Advisory Committee Note accompanying Rule 608(a) states: "Opinion or reputation that the witness is untruthful specifically qualifies as an attack, and evidence of misconduct, including conviction of crime, and of corruption also fall within this category. Evidence of bias or interest does not. Whether evidence in the form of contradiction is an attack upon the character of the witness must depend upon the circumstances."

n. 8.
Fed. R. Evid. 608(a) advisory committee note.

n. 9.
Fed. R. Evid. 608(a) and advisory committee note.

n. 10.
Fed. R. Evid. 608(a) advisory committee note.

n. 11.
Fed. R. Evid. 608(a) advisory committee note;

Add in sentence following footnote 12, before "response":

, direct

n. 15.
Fed. R. Evid. 608(a) advisory committee note;

n. 16.
Fed. R. Evid. 608(a) advisory committee note;

n. 19.
Fed. R. Evid. 608(a) advisory committee note

n. 21.
U.S. v. Drury, 344 F.3d 1089 (11th Cir. 2003), reh'g en banc granted, opinion vacated, 358 F.3d 1280 (11th Cir. 2004)

and opinion superseded, 396 F.3d 1303 (11th Cir. 2005)

n. 24.
    Delete first sentence of footnote.
Wolfson v. Baker, 444 F. Supp. 1124, 1129 n.3 (M.D. Fla. 1978), judgment aff'd, 623 F.2d 1074 (5th Cir. 1980)

n. 28.
    Delete cross-reference to footnote 25 at beginning of footnote.

n. 36.
    Delete cross-reference to footnote at end of second paragraph of footnote.

Replace "such a" in tenth sentence of paragraph containing footnotes 32-38 with:

an express

n. 37.
    Add after first sentence of footnote:
The Advisory Committee Note accompanying the 2014 amendment of Rule 801 recognizes that "consistent statements . . . [can] be probative to rebut a charge of faulty memory." State

v. Wright, 383 S.W.2d 1, 7 (Mo. App. 2012) takes the position that "once a witness's credibility has been attacked, prior consistent statements may be used for any rehabilitative purpose, not only in response to charges of recent fabrication or improper influence."

n. 39.
Delete cross-reference to footnote 25 at end of footnote.

n. 41.
Replace "390" in footnote cross-reference with:

39
Replace cross-reference to Quinto in footnote with:
U.S. v. Quinto, 582 F.2d 224, 3 Fed. R. Evid. Serv. 1097, 47 A.L.R. Fed. 621 (2d Cir. 1978).

Add after footnote 41:
When the proponent offers the evidence in this manner, on request under Rule 105 the trial judge would give the jury a limiting instruction about the proper use of the evidence.

§ 48   Attacking the supporting character witness

n. 1.
Add in second paragraph of footnote, after "content":
to the former Rule

n. 2.
Delete cross-reference to footnote.

Replace first instance of "witness" with "witness's" in last sentence of paragraph containing footnote 8, adding the following after "untruthfulness":

or suggests the witness's bias

Start new paragraph with and add in sentence ending in footnote 9, after "good faith basis":

in fact

Add after footnote 9:
If the opposing attorney objects and at sidebar the cross-examiner cannot demonstrate a good basis, the judge should bar the inquiry.

n. 10.
Bright, 588 F.2d at 511-512

§ 49   Contradiction: Collateral and non-collateral matters; good faith basis

n. 5.
; Imwinkelried, Formalism Versus Pragmatism in Evidence: Use of Extrinsic Evidence to Prove Impeaching, Untruthful Acts That Have Not Resulted in a Conviction, 48 Creighton L. Rev. 213, 232 (2015).

n. 11.
Add in third paragraph of footnote, after "content":

to the former Rule
Add after third paragraph of footnote:
See Imwinkelried, Formalism Versus Pragmatism in Evidence: Reconsidering the Absolute Ban on the Use of Extrinsic Evidence to Prove Impeaching, Untruthful Acts That Have Not Resulted in a Conviction, 48 Creighton L. Rev. 213 (2015) (on the

one hand, the article notes that Rule 608(b) impeachment has been singled out for a virtually absolute ban on extrinsic evidence; on the other hand, after analyzing the probative value of the various impeachment techniques, the article argues that the differential treatment of 608(b) impeachment is unjustifiable; the article contends that the trial judge should have discretion to determine whether the extrinsic evidence is sufficiently probative to be admitted; however, the article concedes that it would be necessary to amend Rule 608(b) to confer such discretion on trial judges).

Add in sentence following footnote 11, after "On the one hand,"

even under the general rule

Add in fifth sentence of third paragraph following heading "When Is a Particular Topic Deemed Collateral?", after "bolstering":

and character

Add after fifth sentence in third paragraph following heading "When Is a Particular Topic Deemed Collateral?"
In effect, the accused has forfeited the protection of the general rule.

n. 13.
   Add at beginning of footnote:
U.S. v. Delgado-Marrero, 744 F.3d 167, 93 Fed. R. Evid. Serv. 938 (1st Cir. 2014) (the evidence was not collateral because it also corroborated pivotal elements of the defendant's entrapment defense on the historical merits); Saltzburg, The Limitation on Exclusion of Extrinsic Evidence, 29 Crim. Just., Fall 2014, at 43, 55 (the article discusses *Delgado-Marrero*; "If the officer denies the acts relied on to prove entrapment, [extrinsic] evidence that the acts occurred might have the incidental effect of impeaching the officer, but as long as the acts are offered to prove entrapment they are offered for a permissible [substantive] purpose"; in other words, the evidence had dual relevance to the merits as well as credibility);

Replace sixth paragraph following heading "When Is a Particular Topic Deemed Collateral?" with:
Consider the following illustration. An accident occurred on Apple Street at the intersection at its intersection with Maple Street. Bob is called to testify that the color of the traffic light facing Apple Street was red at the time of an automobile accident he witnessed at the corner of Apple and Maple. On direct examination, Bob testifies that he distinctly recalls that when he witnessed the accident, he was driving "west on Apple, the street Piagano's Pizza Restaurant is situated on," and indeed was heading toward the restaurant. He adds that Piagano's is located on the corner of Apple and Peach. On cross-examination counsel asks, "Isn't it true that Piagano's Pizza Restaurant is located on Apple three blocks east of Peach at *Maple*?" This cross-examination question is permissible as potentially affecting the jury's assessment of Bob's powers of perception and recollection.

However, if Bob continues to maintain that the cross street for the restaurant is Peach Street, extrinsic evidence may not be offered during the cross-examiner's case in chief as to the cross street. The matter is collateral because the cross street at which the restaurant is located is not relevant in the litigation other than to contradict Bob's testimony. Even if Bob denied on cross-examination making a prior statement in which he allegedly said that the restaurant was on Apple and Maple, extrinsic evidence of the prior statement would be inadmissible because the matter is collateral. Even if Bob is mistaken about the cross street, his testimony on the historical merits about the accident on Apple Street could still be completely accurate.

Replace eighth paragraph following heading "When Is a Particular Topic Deemed Collateral?" with:

Finally, vary the initial illustration. Again, on direct Bob testified that when he witnessed an accident, he was driving "west on Apple, the street on which Piagano's is located." Now the specific contradiction evidence is that Piagano's Pizza Restaurant is situated on Main Street that parallels Apple. If Bob was on Main, not Apple, extrinsic evidence of the location of the restaurant would be admissible. In this variation of the illustration, an error as to the location of the restaurant brings into question the trustworthiness of Bob's testimony on the historical merits of the case. The mistake no longer relates only to the cross street. If Bob was on Main Street, he may have seen another accident; but he could not have witnessed the accident on Apple. Bob may have seen the light facing Main, not the light facing Apple. The location of the restaurant would now be considered a "linchpin" fact, and extrinsic evidence would therefore be admissible to impeach Bob. A fact negating the fundamental assumption that the witness was in the right place at the right time to observe what he testified to is a classic example of a "linchpin" fact.

§ 50   Exclusion and separation of witnesses

n. 5.

Replace first sentence of footnote up to quote with:
Unif. R. Evid. 615 provides:

n. 6.
4 Weinstein's Federal Evidence § 615. 02[2][a], at 617-7-8 (rev. 2013)

n. 15.
Add at end of footnote:

As noted in § 15, there are two forms of the hypothesis in a hypothetical question. In the long form, the questioner specifies the facts in the hypothesis. In the short form, the questioner simply asks the witness to assume the truth of the testimony of a witness or witnesses who have testified about the facts.

Title 3 ADMISSION AND EXCLUSION

Chapter 6

The Procedure of Admitting and Excluding Evidence

> **KeyCite®:** Cases and other legal materials listed in KeyCite Scope can be researched through the KeyCite service on Westlaw®. Use KeyCite to check citations for form, parallel references, prior and later history, and comprehensive citator information, including citations to other decisions and secondary materials.

§ 51   Presentation of evidence: Offer of proof

Add in sentence ending in footnote 5, after "marked by the":

court reporter or

Add in second sentence of third paragraph, preceding "jurisdictions":

courtrooms in most

Replace "an offer of proof." in first sentence of sixth paragraph with:

"an offer of proof" or avowal.

n. 11.
Add in second sentence of footnote, after "content":

to the former Rule
Delete cross-reference to footnote.

Add in sentence ending in footnote 12, preceding "claim":

proponent's

Start new paragraph and replace sentence ending in footnote 15 with:
The offer of proof is not only a traditional common law practice, Federal Rules of Evidence 103(a) to (b) impose the requirement for an offer of proof.

n. 15.
Replace cites at beginning of footnote with:
Fed. R. Evid. 103(a) to (b).
Delete cross-reference to footnotes in second paragraph.

n. 17.
Delete cross-reference to footnote in second paragraph.

n. 18.
Lamonica v. Safe Hurricane Shutters, Inc., 711 F.3d 1299, 90 Fed. R. Evid. Serv. 1128 (11th Cir. 2013) ("In this case, the substance of Leiva's proffered testimony was obvious from its context. Ibacache had already been questioned about his alleged conversation with Leiva, and the question Defendants' counsel posed to Leiva was obviously directed at that same conversation.");

n. 19.
Kane v. Carper-Dover Mercantile Co., 206 Ark. 674, 177 S.W.2d 41 (1944) (overruled on other grounds by, Sharp v. Great Southern Coaches, Inc., 256 Ark. 773, 510 S.W.2d 266 (1974))

Add at end of seventh paragraph:
The Advisory Committee Note accompanying the 2000 amendment points out that even before the amendment, some courts had distinguished offers of proof from objections and not required a proponent to renew an offer at trial.

Replace "a part" in sentence after footnote 24 with:

another part

Replace "methodology" in sentence ending in footnote 26 with:

procedure

Replace "in court" in sentence following sentence ending in footnote 26 with:

on the witness stand

§ 52   Objections

Replace "rejected" in first sentence of section with:

excluded

n. 2.

Replace first sentence of footnote up to quote with:
Unif. R. Evid. 103(a)(1) embodies the principles set forth in this paragraph of the text:

n. 3.

Add after "But see":
U.S. v. Adejumo, 772 F.3d 513, 524, 95 Fed. R. Evid. Serv. 1487 (8th Cir. 2014), petition for certiorari filed, 135 S. Ct. 1869, 191 L. Ed. 2d 742 (2015) ("In the case at hand, . . . defense

counsel did not wait until the end of Detective Breachane's testimony, nor until the close of all the evidence. Instead, it appears from the record that counsel raised her objection mere moments after Exhibit 222 was introduced. There was still ample opportunity for the judge to prevent further potential damage.");

n. 4.

Replace cross-reference to footnote 31 with cross-reference to footnote 3.

Replace sentence following footnote 5 with:
In that event, the counsel may move to strike the answer for the purpose of interposing an objection to the question; if the judge thinks that the witness prematurely "jumped the gun" and grants the motion, the counsel is then permitted to state her objection to the question.

n. 9.

Replace cross-reference in second paragraph with:
§§ 58 to 59

n. 11.

Capra & Greenberg, The Form of the Question Ch. 18 (2014);

Add at beginning of paragraph following header "Pretrial Motions in Limine":
Although the Federal Rules of Evidence do not expressly authorize in limine motions, federal courts have inherent procedural authority to entertain such motions.[12.50]

[12.50]United States v. Holland, 41 F.   Supp. 3d 82, 89 (D.D.C. 2014).

Add in sentence following footnote 13, after "motion":

offensively

Add in next sentence, starting with "However", after "motion":

defensively

n. 21.

Oakes, 565 F.2d at 173
But see U.S. v. Ulbricht, 79 F. Supp. 3d 466, 96 Fed. R. Evid. Serv. 348 (S.D. N.Y. 2015) (stating that a trial

judge should exclude evidence on an in limine motion only when the evidence is clearly inadmissible on all potential grounds).

Add new footnote at end of second sentence in second paragraph following header "Pretrial Motions in Limine":

First, the judge can refuse to entertain the motion and defer the issue until trial.[21.50]

[21.50]United States v. Slough, 22 F. Supp. 3d 29, 32, 94 Fed. R. Evid. Serv. 990 (D.D.C. 2014) (the trial judge ordinarily may wait until trial to rule on an evidentiary issue).

Add new footnote at end of fourth sentence in second paragraph following header "Pretrial Motions in Limine":
By way of example, suppose that the opponent moves to exclude an item of evidence as unduly prejudicial under Rule 403.[22.30]

[22.30]*See* Graham, Prior Conviction Impeachment: "People v. Patrick"—Ameliorating the Risk of Undue Prejudice, 50 Crim. L. Bull. 952, 975, 979 (2014) (according to People v. Patrick, 233 Ill. 2d 62, 330 Ill. Dec. 149, 908 N.E.2d 1 (2009), "the trial judge will in all but the most complicated cases have enough information before trial to weigh the probative value of admitting the prior conviction against the danger of unfair prejudice to the defendant").

Add at end of second paragraph following header "Pretrial Motions in Limine":
(However, even when the judge makes a purportedly definitive ruling, the judge has the power to reconsider and change the ruling at trial.[22.50])

[22.50]The Advisory Committee Note accompanying the 2000 amendment to Rule 103 states that the trial judge may "revisit its decision when the evidence is to be offered." *See* McConnell v. Wal-Mart Stores, Inc., 995 F. Supp. 2d 1164, 1168 (D. Nev. 2014) ("In limine motions are preliminary and therefore 'are not binding on the trial judge [who] may always change his mind during the course of a trial.' Ohler v. United States, 529 U.S. 753, 758 n.3, 120 S. Ct. 1851, 146 L. Ed. 2d 826 (2000); *accord Luce,* 469 U.S. at 41, 105 S. Ct. 460 (noting that in limine rulings are always subject to change, especially if the evidence unfolds in an unanticipated manner)."); Euroholdings Capital & Inv. Corp. v. Harris Trust & Sav. Bank, 602 F. Supp. 2d 928, 935 (N.D. Ill. 2009) ("[T]he [in limine] ruling is subject to change when the case unfolds . . . . 'Indeed, even if nothing unexpected happens at trial, the district judge is free, in the exercise of sound judicial discretion, to alter a previous in limine ruling.' ").

n. 27.
U.S. v. Wilson, 788 F.3d 1298, 97 Fed. R. Evid. Serv. 999 (11th Cir. 2015), cert. denied, 136 S. Ct. 518, 193 L. Ed. 2d 408 (2015) (the trial judge used equivocal language, "[k]eeping in mind that none of this evidence has been actually offered yet," "should [the co-conspirator] testify," and "I think"); Long v. Fairbank Reconstruction Corp., 701 F.3d 1 (1st Cir. 2012) (the judge's comments did not constitute a definitive ruling); U.S. v. Hargrove, 625 F.3d 170, 177 (4th Cir. 2010);

n. 31.
Add after first paragraph of footnote:
A litigant's pretrial conduct can also result in a waiver of the right to make an objection at trial. *See* Fed. R. Civ. P. 26(a)(3) ("Unless the court orders otherwise, a party may serve and promptly file a list of the following objections: any objections to the use under Rule 32(a) of a deposition

designated by another party under Rule 26(a)(3)(A)(ii); and any objection, together with the grounds for it, that may be made to the admissibility of materials identified under Rule 26(a)(3)(A)(iii). An objection not so made—except for one under Federal Rule of Evidence 402 or 403—is waived unless excused by the court for good cause").

n. 32.
Add after "See also, e.g.,":

U.S. v. Lewis, 796 F.3d 543, 546, 98 Fed. R. Evid. Serv. 142 (5th Cir. 2015) ("'A loosely formulated and imprecise objection will not preserve error. Rather, a trial court judge must be fully apprised of the grounds of an objection.'");

n. 39.
Delete cross-reference to footnote.

Add in sentence ending in footnote 41, after "substituted other":

admissible

n. 53.
Delete cross-reference to footnote.

Add new footnote to end of first sentence of fifth paragraph after heading "General and Specific Objections":
To make a sufficiently specific objection, the opponent should name the generic evidentiary rule being violated: "calls for information protected by the attorney-client privilege," "lack of authentication," "not the best evidence," or "hearsay"—the level of specificity found in the phrasing of the titles of the various articles in the Federal Rules of Evidence.[49.50]

[49.50]The title of Article VII is "Opinions and Expert Testimony," Article VIII "Hearsay," and Article IX "Authentication and Identification."

n. 55.
People v. Wright, 48 Cal. 3d 168, 255 Cal. Rptr. 853, 768 P.2d 72 (1989), reh'g granted, opinion not citeable, (Apr. 26, 1989) and opinion vacated on other grounds, 52 Cal. 3d 367, 276 Cal. Rptr. 731, 802 P.2d 221 (1990), as modified on denial of reh'g, (Feb. 20, 1991) and (disapproved of on other grounds by, People v. Williams, 49 Cal. 4th 405, 111 Cal. Rptr. 3d 589, 233 P.3d 1000 (2010))

Replace last sentence of fifth paragraph after heading "General and Specific Objections":
Understandably, the judge demands greater precision in objections in the pretrial context.

n. 59.
Delete cross-reference to footnote.

Delete sentence ending with footnote 60 and footnote.

Add at beginning of third sentence of eighth paragraph after heading "General and Specific Objections":
However,

Replace "judge" in next sentence with:

judge's interference

Add in sentence ending with footnote 62, after "Instead,"

under Federal Rule of Evidence 105,

n. 62.
Finley, 240 Ark. at 324;

Add new paragraph after footnote 62:

Ordinarily, to obtain a reversal on appeal, the litigant must not only have made a specific objection in the trial court; the litigant must also rely on the same ground on appeal. A "hearsay" objection does not preserve the contention that the admission of the statement violates the Sixth Amendment confrontation clause.[62.20] Likewise, a general "relevance" objection does not raise the objection that the admission of the evidence would violate Rule 403[62.40] or the character rules.[62.60] If the litigant attempts to shift to another ground on appeal, the court will apply the plain error doctrine codified in Federal Rule 103(e);[62.80] and appellate courts rarely find plain error.

[62.20]U.S. v. Keita, 742 F.3d 184 (4th Cir. 2014); U.S. v. Cabrera-Beltran, 660 F.3d 742, 751, 86 Fed. R. Evid. Serv. 1475 (4th Cir. 2011); U.S. v. Meises, 645 F.3d 5 (1st Cir. 2011); U.S. v. Arbolaez, 450 F.3d 1283, 1291 n.8, 70 Fed. R. Evid. Serv. 290 (11th Cir. 2006). *See also* Saltzburg, The Right Objection, 25 Crim. Just., Wint. 2011, at 54 (discussing the relationship between the hearsay and lack of personal knowledge objections).

[62.40]U.S. v. Eagle, 515 F.3d 794, 803, 75 Fed. R. Evid. Serv. 730 (8th Cir. 2008).

[62.60]U.S. v. Iwuala, 789 F.3d 1, 6-7, 97 Fed. R. Evid. Serv. 1045 (1st Cir. 2015), cert. denied, 136 S. Ct. 913 (2016).

[62.80]Fed. R. Evid. 103(e): "A court may take notice of a plain error affecting a substantial right, even if the claim of error was not properly preserved."

Add at end of paragraph that starts with sub-heading "Specificity as to party":

There is a division of authority over "vicarious" objections; while some appellate courts allow one co-party to urge a co-party's trial objection, other courts are contra.[64.50]

[64.50]U.S. v. Irving, 665 F.3d 1184, 1206-07, 86 Fed. R. Evid. Serv. 1647   (10th Cir. 2011).

Replace "the objection" in sentence following footnote 72 with:

the initial objection

Replace "Objections" at beginning of sentence ending with footnote 78 with:
On net, objections

n. 85.   tee note.
Fed. R. Evid. 103(d) advisory commit-

Add in sentence ending with footnote 93, after "reluctance":

to reverse

n. 93.
Delete cross-reference to footnote.

§ 53   Preliminary questions of fact arising on objections

Add in second sentence of section, preceding "rule":

best evidence

n. 5.
Replace first sentence of footnote, up to quote with:
Unif. R. Evid. 104(a) provides:
Delete cross-reference to footnote.

n. 7.
Robinson v. U.S., 144 F.2d 392 (6th Cir. 1944), judgment aff'd, 324 U.S. 282, 65 S. Ct. 666, 89 L. Ed. 944 (1945)

n. 8.
Replace third sentence in footnote, up to quote, with:
As to keeping preliminary fact matter from coming to the jury's attention, former Fed. R. Evid. 104(c) provided:

Add in fourth sentence of footnote, after "content":
to the former Rule

Add at end of seventh sentence following heading "Foundational Facts Conditioning the Application of Technical Exclusionary Rules", after "establish":

, not the historical merits

Add after next sentence that begins with "Between":
With the exception of the privilege rules, the technical exclusionary rules do not apply to foundational testimony; and the judge may thus consider any unprivileged testimony, even hearsay.[9.50]

[9.50]Fed. R. Evid. 104(a); In re Intern. Management Associates, LLC, 781 F.3d 1262, 1268 (11th Cir. 2015); U.S. v. Banks, 93 F. Supp. 3d 1237, 1247, 96 Fed. R. Evid. Serv. 1118 (D. Kan. 2015). The Advisory Committee Note accompanying Rule 104 points out that the conventional wisdom is that the courts developed the common law exclusionary rules such as hearsay to compensate for the lay jurors' suppos-edly limited competence to critically evaluate testimony. However, when Rule 104(a) governs, the judge is the factfinder. Indeed, when the judge is ruling on an in limine motion, the jury has not even been selected yet. It therefore makes little sense to apply the technical exclusionary rules to foundational testimony proffered under 104(a). Although the rule stated in 104(a) is now the prevailing view in the United States, a minority of jurisdictions are contra and apply the exclusionary rules to foundational testimony. Imwinkelried & Leach, California Evidentiary Foundations § 1.C[1] (4th ed. 2009).

Add to end of sentence ending with footnote 10, following footnote:

,[10] and ordinarily applies the preponderance of the evidence standard of proof.[10.50]

---

[10]Imwinkelried, Trial Judges—Gatekeepers or Usurpers? Can the Trial Judge Critically Assess the Admissibility of Expert Testimony Without Invading the Jury's Province to Evaluate the Credibility and Weight of the Testimony?, 84 Marq. L. Rev. 1 (2000).

[10.50]Gilmore v. Palestinian Interim Self-Government Authority, 53 F. Supp. 3d 191 (D.D.C. 2014). *See also* Bourjaily v. U.S., 483 U.S. 171, 107 S. Ct. 2775, 97 L. Ed. 2d 144, 22 Fed. R. Evid. Serv. 1105 (1987).

n. 11.
Fed. R. Evid. 104(b) advisory committee note.

Create bulleted list at end of second paragraph following heading "Foundational Facts Conditioning the Logical Relevance of the Evidence" using the next two paragraphs:

In effect, there is a two-step procedure:

- The judge requires the proponent to bring forward evidence from which a rational jury could find the existence of the preliminary fact. At this point, the judge plays a limited, screening role. The judge cannot pass on the credibility of the foundational testimony. Rather, the test is a hypothetical jury finding. The judge must accept the testimony at face value and ask only this question: If the jury decides to believe the testimony, is there a rational, permissive inference of the existence of the preliminary fact? When the judge determines that the jury could not find the existence of the preliminary fact, she excludes the evidence.

- Otherwise, the question is for the jury. The jury makes the real factual determination whether the witness has personal knowledge or whether the letter is authentic. Although in fact some trial judges permit the opponent to conduct voir dire on conditional relevance issues, strictly speaking the opponent has no right to voir dire on this type of issue. When the opponent has contrary evidence, the opponent submits it to the jury rather than the judge. On request, in the final instructions the judge directs the jury to determine the existence of the foundational fact and to disregard the evidence if they find that the foundational fact has not been proven. Unlike the judge at the first step, the jury considers the credibility of the testimony.

n. 13.

　Add at end of first paragraph of footnote:
; Grandoe Corp. v. Gander Mountain Co., 761 F.3d 876, 883 (8th Cir. 2014)

("[The court submits the preliminary question to the jury as long as a reasonable jury could find that the preliminary fact exists").

　Replace next to last sentence of sixth paragraph, starting with "These preliminary facts" with:

These preliminary facts condition the logical relevance of the evidence in a fundamental sense that is obvious even to lay jurors who lack legal training but have common sense; the jury has determined that the witness "doesn't know what he is talking about" or the exhibit "is not worth the paper it's written on." Once the jurors have made that determination, their common sense will naturally lead the jurors to disregard the evidence during the balance of their deliberations. In short, it is safe to allow the jurors to make these determinations.

n. 14.

　Replace first sentence of footnote with:
In *Huddleston*, the Court held that Rule 104(b) governs the foundational question of whether the accused committed an act of uncharged misconduct proffered under Rule 404(b), for example, another murder allegedly committed with the same distinctive modus operandi. Huddleston, 485 U.S. at 689.

n. 17.

　Replace second sentence of first paragraph of footnote, up to quote, with:
It should, however, be noted that Uniform Rule 104(f) provides:

　Delete "described in note 16 supra" from third paragraph of footnote.

　Add in third sentence of eleventh paragraph, preceding "decide":

initially

　Add in sentence following footnote 18, preceding "litigate":

later

　Replace "Rule 1008" in sentence including footnotes 19-20 with:

Rule 1008(a)

n. 20.

　Replace first sentence of footnote, up to quote, with:
Unif. R. Evid. 1008 provides:

n. 21.

Fed. R. Evid. 602, 901 advisory committee notes.

§ 54　Availability as proof of evidence admitted without objection

n. 6.

People v. McCoy, 101 Ill. App. 2d 69, 242 N.E.2d 4 (4th Dist. 1968), judgment rev'd on other grounds, 44 Ill. 2d 458, 256 N.E.2d 449 (1970)

　Replace cross-reference to footnote in second sentence of footnote with:
See note 5 supra for contrary view.

§ 55   Waiver of objection

n. 1.
U.S. v. Irving, 665 F.3d 1184, 1206–1207 (10th Cir. 2011).

n. 2.
Brumfield v. Stinson, 297 F. Supp. 2d 607, 619–20 (W.D.N.Y. 2003).

n. 3.
Add at end of footnote:
The Advisory Committee Note ac-

companying the 2000 amendment to Rule 103 states: "The *Luce* principle has been extended by many lower courts to other situations." The Note then cites examples involving objections under Rules 403, 404, and 608. As previously stated, 404(b) evidence is usually offered as substantive evidence on the merits.

Add in sentence ending in footnote 4, after "some jurisdictions":

a detailed offer of proof[3.50] or

[3.50]Heidelberg v. State, 584 So. 2d 393, 395 (Miss. 1991).

n. 17.
Delete cross-reference to footnote.

n. 26.
See generally S.M. v. Los Angeles Unified School District, 192 Cal. Rptr. 3d 769, 783 (Cal. App. 2d Dist. 2015), as modified on denial of reh'g, (Oct. 7, 2015) and review filed, (Oct. 27, 2015)

("the 'defensive acts' doctrine . . . permits a party to introduce evidence she has previously unsuccessfully objected to, in an attempt to preemptively address the evidence").

n. 28.
Wisniewski v. Weinstock, 130 N.J.L. 58, 31 A.2d 401 (N.J. Sup. Ct. 1943), judgment aff'd, 135 N.J.L. 202, 50 A.2d 894 (N.J. Ct. Err. & App. 1947)

§ 56   The effect of the introduction of part of a writing or conversation

n. 7.
Add to second paragraph of footnote, after "content":
to the former Rule

Replace Rainey cite in third paragraph with:
Rainey, 488 U.S. at 171

Add at end of third paragraph:
; Stehn v. Cody, 74 F. Supp. 3d 140, 148, 95 Fed. R. Evid. Serv. 1471 (D.D.C. 2014) (the pedestrian could still offer the motorist's original interrogatory answers even though the motorist had amended the answers; however, under the rule of completeness, the pedestrian was required to offer the motorist's supplemental interrogatory answers as well).

Add in fourth paragraph:
; State v. Steinle, 345 P.3d 408 (Ariz. App. 2015) (a "cropped" video).

Add in seventh paragraph, preceding cite to U.S. v. Sweiss:

U.S. v. Johnson, 579 Fed. Appx. 867, 95 Fed. R. Evid. Serv. 421 (11th Cir. 2014);

Add after third sentence in eighth paragraph:
U.S. v. Liera-Morales, 759 F.3d 1105, 1111 (9th Cir. 2014) ("our cases have applied the rule only to written and recorded statements. Nevertheless, at least two of our sister circuits have recognized that the principle underlying Rule 106 also applies to oral testimony by virtue of Fed. R. Evid. 611(a) . . . .");

U.S. v. Bauzo-Santiago, 49 F. Supp. 3d 155, 158 (D.P.R. 2014);

n. 9.
Add after "See also":
U.S. v. Ford, 761 F.3d 641 (6th Cir. 2014), cert. denied, 135 S. Ct. 771, 190 L. Ed. 2d 640 (2014) (inadmissible exculpatory hearsay); U.S. v. Hassan, 742 F.3d 104, 93 Fed. R. Evid. Serv. 758 (4th Cir. 2014), cert. denied, 134

S. Ct. 2737, 189 L. Ed. 2d 774 (2014) and petition for certiorari filed, 135 S. Ct. 157, 190 L. Ed. 2d 115 (2014) (the defendant's self-serving exculpatory hearsay statements did not fall within any hearsay exception);

n. 12.
U.S. v. Catano, 65 F.3d 219, 43 Fed.

R. Evid. Serv. 88 (1st Cir. 1995), opinion supplemented, 66 F.3d 306 (1st Cir. 1995)
U.S. v. Ailsworth, 948 F. Supp. 1485 (D. Kan. 1996), aff'd, 138 F.3d 843 (10th Cir. 1998)

n. 17.
Delete cross-reference to footnote.

§ 57 Fighting fire with fire: Inadmissible evidence as opening the door

n. 14.
Delete cross-reference to footnote.

§ 58 Admissibility of evidence dependent on proof of other facts: "Connecting up"

n. 10.
Replace beginning of first sentence of footnote, up to "provide" with:
Uniform Rule 104(c) provides

n. 12.
Caley v. Manicke, 29 Ill. App. 2d 323,

173 N.E.2d 209 (2d Dist. 1961), judgment rev'd on other grounds, 24 Ill. 2d 390, 182 N.E.2d 206 (1962)

Replace sentence ending in footnote 13 with:
The failure should become apparent to the objecting party when the offering party completes the particular stage of the case[12.50] in which the evidence was offered.

[12.50] As § 4 pointed out, the major stages of a trial are: the plaintiff's or prosecutor's case-in-chief, the defense case-in-chief, the plaintiff's or prosecutor's rebuttal, and the defense sur-rebuttal or rejoinder.

Add at end of sentence following sentence ending with footnote 13, after "condition":

either during the trial or on appeal

§ 59 Evidence admissible for one purpose, inadmissible for another: "Limited admissibility"

n. 5.
Replace beginning of sentence, up to quote, with:
Unif. R. Evid. 105 provides:

n. 6.
Add at end of footnote:
But see Sklansky, Evidentiary Instructions and the Jury as Other, 65 Stan. L. Rev. 407, 410, 414-19, 424-30, 451 (2013) (the author surveys 33 pub-

lished studies of the efficacy of instructions; in his view, the assertions about the ineffectiveness of instructions are "at best greatly exaggerated. Evidentiary instructions probably do work although imperfectly and better under some circumstances than others"; "The conventional wisdom about evidentiary instructions—'of course they don't work'—" is "unduly pessimistic").

n. 8.
State v. Goebel, 40 Wash. 2d 18, 240 P.2d 251 (1952) (overruled on other

grounds by State v. Lough, 125 Wash. 2d 847, 889 P.2d 487 (1995))

Add in sentence ending with footnote 10, after "consider":

the evidence

n. 10.
American Medical Ass'n v. U.S., 130 F.2d 233 (App. D.C. 1942), judgment

aff'd, 317 U.S. 519, 63 S. Ct. 326, 87 L. Ed. 434 (1943).

Replace sentence ending with footnote 11 with:
But it may be inadmissible against the defendant. For instance, the confession might not qualify as a vicarious, co-conspirator admission against the defendant because a codefendant made the statement after he had been arrested and ceased being an active member of the conspiracy with the defendant.[11]

n. 14.
Harrington, 395 U.S. at 254;

§ 60   Admission and exclusion of evidence in bench trials without a jury

Replace "states" in sentence ending with footnote 2 with:

famously described

n. 4.
Clark v. U.S., 61 F.2d 695 (8th Cir. 1932), aff'd, 289 U.S. 1, 53 S. Ct. 465, 77 L. Ed. 993 (1933);

Replace second paragraph of footnote with:
It must be conceded that the rules contain no special provision for judge-tried cases. However, given Rules 102 (statement of purpose), 103 (error in admitting or excluding must affect substantial right), and 611 (broad powers to control trial), the case can be made that failure to follow the earlier case law would violate the spirit and to a degree the letter of the Rules.

n. 5.
Add preceding cross-reference at end of footnote:
The court in Gipson v. State, 844 S.W.2d 738 (Tex. Crim. App. 1992) abrogated the *Tolert* decision. *Gipson* held that Texas Rule of Appellate Procedure 81(b)(2) governs and that the rule "does not distinguish trials before juries and trials before the court." The *Gipson* court reasoned that the rule "implicitly voided the presumption" that at a bench trial the judge based his or her factual findings on only admissible evidence.

Delete cross-reference to footnotes.

Add in sentence ending with footnote 8, after "take the form of":

the judge's

81

Title 4 COMPETENCY

Chapter 7

The Competency of Witnesses

> **KeyCite®:** Cases and other legal materials listed in KeyCite Scope can be researched through the KeyCite service on Westlaw®. Use KeyCite to check citations for form, parallel references, prior and later history, and comprehensive citator information, including citations to other decisions and secondary materials.

§ 62   Mental incapacity and immaturity: Oath or affirmation

n. 1.
3 Weinstein's Federal Evidence § 601. 04[1] (rev. 2013)

n. 2.
Add at end of footnote:
The decision in Harris v. Thompson, 698 F.3d 609, 633 n.13, 646 n.15, 647 n.17 (7th Cir. 2012), is particularly noteworthy. The court not only held that a five-year-old, the defendant's son, was competent to testify; even more significantly, the court held that the trial judge had violated the defendant's constitutional right to present evidence by barring the defendant's son from testifying. The son was the only eyewitness to the death of the defendant's other son. The court collected numerous Illinois cases finding four-, five-, six-, and nine-year old children competent to be witnesses. In the court's words, "Courts commonly find children competent to testify despite their expressed belief in Santa Claus and other fictitious characters" such as the tooth fairy.

n. 4.
State v. Barker, 410 S.W.3d 225 (Mo. Ct. App. W.D. 2013) (a seven-year-old boy was ruled a competent witness despite expert testimony that a police sergeant's pretrial suggestive questioning of the boy likely affected the boy's memory of the relevant events);
Add at end of footnote:
At the polar extreme, the courts routinely find very elderly persons to be competent witnesses. State v. Vondenkamp, 141 Idaho 878, 119 P.3d 653 (Ct. App. 2005) (a 96-year-old grand theft victim).

n. 5.
Add at end of first sentence of third paragraph of footnote:
Gilley v. State, 418 S.W.3d 114 (Tex.

Crim. App. 2014), petition for certiorari filed, 135 S. Ct. 57, 190 L. Ed. 2d 56 (2014) (the trial judge conducted the competency examination in camera).

Add preceding "But see" in third paragraph of footnote:
The courts are divided over the question of whether the judge must conduct the hearing out of the jury's presence. Ex parte Brown, 74 So. 3d 1039 (Ala. 2011); State v. Fleming, 280 Neb. 967, 792 N.W.2d 147 (2010).

n. 9.
Houff v. Blacketter, 402 Fed. Appx. 167 (9th Cir. 2010) (a hearsay statement by a four-year-old victim); Walters v. McCormick, 122 F.3d 1172 (9th Cir. 1997)

n. 12.
Sinclair v. City of Grandview, 973 F. Supp. 2d 1234, 1253-54 (E.D. Wash. 2013) (the witness had been medicated and was unable to recall certain events);

Replace first sentence of paragraph following footnote 15 with:
The major reason for the severe, early common law disqualification standards was the judges' distrust of a lay jury's ability to critically assess the words of a small child or a deranged person.

n. 17.
Barton v. American Red Cross, 829 F. Supp. 1290 (M.D. Ala. 1993), aff'd, 43 F.3d 678 (11th Cir. 1994) and aff'd, 43 F.3d 679 (11th Cir. 1994)
Add new paragraph at end of footnote:
    Although most states have adopted a version of Rule 601, in some cases the text of the state rule differs significantly from that of the federal statute. By way of example, Montana Rule of Evidence 601(b) reads: "A person is disqualified to be a witness if the court finds that (1) the witness is incapable of expression concerning the matter so as to be understood by the judge and jury either directly or through interpretation by one who can understand the witness or (2) the witness is incapable of understanding the duty of a witness to tell the truth."

While the language of the federal statute seems to sweep away the common law requirements, rules such as Montana Rule 601 largely preserve those requirements.

n. 18.
    Add to end of second sentence in footnote:
to the former Rule

n. 19.
    Add to end of sentence following quote in footnote:
to the former Rule

n. 22.
    Delete cross-reference to footnote.

n. 24.
    Add to end of second sentence in footnote:
to the former Rule

Replace "The statutes expressly require" in fifth sentence of paragraph ending including footnotes 24-26 with:
Rule 602 expressly requires

Replace "argument runs" in sixth paragraph with:

proponents of the intermediate position argue

n. 28.
Fed. R. Evid. 601 advisory committee

note.

Replace "could" in sentence ending in footnote 31 with:

might

Add after footnote 31:
Admittedly, in assessing the probative value of an item of evidence for purposes of Rule 403, the trial judge ordinarily may not consider the credibility of the source of the evidence.[31.50]

Replace sentence following footnote 31:
However, if the contents of the prospective witness's testimony are virtually incoherent, her testimony would have minimal probative value and pose a significant danger of jury confusion.

[31.50]Imwinkelried, The Meaning of Probative Value and Prejudice in Federal Rule of Evidence 403: Can Rule 403 Be Used to Resurrect the Common Law of Evidence?, 41 Vand. L. Rev. 879, 884-88 (1988).

§ 63   Religious belief

Add at end of second sentence, after "could not":

satsify the test

Replace "For example" in sentence including footnotes 4-8:
To do so

n. 6.
Replace first two sentences of footnote with:
See Fed. R. Evid. (1st sentence) and Unif. R. Evid. 601 in § 62, note 17 supra. Fed. R. Evid. 603 confirms the text. Former Fed. R. Evid. 603 provided: "Before testifying, every witness shall be required to declare that the witness will testify truthfully, by oath or affirmation in a form calculated to awaken his conscience and impress the witness' mind with his duty to do so." Unif. R. Evid. 603 is identical in content to the former Rule.

n. 10.
U.S. v. Moore, 217 F.2d 428 (7th Cir. 1954), judgment rev'd on other grounds, 348 U.S. 966, 75 S. Ct. 530, 99 L. Ed. 753 (1955).

§ 64   Conviction of crime

n. 5.
Delete cross-reference to footnote.

n. 6.
Replace cross-reference.
See § 62 supra.

n. 7.
Add at end of footnote:
However, in *Washington,* the majority rejected Justice Harlan's suggestion in his concurrence that the Court remedy the infirmity by allowing Texas to deny the evidence to both sides. Instead, the majority ruled that the defendant had a constitutional right to present the testimony. Imwinkelried & Garland, Exculpatory Evidence: The Accused's Constitutional Right to Introduce Favorable Evidence §§ 1-2[a], 2-2[f], 4-2[a][2] (4th ed. 2015).

§ 65 Parties and persons interested: The dead man statutes

Replace "could" in sentence ending with footnote 2 with:

were permitted to

Replace the sentence following footnote 3 with:
However, the statutes largely operate as a one-way street; there is often a proviso by statute or case law that the surviving party or interested person may testify if called by the adversary, that is, the decedent's executor or administrator. Thus, the proviso abrogates the privilege feature of the common law rule.

Add new footnote to the end of second sentence of bullets in fourth paragraph:
Does the statute apply only to causes of action derived from the decedent such as suits for the decedent's pain and suffering prior to death, or does it also extend to causes of action for wrongful death which are conferred by statute directly on the heirs?[6.50]

[6.50]*See* Knit With v. Knitting Fever, Inc., 742 F. Supp. 2d 568, 83 Fed. R. Evid. Serv. 851 (E.D. Pa. 2010) (under the Pennsylvania Dead Man's Act, the deceased's right must have passed to a party of record who represents the deceased's interests).

n. 9.
Zang v. Alliance Financial Services of Illinois, Ltd., 875 F. Supp. 2d 865, 877 (N.D. Ill. 2012) (the Illinois Act "does not bar testimony regarding 'evidence of facts that the decedent could not have refuted' ").

Add at end of footnote:
See Northern Health Facilities v. Batz, 993 F. Supp. 2d 485, 490 n.2 (M.D. Pa. 2014) (the Pennsylvania Act "applies only to oral testimony . . . .").

Add new footnote to end of second sentence of fourth bullet:
Many statutes lift the bar of the statute when the survivor and the decedent stood in the relationship of employer and employee or partners.[9.50]

[9.50]Batz, 993 F. Supp. 2d at 877 n.2 (the Pennsylvania Act does "not [apply] to agents or employees of a surviving party to a transaction").

n. 13.
Replace cross-reference to footnote:
See § 62 supra.

n. 16.
Delete cross-reference to footnote.

Add in sentence ending with footnote 19, preceding "relevance":

obvious

n. 20.
Add at end of footnote:
; Imwinkelried & Garland, Exculpatory Evidence: The Accused's

Constitutional Right to Introduce Favorable Evidence § 8-7 (4th ed. 2015).

§ 66   Husbands and wives of parties

Add after first sentence of second paragraph:
After the Supreme Court's 2015 decision recognizing a constitutional right to same-sex marriage,[3.50] in all probability the rule's protection will be extended to same-sex couples. However, even before that landmark decision, the rule underwent major change.

Add in sentence ending in footnote 4, after "jurisdictions":

[3.50]Obergefell v. Hodges, 135 S. Ct. 2584, 192 L. Ed. 2d 609 (2015).

n. 4.
2 Wigmore, Evidence § 488 (Chadbourn

rev. 1979)

n. 5.
Replace second sentence in footnote:
See also the sources cited in note 5.

Add after footnote 5:
To distinguish this competency doctrine from the more limited spousal communications privilege, this doctrine is often referred to as the anti-marital fact or spousal testimonial privilege.

n. 6.
Replace cross-reference to note:
n. 7.
Trammel, 445 U.S. at 53.

Henness v. Bagley, 644 F.3d 308, 326-27 (6th Cir. 2011) (Ohio law).

Replace "almost always" in second sentence of third paragraph:

usually

n. 9.
Delete cross-reference to footnote.
Delete second sentence of footnote, including quote.
Replace cross-reference to note in third paragraph of footnote:
note 8 supra

n. 10.
Replace cross-reference to note.
n. 14.
U.S. v. Ramos-Oseguera, 120 F.3d 1028 (9th Cir. 1997) (overruled on other grounds by U.S. v. Nordby, 225 F.3d 1053 (9th Cir. 2000))

Add to first sentence of sixth paragraph, after "Several":

related

n. 16.
Replace cross-reference to footnote:

note 6 supra

Add after footnote 18:
In some but not all jurisdictions, the trial judge must inform the spouse witness of the availability of the privilege.[18.50]

[18.50]Henness v. Bagley, 644 F.3d 308, 326-27 (6th Cir. 2011) (Ohio law).

Replace "applied" in sentence ending in footnote 19 with:

extended

Add in sentence following footnote 23, after "instant":

testimonial

Replace last sentence in section with:
In contrast, the spousal communications privilege has a far more limited procedural effect; while the spouse is on the stand, the communications privilege merely bars the spouse from disclosing certain communications passing between the spouses.

§ 67 Incompetency of husband and wife to give testimony on non-access

Replace "it" in sentence including footnotes 7-8 with:

the doctrine

n. 8.
State ex rel. Worley v. Lavender, 147 W. Va. 803, 131 S.E.2d 752 (1963) (overruled on other grounds by, State ex rel. Toryak v. Spagnuolo, 170 W. Va. 234, 292 S.E.2d 654 (1982)).

n. 10.
Add at end of footnote:
However, in Melvin v. Kazhe, 1971-NMSC-128, 83 N.M. 356, 492 P.2d 138 (1971), the court held that both the mother and the father are competent to testify regarding the husband's non-access to rebut the presumption of legitimacy of children born during wedlock.

n. 11.
Biggs v. Biggs, 253 N.C. 10, 116 S.E.2d 178 (1960) (overruled in other part by, Hicks v. Hicks, 271 N.C. 204, 155 S.E.2d 799 (1967))

§ 68 Judges, jurors and lawyers

n. 3.
Hamilton v. Vasquez, 17 F.3d 1149 (9th Cir. 1994), amended (Mar. 22, 1994)
Steele v. Duckworth, 900 F. Supp. 1048 (N.D. Ind. 1994), aff'd, 62 F.3d 1419 (7th Cir. 1995);

Delete second paragraph of footnote.

Start new paragraph after footnote 8.

Start new paragraph with sentence ending in footnote 10.

n. 11.

Delete reference to Fed. R. Evid. 605 from beginning of note.

Add at end of first paragraph of footnote:

Effective December 1, 2011, Fed. R. Evid. 605 reads: "The presiding judge may not testify as a witness at the trial. A party need not object to preserve the issue."

Add new paragraph after footnote 12:

It is ordinarily easy to recognize this issue. The problem is obvious when the judge attempts to slide from the bench onto the witness stand. However, it can be more difficult to recognize the issue in another setting. Suppose that during trial, the judge injects her personal knowledge of facts that are not judicially noticeable. In effect, the judge has become a witness; and in principle the judge's conduct is objectionable under Rule 605.[12.50]

[12.50]U.S. v. Berber-Tinoco, 510 F.3d 1083, 1089-93, 75 Fed. R. Evid. Serv. 399 (9th Cir. 2007) (at a suppression hearing, the judge improperly injected his own observation regarding the location of stop signs along a certain road near the border and the narrowness of the road; those facts were not in the record, and they were not reasonable inferences from the record; "[a] trial judge is prohibited from relying on his personal experience to support the taking of judicial notice"); U.S. v. Nickl, 427 F.3d 1286, 1292-94, 68 Fed. R. Evid. Serv. 837 (10th Cir. 2005) (an accomplice testified at the defendant's trial; in a previous proceeding, the judge had taken the accomplice's guilty plea; during cross-examination, the defense counsel asked the accomplice whether she had pleaded guilty just to get the matter behind her; at that point, the judge improperly interjected the comment that he would never have accepted her guilty plea unless she had convinced him that she had the requisite *mens rea*); U.S. v. Lewis, 833 F.2d 1380, 1385, 24 Fed. R. Evid. Serv. 432 (9th Cir. 1987) (the trial judge's personal experience with "a general anesthetic").

Similarly, the problem can arise if one of the counsel attempts to read into the record the judge's statements at a prior hearing. U.S. v. Blanchard, 542 F.3d 1133, 1147-49, 77 Fed. R. Evid. Serv. 532 (7th Cir. 2008) (the prosecutor read into the record the judge's comments at a prior suppression hearing; "While it is true that the

prosecutor, rather than the trial judge, read the . . . comments into the record at trial, this in no way alters our conclusion . . . In the presence of the jury, the trial judge acknowledged that the . . . comments were his own . . . . Under such circumstances, Rule 605 is violated; the rule would serve little purpose if it were violated only where a judge observes all the formalities— taking of an oath, sitting in the witness chair, etc.—of an ordinary witness.").

n. 13.

Add at end of footnote:
But see People v. Morris, 239 Cal. App. 4th 276, 190 Cal. Rptr. 3d 803 (2d Dist. 2015) (the witness was a juror who had been excused in the case; the prosecution called the witness to testify to an incriminating statement that he had overhead the defendant make in the courthouse; the appellate court held that the presentation of the excused juror's testimony violated the defendant's due process right to a fair trial; there was a significant risk that the other jurors would regard the excused juror's testimony with a favorable bias, since they had served on the same juror with him).

n. 14.

Add to end of sentence following quote in footnote:
to the former Rule

n. 20.
Tanner, 483 U.S at 119
People v. Force, 89 Cal. Rptr. 3d 50,

68-70 (Cal. App. 4th Dist. 2009), review granted and opinion superseded, 93 Cal. Rptr. 3d 536, 207 P.3d 1 (Cal. 2009)

Delete cross-reference to footnote at end.

Replace "the objective event" in sentence ending in footnote 24 with:

objective events

n. 24.
Bouret-Echevarria v. Caribbean Aviation Maintenance Corp., 784 F.3d 37, 45, 91 Fed. R. Serv. 3d 569 (1st Cir. 2015) ("its 'probable effect on a hypothetical average juror'");

n. 25.
Add to end of sentence following quote in footnote:
as the former Rule
Add at end of third paragraph of footnote:
See Warger v. Shauers, 721 F.3d 606,

610, 91 Fed. R. Evid. Serv. 1395 (8th Cir. 2013), cert. granted, 134 S. Ct. 1491, 188 L. Ed. 2d 374 (2014) (the Federal Rules codify "very strict" requirements limiting the admissibility of testimony by or affidavits from jurors).
McDowell v. Calderon, 107 F.3d 1351, 46 Fed. R. Evid. Serv. 749 (9th Cir. 1997), opinion amended and superseded in part on other grounds, 116 F.3d 364 (9th Cir. 1997) and judgment vacated in part on reh'g, 130 F.3d 833 (9th Cir. 1997);

Add in sentence ending in footnote 26, after "testify":

or supply an affidavit or declaration

Add in sentence ending in footnote 27 after "addition to":

barring evidence of

n. 28.
Dobbs v. Zant, 720 F. Supp. 1566 (N.D. Ga. 1989), aff'd, 963 F.2d 1403, 1566-71 (11th Cir. 1991), cert. granted, judgment rev'd on other grounds, 506 U.S. 357, 113 S. Ct. 835, 122 L. Ed. 2d 103 (1993).

Add after second sentence of footnote:
Imwinkelried & Garland, Exculpatory Evidence: The Accused's Constitutional Right to Introduce Favorable Evidence § 12-3[e] (4th ed. 2015);

Replace Rule cite in second sentence after footnote 29, which begins with "While that rule . . ." with the following, and add a new footnote at the end of the sentence:
While that rule barred juror testimony and affidavit only when it was offered to impeach a verdict, the wording of 606(b)(1) is so expansive that it seemingly applies whether the evidence is offered to impeach or support the verdict.[29.50]

[29.50]Rule 606(b)(1) states that a juror "may not testify" "[d]uring an inquiry into the validity of a verdict or indictment . . . ." The statutory language does not include the further limitation that the juror may not testify "in order to impeach" the verdict or indictment.
n. 30.
Delete cross-reference to footnote.

U.S. v. Elias, 269 F.3d 1003, 1020 (9th Cir. 2001), opinion supplemented, 27 Fed. Appx. 750 (9th Cir. 2001) and as modified, (Dec. 21, 2001)

Authority, 277 F. Supp. 2d 163, 170-71 (E.D. N.Y. 2003), order aff'd, 381 F.3d 99, 65 Fed. R. Evid. Serv. 223 (2d Cir. 2004)

n. 33.
Munafo v. Metropolitan Transp.

Add after footnote 33:
Amended Rule 606(b)(2)(C) permits the use of juror testimony and affidavits to prove that "a mistake was made in entering the verdict on the verdict form."

n. 34.
Replace cite:

Fed. R. Evid. 606(b) advisory committee note.

Add new paragraph after paragraph including footnotes 26-34:
In its 2014 decision, *Warger v. Shauers,*[34.30] a lawsuit arising from a motor vehicle accident, the Supreme Court dealt with another limitation on the scope of the doctrine, recognized in some jurisdictions. As Justice Sotomayor noted in her opinion, "[a]lthough some common-law courts . . . permit[ ] evidence of jury deliberations to be introduced to demonstrate juror dishonesty during voir dire, the majority do not . . . ." The courts allowing such evidence reason that the exclusionary rule bars the use of the evidence to demonstrate jury misconduct during deliberations, but not during voir dire. However, the Court adopted the majority view that the language of Rule 606(b) is sweeping enough to preclude the use of the evidence to prove a panelist's lie during jury selection. In dictum in footnote three, the justice stated that in rare cases, the evidence might demonstrate a "juror bias so extreme that . . . the [constitutional] jury trial right has been abridged. If and when such a case arises, the Court can consider whether the usual safeguards are . . . sufficient to protect the integrity of the process." In *Warger,* the evidence did not tend to establish an invidious, intense bias such as racism.[34.50] Rather, the evidence tended to show only that the jury foreperson's daughter had been at fault in a motor vehicle accident and that the lawsuit based on that accident had adversely affected the daughter's life. In the Court's view, that evidence was insufficient to invalidate the judgment on constitutional grounds.

[34.30]Warger v. Shauers, 135 S. Ct. 521, 190 L. Ed. 2d 422, 96 Fed. R. Evid. Serv. 186 (2014).

[34.50]Imwinkelried & Garland, Exculpatory Evidence: The Accused's Constitutional Right to Introduce Favorable Evidence § 12-3[e], at 623-24 n.229 (4th ed. 2015) (the text surveys the relevant cases and states that

"[t]here is a large and growing body of precedent that . . . [on constitutional grounds] the privilege must yield when the moving party seeks to establish a juror's racial bias").

n. 37.
; U.S. v. Perry, 30 F. Supp. 3d 514, 536 (E.D. Va. 2014) (" 'there is no rule of evidence absolutely excluding the

testimony of a lawyer on behalf of his client' "; "the witness advocate rule 'does not render an attorney incompetent to testify, but merely vests the Court with discretion to determine whether counsel may appear as a witness without withdrawing from the case' ").

n. 39.
; U.S. v. Lucio, 996 F. Supp. 2d 514, 526-28 (S.D. Tex. 2013) (the court applied Restatement (Third) of the Law Governing Lawyers § 108; that provision forbids the attorney from testifying adversely to his or her client; in addition, the provision allows an at-

torney to testify on behalf of his or her client only when the testimony "relates to an uncontested issue" or "the attorney's disqualification would result in a substantial hardship on the client"; in the instant case, the defendant wanted to call the defense counsel; however, the proposed testimony did not relate to an uncontested matter or formality, and the defense did not make a showing of the requisite prejudice; the defense made only a "bare conclusory statement" and did "not submit[ ] affidavits or any other evidence in support of the" claim of prejudice).

Add toward end of sentence ending in footnote 40, preceding "avoided":

foreseen and

n. 40.
RFF Family Partnership, LP v. Link Development, LLC, 68 F. Supp. 3d 260, 261 (D. Mass. 2014) ("soliciting trial testimony from opposing counsel is strongly disfavored"); U.S. v. Rodella, 59 F. Supp. 3d 1331, 1345-46 (D.N.M. 2014) (" 'The government has a substantial interest in not allowing its prosecutors to testify because doing so generally requires disqualification of the prosecutor' "; "The Tenth Circuit has held that a 'district court may

decline to allow the defendant to call the prosecutor as a witness if it does not appear the prosecutor possesses information vital to the defense.' Many courts have held that a prosecutor's testimony is not vital to the defense . . . if the defendant can obtain the evidence from another source other than the prosecutor's testimony");

n. 41.
Delete cross-references to footnotes.

Add at end of paragraph under the heading "Lawyers":
Rule 403 authorizes the trial judge to exclude logically relevant evidence when its probative value is substantially outweighed by probative dangers such as "confusing the issues."

Add at end of section:
In most cases, it is easy to recognize this issue: There is a red flag when a party calls a trial attorney in the case to the witness stand. However, it is more difficult to identify some variations of the problem. Suppose that before trial, the trial attorney interviewed the witness who is now on the stand. The trial attorney believes that the witness has testified inconsistently with his or her pretrial statements to the attorney. In principle, the same restrictions come into play if in open court the attorney then inquires whether the witness's testimony is at odds with what "you told us" or "said to us" before trial. Even though the attorney has not attempted to take the witness stand, the op-

ponent should object that the attorney has in effect become a rebuttal witness.[47]

[47]U.S. v. Rangel-Guzman, 752 F.3d 1222 (9th Cir. 2014); Saltzburg, Advocate Yes, Witness No, 29 Crim. Just. 34 (Winter 2015) (discussing *Rangel-Guzman*).

§ 70   The procedure of disqualification

n. 4.
Replace cross-reference to footnote
See the rule in § 62 supra.

Add new footnote at end of sentence following footnote 5:
Hence, under the new statutes, there appears to be only one case in which the opponent must routinely follow the common law procedure; in federal criminal cases, objections based on the spouse witness's privilege not to be called by the prosecution must still arguably be asserted before the spouse witness takes the oath.[5.50]

[5.50]In some cases, the objecting party may have a legitimate excuse for not objecting at that point. If the witness did not use the same surname as the defendant, the objecting party may not have realized that the defendant and witness were married. Even then, unless there was an extremely limited opportunity for pretrial discovery, the objecting party should ordinarily have discovered the spousal relationship before trial.

Add in sentence ending in footnote 6, preceding "challenge":
potential

n. 6.
Delete first paragraph of footnote.
Delete cross-reference to footnote in first sentence of second paragraph.

n. 7.
.Add after cross-reference:
In some jurisdictions, after eliciting the testimony about the witness's qualifications, it is customary for the proponent to pause and formally "tender" the witness as an expert on a certain subject. Ingram v. State, 178 Ga. App. 292, 342 S.E.2d 765 (1986) (the preferred practice). However, a growing number of courts are abandoning that practice. If there is no pending objection, there is no need for the trial judge to intervene and make a ruling. U.S. v. Bartley, 855 F.2d 547, 552 (8th Cir. 1988). Moreover, as *Bar-*tley notes, there is a danger that the judge's express acceptance of the witness as an expert will unfairly enhance the witness's stature in the jurors' minds. The clear trend is to discontinue the practice. Standard 17 of the A.B.A. Litigation Section's Civil Trial Practice Standards reads: "Except in ruling on an objection, the court should not, in the presence of the jury, declare that a witness is qualified as an expert, and counsel should not ask the court to do so." The official commentary to Ky. R. Evid. 702 declares that "the practice of tendering a witness [as an expert] should be discontinued." The commentary asserts that the judge's "anointing" or "approbation of the witness . . . improperly conveys the impression that the witness's testimony is especially believable."

Add in sentence ending in footnote 8, after "whether":

under Rule 602

Add in sentence ending in footnote 8, after "whether":

under Rule 501

Title 5 PRIVILEGE: COMMON LAW AND STATUTORY

Chapter 8

The Scope and Effect of the Evidentiary Privileges

KeyCite®: Cases and other legal materials listed in KeyCite Scope can be researched through the KeyCite service on Westlaw®. Use KeyCite to check citations for form, parallel references, prior and later history, and comprehensive citator information, including citations to other decisions and secondary materials.

---

§ 72   The purposes of rules of privilege: (a) Other rules of evidence distinguished

n. 9.   (1976)

Comment, 9 U.C. Davis L. Rev. 477

§ 73.1   Procedural recognition of rules of privilege: (a) Who may assert?

n. 3.

Mayer v. Albany Medical Center Hospital, 56 Misc. 2d 239, 288 N.Y.S.2d 771 (Sup 1968), judgment aff'd as modified, 37 A.D.2d 1011, 325 N.Y.S.2d 517 (3d Dep't 1971)

§ 74   Limitations on the effectiveness of privileges: (a) Risk of eavesdropping and interception of letters

n. 3.

U.S. v. Neal, 532 F. Supp. 942, 10 Fed. R. Evid. Serv. 968 (D. Colo. 1982), aff'd, 743 F.2d 1441, 16 Fed. R. Evid. Serv. 979 (10th Cir. 1984)

n. 5.
3 Weinstein & Berger, Evidence ¶ 503.
15[3] (2015)

A.3d 882, 894 (2014) (New Jersey statute prevents disclosure of marital communications obtained by legal wiretap)

n. 9.
; State v. Terry, 218 N.J. 224, 245, 94

§ 75   The sources of privilege

n. 26.
2 Weinstein and Berger, Evidence

§§ 502-510 (2015)

§ 76.1   The current pattern of privilege: (a) Privilege in federal courts; what law applies?

Delete footnote 2.

n. 3.
  Add at end of footnote:
See generally Broun, Evidentiary Privileges in Federal Courts—Survey Rules (West Academic 2015).

n. 4.
Imwinkelried, An Hegelian Approach

to Privileges Under Federal Rule of Evidence 501: The Restrictive Thesis, the Expansive Antithesis, and the Contextual Synthesis, 73 Neb. L. R. 511 (1994)

§ 76.2   The current pattern of privilege: (b) State patterns of privilege; recognizing new privileges

n. 8.
Ariz. Rev. Stat. § 12-2233

n. 14.
People v. Burnidge, 279 Ill. App. 3d 127, 216 Ill. Dec. 19, 664 N.E.2d 656 (2d Dist. 1996), aff'd, 178 Ill. 2d 429, 227 Ill. Dec. 331, 687 N.E.2d 813 (1997)

n. 21.
  Add at end of footnote:
See also U.S. v. Sterling, 724 F.3d 482 (4th Cir. 2013), cert. denied, 134 S. Ct. 2696, 189 L. Ed. 2d 739 (2014) (finding no reporter's privilege under Constitution or common law in criminal case). *See generally* Greenberg, The Federal Media Shield Folly, 91 Wash. U. L. Rev. 437 (2013); Jones, Rethinking Reporter's Privilege, 111 Mich. L. Rev. 1221 (2013).

n. 26.
  Delete State v. Rinaldo cite and parenthetical.

n. 34.
Under Seal v. U.S., 755 F.3d 213, 94 Fed. R. Evid. Serv. 998 (4th Cir. 2014) (adoption of parent-child privilege unwarranted);

n. 35.
  Add after "See":
Adams, The Tension Between Research Ethics and Legal Ethics: Using Journalist's Privilege State Statutes as a Model for a Proposed Researcher's Privilege, 27 Geo. J. Legal Ethics 335 (2014);

Chapter 9

The Privilege for Marital Communications

§ 79   What is privileged: Communications only, or acts and facts?
§ 80   The communication must be confidential
§ 81   The time of making the communication: Marital status
§ 82   Hazards of disclosure to third persons against the will of the communicating spouse
§ 83   Who is the holder of the privilege? Enforcement and waiver
§ 84   Controversies in which the privilege is inapplicable

KeyCite®: Cases and other legal materials listed in KeyCite Scope can be researched through the KeyCite service on Westlaw®. Use KeyCite to check citations for form, parallel references, prior and later history, and comprehensive citator information, including citations to other decisions and secondary materials.

---

§ 79   What is privileged: Communications only, or acts and facts?

n. 16.

Delete cross-reference.

Add in cites after "See also":
State v. Terry, 218 N.J. 224, 94 A.3d 882 (2014) (no exception to marital privilege for statements in furtherance of crime or fraud; amendment to Rule establishing such an exception proposed);

§ 80   The communication must be confidential

n. 6.

Add after "see" in first sentence of footnote:
U.S. v. Hamilton, 701 F.3d 404, 407-09 (4th Cir. 2012) (emails sent to wife on workplace computer were not found to be privileged);

n. 7.
Stafford v. State, 1983 OK CR 131, 669 P.2d 285 (Okla. Crim. App. 1983), cert. granted, judgment vacated on other grounds, 467 U.S. 1212, 104 S. Ct. 2652, 81 L. Ed. 2d 359 (1984)

§ 81   The time of making the communication: Marital status

n. 4.
; Schaffzin, Beyond Bobby Jo Clary: The Unavailability of Same-Sex Marital Privileges Infringes the Rights of So Many More than Criminal Defendants, 63 U. Kan. L. Rev. 103

(2014)

n. 6.
Replace cross-reference to footnote with:
People v. Godines, 17 Cal. App. 2d 721, 62 P.2d 787 (2d Dist. 1936)

n. 7.

Replace cross-reference to footnote with:
People v. Mabry, 71 Cal. 2d 430, 78 Cal. Rptr. 655, 455 P.2d 759 (1969) Comment, 9 U.C. Davis L. Rev. 569,

600 (1976)

n. 10.
People v. Fields, 38 A.D.2d 231, 328 N.Y.S.2d 542 (1st Dep't 1972), order aff'd, 31 N.Y.2d 713, 337 N.Y.S.2d 517, 289 N.E.2d 557 (1972)

§ 82   Hazards of disclosure to third persons against the will of the communicating spouse

n. 14.
U.S. v. Neal, 532 F. Supp. 942, 10 Fed. R. Evid. Serv. 968 (D. Colo. 1982),

aff'd, 743 F.2d 1441, 16 Fed. R. Evid. Serv. 979 (10th Cir. 1984)

§ 83   Who is the holder of the privilege? Enforcement and waiver

n. 10.
U.S. v. Brock, 724 F.3d 817, 821 (7th Cir. 2013) (privilege waived where wife testified to communications at detention hearing and husband failed to object);

Luick v. Arends, 21 N.D. 614, 132 N.W. 353, 362, 363 (1911); Coles v. Harsch, 129 Or. 11, 276 P. 248, 253-255 (1929); Patterson v. Skoglund, 181 Or. 167, 180 P.2d 108 (1947).

n. 12.
Replace contents of footnote with:

§ 84   Controversies in which the privilege is inapplicable

n. 4.
People v. McCormack, 278 A.D. 191, 104 N.Y.S.2d 139, 143 (1st Dep't 1951), judgment aff'd, 303 N.Y. 782, 103 N.E.2d 895 (1952)

n. 6.
Add after "See also":
U.S. v. Breton, 740 F.3d 1, 93 Fed. R.

Evid. Serv. 350 (1st Cir. 2014) (exception applies for offenses against a spouse's child);

n. 9.
Delete cross-reference after first sentence in footnote.

Chapter 10

The Client's Privilege: Communications Between Client & Lawyer

---

KeyCite®: Cases and other legal materials listed in KeyCite Scope can be researched through the KeyCite service on Westlaw®. Use KeyCite to check citations for form, parallel references, prior and later history, and comprehensive citator information, including citations to other decisions and secondary materials.

---

§ 87 Background and policy of the privilege: (a) Theoretical considerations

n. 18.

Add at end of footnote:
See also Natali, Should We Amend or Interpret the Attorney-Client Privilege to Allow for an Innocence Exception, 37 Am. J. Trial Advoc. 93 (2013).

§ 87.1 Background and policy of the privilege: (b) Applications in corporate, governmental and other entity settings

n. 8.
Harper & Row Publishers, Inc. v. Decker, 423 F.2d 487, 13 Fed. R. Serv. 2d 984, 9 A.L.R. Fed. 674 (7th Cir.

1970), judgment aff'd, 400 U.S. 348, 91
S. Ct. 479, 27 L. Ed. 2d 433 (1971)

n. 13.
See also In re Kellogg Brown & Root,
Inc., 756 F.3d 754, 94 Fed. R. Evid.
Serv. 1078, 94 Fed. R. Evid. Serv. 1129
(D.C. Cir. 2014) (corporation's investigation into possible fraud against
government was protected by attorney-
client privilege even if undertaken as
part of a mandatory compliance
program).

n. 17.
*Delete cross-reference in second para-
graph of footnote.*

§ 88   The professional relationship

n. 2.
Richardson v. State, 744 S.W.2d 65
(Tex. Crim. App. 1987), cert. granted,
judgment vacated on other grounds,
492 U.S. 914, 109 S. Ct. 3235, 106 L.
Ed. 2d 583 (1989)

n. 11.
Aetna Cas. and Sur. Co. v. Certain
Underwriters at Lloyd's London, 176
Misc. 2d 605, 676 N.Y.S.2d 727 (Sup
1998), aff'd, 263 A.D.2d 367, 692

n. 29.
Saltzburg, Martin & Capra, Federal
Rules of Evidence Manual, § 501.
02[5][l][ii] (11th ed. 2015)
*Add at end of first paragraph of foot-
note:*
; Note, An Uncertain Privilege:
Reexamining Garner v. Wolfinbarger
and Its Effect on Attorney-Client Privi-
lege, 35 Cardozo L. Rev. 1217 (2014)

N.Y.S.2d 384 (1st Dep't 1999)

n. 19.
Delete cross-reference in footnote.

n. 26.
Prichard v. U.S., 181 F.2d 326 (6th
Cir. 1950), judgment aff'd, 339 U.S.
974, 70 S. Ct. 1029, 94 L. Ed. 1380
(1950)

n. 27.
Delete law review citations.

§ 89   Subject-matter of the privilege: (a) Communications

n. 6.
Delete cross-reference.

n. 10.
Add at end of footnote:
; U.S. v. Bey, 772 F.3d 1099, 1101 (7th
Cir. 2014) (admission of defense counsel's letter notifying defendant of date
of self-surrender did not violate
attorney-client privilege)

n. 11.
Manning v. State, 766 S.W.2d 551

(Tex. App. Dallas 1989), judgment
aff'd, 773 S.W.2d 568 (Tex. Crim. App.
1989) and petition for discretionary
review granted, (June 28, 1989)

n. 12.
In re Ryder, 263 F. Supp. 360 (E.D.
Va. 1967), judgment aff'd, 381 F.2d
713 (4th Cir. 1967)

§ 90   Subject-matter of the privilege: (b) Fact of employment and identity of the client

n. 2.
People ex rel. Vogelstein v. Warden of
County Jail of New York County, 150
Misc. 714, 270 N.Y.S. 362 (Sup 1934),
aff'd, 242 A.D. 611, 271 N.Y.S. 1059
(1st Dep't 1934)

n. 6.
*Delete signal and cite from first
paragraph.*

n. 7.
People ex rel. Vogelstein v. Warden of
County Jail of New York County, 150
Misc. 714, 270 N.Y.S. 362 (Sup 1934),

aff'd, 242 A.D. 611, 271 N.Y.S. 1059 (1st Dep't 1934)

n. 15.

People ex rel. Vogelstein v. Warden of

County Jail of New York County, 150 Misc. 714, 270 N.Y.S. 362 (Sup 1934), aff'd, 242 A.D. 611, 271 N.Y.S. 1059 (1st Dep't 1934)

§ 91 The confidential character of the communications: Communications intended to be made public; presence of third persons and agents

n. 8.

Rice, et al., Attorney-Client Privilege

in the United States § 5:13 (2015-2016 ed.)

§ 91.1 The confidential character of the communications: Joint consultations and employments; controversies between client and attorney

n. 6.

Liberty Mut. Ins. Co. v. Engels, 41 Misc. 2d 49, 244 N.Y.S.2d 983 (Sup 1963), order aff'd, 21 A.D.2d 808, 250 N.Y.S.2d 851 (2d Dep't 1964)

n. 7.

Add in cites after "See also":

; Giesel, End the Experiment: The Attorney-Client Privilege Should Not Protect Communications in the Allied Lawyer Setting, 95 Marq. L. Rev. 475 (2012)

§ 93 Waiver

n. 6.

In re Grand Jury Proceedings Involving Berkley and Co., Inc., 466 F. Supp. 863 (D. Minn. 1979), aff'd as modified, 629 F.2d 548, 6 Fed. R. Evid. Serv. 1165 (8th Cir. 1980)

n. 17.

; McLoughlin, Bloomfield, et al, Navigating Implied Waiver of the Attorney-Client Privilege After Adoption of Federal Rule 502 of the Federal Rules of Evidence, 67 N.Y.U. Ann. Surv. Am. L. 693 (2012)

n. 23.

Seneca Ins. Co., Inc. v. Western Claims, Inc., 774 F.3d 1272 (10th Cir. 2014) (waiver of privilege by relying on "advice of counsel," applying state law

in a diversity case);

n. 43.

Fed. R. Evid. 612 advisory committee note

n. 45.

In re Kellogg Brown & Root, Inc., 796 F.3d 137, 146, 98 Fed. R. Evid. Serv. 149 (D.C. Cir. 2015) (privileged and work product protected documents improperly ordered produced under Rule 612 where no basis for balancing test and court failed to give due weight to privilege and work product protection);

n. 48.

Matison v. Matison, 95 N.Y.S.2d 837 (Sup 1950), judgment aff'd, 277 A.D. 770, 97 N.Y.S.2d 550 (1st Dep't 1950)

§ 94 The effect of the death of the client

n. 18.

Add at end of footnote:
See also Natali, Should We Amend or

Interpret the Attorney-Client Privilege to Allow for an Innocence Exception, 37 Am. J. Trial Advoc. 93 (2013).

§ 95   Consultation in furtherance of crime or fraud

n. 8.
See also In re Grand Jury Subpoena, 745 F.3d 681 (3d Cir. 2014), cert. denied, 135 S. Ct. 510, 190 L. Ed. 2d 361 (2014) (*Zolin* standard applied where unmemorialized communications were at issue).

n. 14.
; Lipman, Invoking the Crime Fraud Exception: Why Courts Should Heighten the Standard in Criminal Cases, 52 Am. Crim. L. Rev. 595 (2015)

§ 96   Protective rules relating to materials collected for use of counsel in preparation for trial: Reports of employees, witness-statements, experts' reports, and the like

n. 5.
6 Moore, Federal Practice ¶ 26.02 (2015)
Wright & Kane, Law of Federal Courts § 81 (7th ed. 2011)

n. 28.
Wright & Kane, Law of Federal Courts § 82 (7th ed. 2011)

n. 36.
Fed. R. Civ. P. 26 advisory committee note to 1993 amendment

n. 38.
Fed. R. Civ. P. 26 advisory committee note to 1993 amendment

§ 97   Discovery in criminal cases: Statements by witnesses

n. 2.
Wright and Miller's Federal Practice and Procedure, Criminal § 251 (2015)

n. 9.
4 Weinstein & Berger, Evidence

§ 612[02] (2015)

n. 22.
Mueller and Kirkpatrick, Federal Evidence § 6:97 (4th ed.)

Chapter 11

The Privilege for Confidential Information Secured in the Course of the Physician-Patient Relationship

> **KeyCite®:** Cases and other legal materials listed in KeyCite Scope can be researched through the KeyCite service on Westlaw®. Use KeyCite to check citations for form, parallel references, prior and later history, and comprehensive citator information, including citations to other decisions and secondary materials.

§ 98   The statement of the rule and its purpose

n. 24.
U. S. ex rel. Edney v. Smith, 425 F.

Supp. 1038 (E.D. N.Y. 1976), aff'd, 556 F.2d 556 (2d Cir. 1977)

§ 99   Relation of physician and patient

n. 8.
Arizona & N. M. Ry. Co. v. Clark, 207 F. 817 (C.C.A. 9th Cir. 1913), aff'd, 235

U.S. 669, 35 S. Ct. 210, 59 L. Ed. 415 (1915)

§ 101   The confidential character of the disclosure: Presence of third persons and members of family; information revealed to nurses and attendants; public records

n. 8.

Add at end of footnote:
See also Goodman, When Privacy Is Not An Option: Codifying the Contours of Necessary Third Parties in Emergency Medical Situations, 63 Syracuse L. Rev. 399 (2013).

n. 14.
Volkman v. Miller, 41 N.Y.2d 946, 394 N.Y.S.2d 631, 363 N.E.2d 355 (1977)

n. 15.
People v. Lay, 254 A.D. 372, 5 N.Y.S.2d 325 (2d Dep't 1938), judgment aff'd, 279 N.Y. 737, 18 N.E.2d 686 (1939)

n. 17.

Add at end of footnote:
See also People v. Rivera, 25 N.Y.3d 256, 11 N.Y.S.3d 509, 33 N.E.3d 465 (2015) (statements to psychiatrist

concerning the abuse of a child was protected by privilege even though psychiatrist was required to report the incident to authorities).

§ 102 Rule of privilege, not incompetency: Privilege belongs to the patient, not to an objecting party as such; effect of the patient's death

n. 10.
Cooksey v. Landry, 295 Ga. 430, 433, 761 S.E.2d 61, 65 (2014) (patient-psychiatrist privilege survives death of patient; deceased patient's representative cannot waive);

Delete history from U.S. v. Hansen cite.

U.S. v. Hansen, 955 F. Supp. 1225 (D. Mont. 1997)

n. 11.
Fleet Messenger Service, Inc. v. Life Ins. Co. of North America, 205 F. Supp. 585 (S.D. N.Y. 1962), judgment aff'd, 315 F.2d 593 (2d Cir. 1963)

§ 103 What constitutes a waiver of the privilege?

n. 5.

Add in second paragraph of footnote:
U.S. v. Bolander, 722 F.3d 199, 91 Fed. R. Evid. Serv. 1138 (4th Cir. 2013) (patient waived privilege by producing covered documents without asserting privilege);

n. 15.
; Anderson, The Psychotherapist Privilege: Privacy and "Garden Variety" Emotional Distress, 21 Geo. Mason L. Rev. 117 (2013)

n. 16.
; Mitchell v. Eighth Judicial Dist.

Court of State ex rel. County of Clark, 359 P.3d 1096, 131 Nev. Adv. Op. No. 21 (Nev. 2015) (no waiver where plaintiff put defendant's drug addiction in issue)

n. 18.
Youngs v. Peacehealth, 179 Wash. 2d 645, 653, 316 P.3d 1035 (2014) (defendant's counsel may conduct privileged ex parte communications with plaintiff's treating physicians employed by defendant only where the physician has direct knowledge of the events and the communication concerns the facts of the alleged negligent conduct);

§ 105 The policy and future of the privilege

n. 1.
Delete cross-reference to footnote at end of note.

Chapter 12

Privileges for Governmental Secrets

> **KeyCite®:** Cases and other legal materials listed in KeyCite Scope can be
> researched through the KeyCite service on Westlaw®. Use KeyCite to check
> citations for form, parallel references, prior and later history, and comprehen-
> sive citator information, including citations to other decisions and secondary
> materials.

§ 107   The common law privileges for military or diplomatic secrets and other facts the disclosure of which would be contrary to the public interest

n. 4.
Maxwell v. First Nat. Bank of Maryland, 143 F.R.D. 590 (D. Md. 1992), aff'd, 998 F.2d 1009 (4th Cir. 1993)

n. 15.
Maxwell v. First Nat. Bank of Maryland, 143 F.R.D. 590 (D. Md. 1992), aff'd, 998 F.2d 1009 (4th Cir. 1993)

Replace paragraph including footnotes 16-17 with:

Congress has enacted statutes that interact with and mirror the state secrets privilege: the national security exemption in the Freedom of Information Act (FOIA),[16] the Classified Information Procedures Act (CIPA),[17] and the Foreign Intelligence Surveillance Act (FISA),[17.30] which applies when state secrets involve electronic surveillance for intelligence purposes.[17.50]

---

[16]5 U.S.C.A. § 552(b)(1). This pro-   vision provides that FOIA does not ap-

ply to information that "(A) is specifically authorized under criteria established by an Executive order to be kept secret in the interest of national defense or foreign policy and (B) are in fact classified pursuant to such Executive order." *See generally* Greenwald, et al., Testimonial Privileges § 9:17 (2012 ed.); United States Dep't of Justice, Justice Dep't Guide to the Freedom of Information Act, available at http://www.justice.gov/oip/exemptio n1.htm (discussing exemption 1).

[17]18 U.S.C.A. App. 3. *See also* Yaroshefsky, Secret Evidence is Slowly Eroding the Adversary System: CIPA and FISA in the Courts, 34 Hofstra L. Rev. 1063 (2006); Yaroshefsky, The Slow Erosion of the Adversary System: Article III Courts, FISA, CIPA and

Ethical Dilemmas, 5 Cardozo Pub. L. Pol'y & Ethics J. 203 (2006).

[17.30]50 U.S.C.A. ch. 36.

[17.50]*See* Jewel v. National Security Agency, 965 F. Supp. 2d 1090, 1104-05 (N.D. Cal. 2013) (ruling that in camera review procedure in FISA applies and preempts the determination of evidentiary preclusion under the state secrets doctrine where electronic surveillance yields potentially sensitive evidence).

n. 22.

United States v. Turi, 2015 WL 5770538 (D. Ariz. 2015) (stating that under *Roviaro*-based balancing test disclosure is required when there is a reasonable probability that the information would change the outcome of the case);

Add new footnote in sentence ending in footnote 26, after "information,":

Upon receiving such notice, the government can seek a ruling that some or all of the information is immaterial, move for substitution of a non-sensitive summary for the information,[25.50]

[25.50]U.S. v. Sedaghaty, 728 F.3d 885, 965-66 (9th Cir. 2013) (ruling that summary should be worded in an even-handed fashion and not shaded to the government's advantage and finding the document substituted in this case violated those neutrality requirements).

§ 108 Qualified privileges for government information: The constitutional presidential privilege; common law privileges for agency deliberations and law enforcement files

n. 20.

Add at end of footnote:
See Judicial Watch, Inc. v. U.S. Dept. of Transp., 950 F. Supp. 2d 213, 218-19 (D.D.C. 2013) (stating that the D.C. Circuit rule is "[w]hen communications between an agency and a non-agency aid the agency's decision-making process and the non-agency did not have an outside interest in obtaining a benefit that is at the expense of competitors, the communication must be considered an intra-agency communication for the purposes of FOIA Exemption 5").

n. 23.
Delete *Town of Norfolk, Hopkins and Florida House of Representatives cites*

from first citation sentence of footnote.
National Sec. Archive v. C.I.A., 752 F.3d 460, 463-65 (D.C. Cir. 2014) (considering an agency's official history as a final agency decision and ruling that information in a draft of the official history is protected because predecisional and deliberative);

Add at end of first paragraph of footnote:
Whether a strictly temporal test is to be applied is subject to disagreement between the circuits. See Cherokee Nation v. Salazar, 986 F. Supp. 2d 1239, 1245-47 (N.D. Okla. 2013) (finding that documents were not predecisional even though created before the decision was formally announced).

n. 27.
Manna v. U.S. Dept. of Justice, 815 F.
Supp. 798, 815 (D.N.J. 1993), aff'd, 51
F.3d 1158 (3d Cir. 1995)

n. 28.
Add at end of footnote:

However, when the privilege is invoked in a FOIA action rather than to resist discovery in civil litigation, the claim need not be made by a department head. *See* Fraternal Order of Police v. District of Columbia, 79 A.3d 347, 357 (D.C. 2013).

Replace "concerned" in sentence ending with footnote 30 with:

at issue in the communication

n. 33.
Delaware Riverkeeper Network v.
Delaware River Basin Com'n, 300
F.R.D. 207, 213-14 (D.N.J. 2014) (ruling that deliberative process privilege remained applicable because the subjective motivation of agency was not challenged by the suit);

Delete Anderson and Scott cites from footnote.

Add at end of footnote:
See also Burbar v. Incorporated Village of Garden City, 303 F.R.D. 9, 14 (E.D. N.Y. 2014) (finding that application of the balancing approach rarely would lead to a different result).

n. 34.
Replace contents of footnote with:
N. L. R. B. v. Sears, Roebuck &
Co., 421 U.S. 132, 161, 95 S. Ct. 1504,

44 L. Ed. 2d 29 (1975); National Council of La Raza v. Department of Justice, 411 F.3d 350, 355 (2d Cir. 2005). *See also* New York Times Co. v. U.S. Dept. of Justice, 2015 WL 5729976 (S.D. N.Y. 2015) (discussing application of "express adoption" doctrine to deliberative process and other privileges).

Similarly, deliberative process privilege does not apply to documents that explain a decision already reached or policy adopted. *See* Sears, Roebuck & Co., *supra*, 421 U.S. at 152 n.19, 95 S. Ct. at 1504, 44 L. Ed. 2d 29; American Civil Liberties Union of North California v. Federal Bureau of Investigation, 2015 WL 7251928 (N.D. Cal. 2015) (ruling that FAQ that reflected the agency's "working law" was not protected by the privilege).

Replace "relatively infrequently" in sentence ending with footnote 35 with:

with growing frequency

n. 37.
Vandelay Entertainment, LLC v.
Fallin, 2014 OK 109, 343 P.3d 1273,
1276-80 (Okla. 2014) (recognizing common law deliberative process privilege as part of governor's executive privilege); City of Garland v. Dallas Morning News, 22 S.W.3d 351, 360 (Tex. 2000) (rejecting party's argument that there was no deliberative process privilege in the state); ; Aland v. Mead, 2014 WY 83, 327 P.3d 752, 763 (Wyo. 2014) (concluding that common law deliberative process exists in the state)

Add in footnote, after "But see":
Popovich v. Indiana Dept. of State Revenue, 7 N.E.3d 406, 415-16 (Ind. Tax Ct. 2014) (stating that no deliberative process privilege is recognized in Indiana);

Add at end of footnote:
See also Valbruna Slater Steel Corp. v. Joslyn Mfg. Co., L.L.C., 2015 WL 6695510 (S.D. Ind. 2015) (finding that Indiana has no state deliberative process privilege and discussing whether to extend the federal privilege to state agency records in federal litigation).

Delete sentence ending with footnote 38.

n. 39.

U. S. v. Mackey, 36 F.R.D. 431, 433 (D. D.C. 1965), judgment aff'd, 351 F.2d 794 (D.C. Cir. 1965)

n. 43.

McQueen v. U.S., 179 F.R.D. 522, 526 (S.D. Tex. 1998), aff'd, 176 F.3d 478 (5th Cir. 1999)

n. 44.

; Friedman v. U.S. Secret Service, 923 F. Supp. 2d 262, 282-83 (D.D.C. 2013) (ruling that Secret Service's status as law enforcement agency was insufficient to establish the privilege without addressing specific document that

may have been of "research nature")

n. 45.

J & C Marketing, L.L.C. v. McGinty, 143 Ohio St. 3d 315, 2015-Ohio-1310, 37 N.E.3d 1183 (2015);

n. 47.

Add after first citation sentence of footnote:
But see Sea Shepherd Conservation Society v. Internal Revenue Service, 89 F. Supp. 3d 81, 95-96 (D.D.C. 2015) (ruling that the government's claim that it may reopen the investigation is insufficient to continue the life of the privilege for a closed investigation).

§ 109   Effect of the presence of the government as a litigant

n. 4.

Restis v. American Coalition Against Nuclear Iran, Inc., 2015 WL 1344479 (S.D. N.Y. 2015) (dismissing private defamation action regarding alleged prohibited business transactions with Iran on government's motion because the trial court was satisfied that allowing the litigation to proceed would inevitably risk disclosure of state secrets);

Delete Black v. U.S. cite

n. 9.

U.S. v. Cotton Valley Operators Committee, 9 F.R.D. 719 (W.D. La. 1949), judgment aff'd, 339 U.S. 940, 70 S. Ct. 793, 94 L. Ed. 1356 (1950)

n. 13.

Edmonds v. U.S. Dept. of Justice, 323 F. Supp. 2d 65, 77-81 (D.D.C. 2004), order aff'd, 161 Fed. Appx. 6 (D.C. Cir. 2005)

§ 110   The scope of the judge's function in determining the validity of the claim of privilege

n. 4.

Maxwell v. First Nat. Bank of Maryland, 143 F.R.D. 590, 598 (D. Md.

1992), aff'd, 998 F.2d 1009 (4th Cir. 1993)

§ 111   The privilege against the disclosure of the identity of an informer

n. 3.

Replace Brennan cite appearing after "See" with:
In re Perez, 749 F.3d 849, 855-56 (9th Cir. 2014)

Replace the last sentence in footnote and cites with:
The privilege may be stronger in civil suits because the countervailing constitutional guarantees afforded to criminal defendants are not present. See Elnashar v. Speedway Super-America, LLC, 484 F.3d 1046, 1053 (8th Cir. 2007).

n. 10.

In re Apollo Group, Inc. Securities Litigation, 251 F.R.D. 12, 34-35 (D.D.C. 2008), aff'd on other grounds, remanded by 329 Fed. Appx. 283 (D.C. Cir. 2009)

n. 11.

U.S. v. Sierra-Villegas, 774 F.3d 1093, 1098-99 (6th Cir. 2014), cert. denied, 136 S. Ct. 34, 193 L. Ed. 2d 47 (2015) (ruling privilege still effective after disclosure of informer's name to defense because of potential retribution from broader disclosure to others where informant contributed to major "meth bust" and may be involved in future investigations)

n. 13.

Delete "See also" and U.S. v. Martinez-Figuroa cite.

§ 112 Statutory privileges for certain reports of individuals to government agencies: Accident reports, tax returns, etc.

n. 1.
3 Weinstein's Federal Evidence §§ 502A.01-502A.07 (2d ed. 2015)

n. 6.
3 Weinstein's Federal Evidence § 502A. 03[2] (2d ed. 2015)

Replace Washington Post Co. cite

with:
Association for Women in Science v. Califano, 566 F.2d 339, 347, 24 Fed. R. Serv. 2d 393 (D.C. Cir. 1977) (observing that "confidential report privilege, like the informer's privilege, is shared by the reporter and the government").

§ 113 The secrecy of grand jury proceedings: Votes and expressions of grand jurors; testimony of witnesses

n. 1.
Beale, Felman, Elston, and Bryson, Grand Jury Law & Practice §§ 5:1 et seq. (2d ed.)

n. 4.
Delete U.S. v. Sigma International cite and parenthetical.

n. 11.
Moore v. Hartman, 102 F. Supp. 3d 35, 108-11 (D.D.C. 2015), appeal dismissed, 2015 WL 6153963 (D.C. Cir. 2015) (ruling that disclosure of witness summaries did not violate grand jury secrecy even though same summaries were presented to grand jury where no secret aspect of grand jury investigation was revealed);

Delete Lockheed Martin Corp. cite from end of footnote.

n. 12.
Beale, Felman, Elston, and Bryson,

Grand Jury Law & Practice § 5:8 (2d ed.)

n. 15.
Beale, Felman, Elston, and Bryson, Grand Jury Law & Practice § 5:8 (2d ed.)

n. 22.
Beale, Felman, Elston, and Bryson, Grand Jury Law & Practice § 5:10 (2d ed.)

n. 29.
Beale, Felman, Elston, and Bryson, Grand Jury Law & Practice § 5:5 (2d ed.)

n. 31.
Beale, Felman, Elston, and Bryson, Grand Jury Law & Practice § 5:5 (2d ed.)

Title 6 PRIVILEGE: CONSTITUTIONAL

Chapter 13

The Privilege Against Self-Incrimination

KeyCite®: Cases and other legal materials listed in KeyCite Scope can be researched through the KeyCite service on Westlaw®. Use KeyCite to check citations for form, parallel references, prior and later history, and comprehensive citator information, including citations to other decisions and secondary materials.

---

§ 118   Asserting the privilege

Add new footnote to end of first sentence of second paragraph:
In some situations, the need to so assert the Fifth Amendment privilege is relaxed.[3.50]

[3.50]According to three members of the Court, the privilege need not be asserted in two situations. One is the criminal defendant who wishes to not testify at trial. The other is where governmental coercion makes forfeiture of the privilege involuntary. Salinas v. Texas, 133 S. Ct. 2174, 2179-80, 136 L. Ed. 2d 376 (2013) (plurality opinion).

§ 124   Limitation of the privilege to compelled "testimonial" activity

n. 20.

Add to end of footnote:
Accord State v. Jamison, 152 Conn. App. 753, 779-80, 99 A.3d 1273,1291 (2014), aff'd in part, rev'd in part on other grounds, 320 Conn. 589 (Conn. 2016) ("handwriting exemplar is a clear example of 'nontestimonial' evidence," and compelling such an exem-

plar does not violate either federal or state constitution).

n. 24.

Add to end of footnote:
Accord State v. Gonzalez, 2014 WI 124, 359 Wis. 2d 1, 14-15, 856 N.W.2d 580, 586-87 (2014).

§ 126   Privilege as applied to an accused in a criminal proceeding: (a) Inferences from and comment upon the accused's reliance upon the privilege in the trial

Add new footnote to end of first sentence of second paragraph, including footnotes 3-4:

In *Griffin v. California*,[3] the Supreme Court held that the Fifth Amendment privilege was violated[4] by a prosecutor's argument which urged the jury to draw an inference of guilt from a defendant's failure to testify when his testimony could reasonably have been expected to deny or explain matters proved by the prosecution and a jury instruction that authorized the jury to draw that suggested inference.[4.50]

[4.50]Several members of the Court have characterized *Griffin* as resting on an "indefensible foundation," because permitting a jury to draw an adverse interest from a defendant's silence does not compel the defendant to be a witness against himself. Salinas v. Texas, 133 S. Ct. 2174, 2184, 136 L. Ed. 2d 376 (2013) (Thomas, J., concurring in the judgment).

Add new footnote after footnote 12:

The prosecution violated *Griffin*, for example, when the lead prosecutor stood in front of the defendant in the courtroom, gestured towards her, and demanded in a loud voice, "Just tell us where you were. That's all we are asking, Noura!"[12.50]

[12.50]State v. Jackson, 444 S.W.3d 554, 589 (Tenn. 2014) (jury would necessarily have taken prosecutor's remark as a comment on the defendant's exercise of her right not to testify).

§ 129   Privilege as applied to an accused in a criminal proceeding: (d) "Waiver" of the privilege by voluntary testimony

Add new footnote in second sentence, after "testifying,":

Unlike the situation of a witness, who loses the privilege only by testifying to incriminating facts, the accused suffers this reduction in his rights merely by testifying,[1] regardless of the incriminatory content of his testimony.

---

[1]A pro se defendant may lose protection by action short of taking the witness stand and testifying. If such a defendant in the course of self-representation makes testimonial statements, the prosecutor may point out the jury that such statements cannot be tested by cross-examination and are not evidence. State v. Tayari-Garrett, 841 N.W.2d 644, 652 (Minn. Ct. App. 2014), review denied, (Mar. 26, 2014) and cert. denied, 135 S. Ct. 167, 190 L. Ed. 2d 50 (2014) (commenting in addition that the defendant's action "came very close" to being so egregious "that the state could have compelled her to take the witness stand and submit to cross-examination").

§ 130   The privilege as applied to a witness: (a) Invoking the privilege

n. 5.

Add to end of footnote:
This was stressed in State v. Rainey, 180 Wash. App. 830, 327 P.3d 56 (2014), in which the trial judge was held to have erred in closing the hearing on a motion for new trial and accepting a witness's representation he would invoke the privilege:

> Requiring a witness claiming the Fifth Amendment privilege to do so openly and in full view of the public subjects the witness to public scrutiny and satisfies the appearance of fairness that would be absent if the assertion could take place behind closed doors. It prevents abuse of the privilege by all participants by holding witnesses accountable for their use of the privilege while also tempering bias and partiality.

180 Wash. App. at 842, 327 P.3d at 61.

§ 135   The privilege as applied to a witness: (f) Effect in a criminal trial of defense witness's invocation of the privilege

n. 2.

Add new paragraph after first paragraph:
The *Smith* court later rejected the suggestion in *Smith* that federal courts have power to grant immunity to defense witnesses. Under certain circumstances, however, the Government's failure to grant immunity to defense witnesses will be prosecutorial misconduct violating due process and a federal district court may dismiss the prosecution. *See* U.S. v. Quinn, 728 F.3d 243, 256-60 (3d Cir. 2013), cert. denied, 134 S. Ct. 1872, 188 L. Ed. 2d 916 (2014).

§ 138   The privilege as related to documents and
         tangible items: (b) Compulsory production and
         incrimination by the "act of production"

n. 18.

Add at end of footnote:
Accord State v. Trant, 2015 WL
7575496 (Me. Dist. Ct. 2015) ("compelling Defendant to divulge the contents
of his mind—either by compelling him
to surrender the passcodes or compelling him to himself open the phones—
would violate his privilege against
self-incrimination protected by the
Federal and Maine Constitutions");
Commonwealth v. Baust, 89 Va. Cir.
267, 2014 WL 10355635 (2014) (where
encrypted smart phone could be en-
tered only with a passcode or fingerprint, defendant would be compelled
to provide fingerprint but not
passcode). *Compare* Com. v. Gelfgatt,
468 Mass. 512, 523, 11 N.E.3d 605,
615 (2014) ("the factual statements
that would be conveyed by the defendant's act of entering an encryption
key in the computers are 'foregone
conclusions' and, therefore, the act of
decryption is not a testimonial communication that is protected by the
Fifth Amendment").

Chapter 14

Confessions

KeyCite®: Cases and other legal materials listed in KeyCite Scope can be
researched through the KeyCite service on Westlaw®. Use KeyCite to check
citations for form, parallel references, prior and later history, and comprehensive citator information, including citations to other decisions and secondary
materials.

---

§ 145   *Corpus delicti* or corroboration requirement: (a) In general

n. 2.

Add at end of footnote:

The Idaho Supreme Court abandoned the *corpus delicti* rule in State
v. Suriner, 154 Idaho 81, 294 P.3d
1093 (2013), adding: "We see no reason to attempt to fashion another rule
to take its place. Instead, the jury can
give a defendant's extrajudicial confession or statement whatever weight it
deems appropriate along with all of
the other evidence when deciding
whether the State has proved guilt beyond a reasonable doubt." 154 Idaho

at 88, 294 P.3d at 1100. Thus, Idaho
now appears to have no corroboration
requirement.

n. 22.

Add new paragraph after cite:

Under the Alaska approach, the
trial judge may—in deciding whether
the state may introduce the confession—consider evidence that is not
admissible at trial. Loggett v. State,
320 P.3d 311, 314-25 (Alaska Ct.. App.
2014) (acknowledging that this is not
the case under the majority conceptualization of the *corpus delicti* rule).

§ 146   *Corpus delicti* or corroboration requirement: (b) Requirement of independent proof of the *corpus delicti*

n. 3.

Replace contents of footnote:
State v. Meyers, 799 N.W.2d 132, 139 (Iowa 2011) ("Corroborating evidence may be either direct or circumstantial." *Accord, e.g.,* Jones v. State, 2010 WY 44, 228 P.3d 867, 870 (Wyo. 2010). Circumstantial evidence merely establishing an opportunity to commit the charged crime is not sufficient. State v. McGill, 50 Kan. App. 2d 208, 220, 328 P.3d 554, 561 (2014), review denied, (Jan. 25, 2016); Allen v. Com., 287 Va. 68, 752 S.E.2d 856. 863 (2014).

One extrajudicial uncorroborated statement, further, cannot be used to corroborate another extrajudicial statement. *E.g.,* Ross v. State, 268 Ind. 471, 376 N.E.2d 1117 (1978); State v. Charity, 587 S.W.2d 350 (Mo. Ct. App. S.D. 1979). One court applying the trustworthiness approach discussed in the next section agreed that a confes-

sion made to law enforcement officers cannot be corroborated by a second confession made to law enforcement officers, but added that evidence that a defendant confessed several times to non-law enforcement individuals providing consistent details bolsters the trustworthiness of the statement. McGill, 50 Kan. App. 2d at 219, 328 P.3d at 561.

n. 19.

Add to end of first paragraph of footnote:
Accord Miller v. State, 457 S.W.3d 919, 927 (Tex. Crim. App. 2015) (Texas recognizes "a closely related crimes exception to strict application of the *corpus delicti* rule," applicable "only when the temporal relationship between the offenses is sufficiently proximate that introduction of the extrajudicial confession does not violate the policies underlying the *corpus delicti* rule.").

§ 147   *Corpus delicti* or corroboration requirement: (c) Requirement of evidence tending to establish truthfulness of statement

n. 4.
State v. Dern, 303 Kan. 384, 362 P.3d 566, 582-83 (2015);
State v. Bishop, 431 S.W.3d 22, 57-61 (Tenn. 2014), cert. denied, 135 S. Ct. 120, 190 L. Ed. 2d 92 (2014);

Add to end of third paragraph:
Accord Miller v. State, 457 S.W.3d

919, 926-27 (Tex. Crim. App. 2015) (*corpus delicti* approach has been applied in state for at least one hundred sixty one years and, as modified by an exception for closely related crimes, "continues to serve an important function").

Add new paragraph following quotation ending in footnote 9:

At least one court has indicated that the trustworthiness approach has the further benefit of providing some protection against convictions based on false confessions to actual crimes.[10] As applied in some cases, the trustworthiness standard stimulates production by the prosecution of evidence confirming not simply the occurrence of crimes but the defendants' identity as the perpetrators.

---

[10]State v. Bishop, 431 S.W.3d 22, 58 (Tenn. 2014), cert. denied, 135 S.

Ct. 120, 190 L. Ed. 2d 92 (2014).

§ 149 Voluntariness, in general

Add after footnote 37:

Of course, state law cannot make admissible statements involuntary under the federal constitutional case law. It can, however, impose additional limits upon admissibility of statements voluntary under due process law. These limits, unlike due process voluntariness, most likely can emphasize reliability as the benchmark for admissibility. A Georgia statute, for example, makes a confession inadmissible if it was "induced by * * * the slightest hope of benefit or remotest fear of injury."[37.30] The Georgia court has construed this statute when applied to confessions voluntary under due process analysis as requiring state law scrutiny focusing on whether hope of benefit or fear of injury affected the reliability of the confessions.[37.50]

[37.30]Ga. Code Ann. § 24-8-824.

[37.50]State v. Chulpayev, 296 Ga. 764, 779-80, 770 S.E.2d 808, 820-21 (2015).

§ 150 Self-incrimination (*Miranda*) requirements: (a) In general

Research References

West's Key Number Digest, Criminal Law ☞517.2, 518

§ 152 Self-incrimination (*Miranda*) requirements: (c) Prohibition against interrogation

n. 27.
Accord Com. v. Bland, 115 A.3d 854, 863 (Pa. 2015) ("to require a suspension of questioning by law enforcement officials on pain of an exclusionary remedy, an invocation of the *Miranda*-based right to counsel must be made upon or after actual or imminent commencement of in-custody interrogation").

§ 154 General right to counsel requirements

Add to end of paragraph beginning with italicized heading "State Constitutional Rights to Counsel":

Several state courts have held state law rights to counsel bar officers from approaching suspects who have accepted representation or requested counsel regarding charges as to which adversary judicial proceedings have begun.[23.50]

[23.50]State v. Camacho, 856 N.W.2d 381, 2014 WL 4628984, at *7 (Iowa App. 2014) (unpublished) (statement should have been suppressed under Iowa Constitution because officer continued to question suspect regarding matter on which adversary judicial proceedings had begun after learning that suspect had a lawyer); State v. Bevel, 231 W. Va. 346, 356, 745 S.E.2d 237, 247 (2013) ("if police initiate interrogation after a defendant asserts his right to counsel at an arraignment or similar proceeding, any waiver of

115

the defendant's right to counsel for that police-initiated interrogation is invalid as being taken in violation of the defendant's right to counsel under article III, section 14 of the Constitution of West Virginia"). One court reached this result under a state statu-tory right to counsel. State v. Lawson, 296 Kan. 1084, 1098, 297 P.3d 1164, 1173 (2013). *Compare* State v. Delebreau, 362 Wis. 2d 542, 561, 864 N.W.2d 852, 862 (2015) (refusing to follow *Bevel* as a matter of state constitutional law).

§ 155   Special problems: Promises made to suspects and deception of suspects

n. 23.

Add after "Accord":
Bussey v. State, 184 So. 3d 1138, 1145-46 (Fla. 2d DCA 2015) (detectives repeatedly referred to death penalty for murder and represented defendant would be charged with robbery rather than murder if he confessed);

n. 26.

Add at end of footnote:
The Kansas court, applying its approach, held a promise not to book the defendant for murder carrying a life sentence "was one that would likely cause the accused to make a false statement." State v. Garcia, 297 Kan. 182, 196, 301 P.3d 658, 668 (2013).

n. 37.

Where a defendant found in possession of marihuana was told by an officer that the officer could not charge him with any other drugs, this misrepresentation rendered ineffective the defendant's waivers in his admission that he possessed other controlled substances in his home. U.S. v. Castor, 598 F. Appx. 700, 703-04 (11th Cir. 2015) (per curiam) (officer "misled Castor regarding the consequences of relinquishing his right to remain silent" and as a result "Castor did not truly understand the nature of his right against self-incrimination or the consequences of waiving it").

n. 48.

; Com. v. Monroe, 472 Mass. 461, 35 N.E.3d 677, 686 (2015) (false representation to assault suspect that police had evidence of suspect's DNA on victim supported court's conclusion that statement was involuntary)

n. 49.

A confession was held involuntary where an interrogating officer told the African-American defendant he should cooperate and confess because if he went to trial the jury would be unfair to him because of his race. Bond v. State, 9 N.E.3d 134, 141 (Ind. 2014) (impermissible to "mislead[ ] a suspect as to his constitutionally guaranteed rights to a fair trial and an impartial jury").

§ 157   Reliability or trustworthiness as admission requirement

n. 9.

Add after "Accord":
; State v. Dubray, 289 Neb. 208, 234-35, 854 N.W.2d 584, 609 (2014) (state-ment coerced by private persons could be challenged as inadmissible because danger of prejudice outweighs probative value)

§ 160   Judicial confessions, guilty pleas, and admissions made in plea bargaining

n. 15.

Add at end of footnote:
Compare State v. Myrick, 354 Wis. 2d 828, 849, 848 N.W.2d 743, 754 (2014) (testimony given at hearing while ne-gotiations were still ongoing was inadmissible).

n. 16.

If a provision refers to statements made in connection with an offer to

plead guilty, this does not require that
the defendant have begun the negotiations with an offer. Coverage exists if
the prosecution begins the negotiations during which the defendant
makes an offer. State v. Myrick, 354
Wis. 2d 828, 848, 848 N.W.2d 743, 753
(2014).

Some provisions do not literally
require the statements to have been
made to an official. Nevertheless, a
statement made by a jailed defendant
in a phone call to his mother concerning pending plea negotiations was held
not to have been made "in connection
with" an offer to plead as required by
the applicable provision. Bass v. State,
147 So. 3d 1033, 1035 (Fla. 1st DCA
2014), review denied 163 So. 3d 507
(Fla. 2015) (stressing that nothing said
by the defendant to his mother in the
conversation was communicated to the
State).

n. 19.

Add after "Accord":
U.S. v. Riedman, 2014 WL 713552, at

*24 (W.D.N.Y. 2014) (defendant had
no objective basis for conclusion that
F.B.I. agent was authorized to engage
in plea negotiations);

n. 20.
People v. Smart, 304 Mich. App. 244,
254-56, 850 N.W.2d 579, 584-85 (2014),
appeal denied, 497 Mich. 950, 857
N.W.2d 658 (2015) (statements made
to officer were protected where prior
meeting with officer had resulted in
plea offer, prosecutor was involved in
setting up meeting with officer, and officer told defendant prosecutor would
be "very interested" in information);

n. 30.
Protections afforded by state provisions are generally regarded as
waivable. *E.g.*, Com. v. Widmer, 2015
PA Super 156, 120 A.3d 1023, 1027
(2015) (although "Pennsylvania courts
have not expressly considered waiver
of the inadmissibility of statements
made during plea negotiations," protection held waivable citing
Mezzanatto).

§ 161   "Tacit" and "adoptive" confessions and admissions

n. 15.

Add after "E.g.,":
Bartley v. Com., 445 S.W.3d 1, 9 (Ky.
2014) (use of silence after *Miranda*
warnings is prohibited, even if warn-
ing were not necessary because suspect was not in custody);

n. 16.

*Delete Salinas v. State cite and
parenthetical.*

Add after eighth paragraph:

A split five justice majority in *Salinas v. Texas*[16.30] held the prosecution's use in its case-in-chief of a defendant's pre-custody and
pre-warning silence did not violate the Fifth Amendment. Justice
Alito's plurality opinion announcing the judgment—joined by two
other members of the Court—reasoned that Salinas could rely on
the Fifth Amendment privilege only if he invoked it and he did
not.[16.50] Thus the plurality did not address whether proved reliance on the privilege could be burdened by using that silence as
evidence of guilt. Justice Thomas, writing for himself and Justice
Scalia, concurred in the judgment on the ground that using
Salinas's silence did not compel him to give self-incriminating
testimony and thus no violation of the Fifth Amendment
occurred.[16.70] Four justices contended the Fifth Amendment
protects against penalizing reliance on the privilege in the pre-
custody and pre-warning context and reliance on the privilege is

shown when—as in *Salinas*—the circumstances justify an inference that a suspect's silence reflects reliance on the privilege.[16.90]

[16.30]Salinas v. Texas, 133 S. Ct. 2174, 136 L. Ed. 2d 376 (2013).

[16.50]Salinas, 133 S. Ct. at 2179-84 (plurality opinion of Alito, J.).

[16.70]Salinas, 133 S. Ct. at 2184

(Thomas, J., concurring in the judgment).

[16.90]Salinas, 133 S. Ct. at 2190 (Breyer, J., dissenting).

Chapter 15

The Privilege Concerning Improperly Obtained Evidence

KeyCite®: Cases and other legal materials listed in KeyCite Scope can be researched through the KeyCite service on Westlaw®. Use KeyCite to check citations for form, parallel references, prior and later history, and comprehensive citator information, including citations to other decisions and secondary materials.

---

§ 165   Policy bases for exclusionary sanctions

n. 5.
; Taslitz, Hypocrisy, Corruption, and Illegitimacy: Why Judicial Integrity

Justifies the Exclusionary Rule, 10 Ohio St. J. Crim. L. 419 (2013)

§ 166   Federal constitutional exclusionary sanctions: (a) Development

n. 3.
   Add at end of footnote:
Compare Re, The Due Process Exclusionary Rule, 127 Harv. L. Rev.

1885 (2014) (arguing that the Due Process Clauses prescribe the remedy for violation of Fourth Amendment procedural rules).

Add new footnote to end of last sentence of paragraph preceding paragraph ending in footnote 18:
It was also undoubtedly influenced by the majority's increasing disenchantment with exclusion of evidence as a constitutional remedy.[17.50]

[17.50]One court held that despite *Hudson* exclusion is required for at least some unreasonable unannounced entries to execute *arrest* warrants. U.S. v. Weaver, 808 F.3d 26 (D.C. Cir. 2015). It relied heavily upon what it regarded as the greater protection of privacy the announcement requirement provides in the arrest warrant context, which permits the suspect to surrender at the door and thus avoid officers' entry into the premises. 808 F.3d at 43-44.

Add new footnote to end of second sentence of paragraph following paragraph that includes footnotes 22-23:

It may in at least some situations allow trial courts to balance on a case-by-case basis the proven law enforcement culpability against the need for deterrence in the type of situation presented.[23.50]

[23.50]Some judges appear to engage in this balancing. *E.g.*, U. S. v. Taylor, 963 F. Supp. 2d 595, 604-05 (S.D.W. Va. 2013) (ordering suppression of evidence despite "heavy toll on the judicial system and society," where unreasonable search was pursuant to "a standard operating procedure" and suppression would have "a strong deterrent effect"); U. S. v. Houston, 965 F. Supp. 2d 855, 871-72 (E.D. Tenn. 2013) (denying suppression of evidence obtained by assumed unconstitutional surveillance where officers without "deliberate, reckless, or grossly negligent disregard for the defendant's Fourth Amendment rights" acted in "good faith reliance on the absence of any judicial decision requiring a search warrant" and therefore "given the facts of this matter, and in particular law enforcement's conduct, the deterrence benefits of suppression do not outweigh the cost to society").

§ 168 State constitutional exclusionary sanctions

n. 12.
Accord Parker v. Com., 440 S.W.3d 381, 388 (Ky. 2014) (language in early cases discussing judicial integrity considerations is "incongruous with our modern search and seizure jurisprudence to the extent that it is interpreted as establishing a broad Kentucky tradition of applying the exclusionary rule for purposes other than police deterrence").

n. 15.
In State v. Scull, 2015 WI 22, ¶ 22, 361 Wis. 2d 288, 300-01, 862 N.W.2d 562, 568 (2015), the lead opinion noted that in prior opinions the court had "cited two rationales in support of its application of the exclusionary rule: assurance of judicial integrity and deterrence of unlawful police conduct." Four of the seven judges, however, "clarif[ied] that the 'assurance of judicial integrity,' standing alone, is not a sufficient basis upon which to employ the exclusionary rule to preclude the prosecution's use of evidence seized when there is no underlying finding of police misconduct." 2015 WI at ¶ 47, 361 Wis. 2d at 311, 862 N.W.2d at 573 (Roggensack, J., concurring).

§ 170 Exclusion for nonconstitutional illegality: (b) Legislative requirements

n. 14.
Accord State v. Hai Kim Nguyen, 419 N.J. Super. 413, 428, 17 A.3d 256, 264 (App. Div. 2011) ("The exclusion of evidence obtained in violation of a statute is justifiable only if the violation

affects privacy rights that the Fourth Amendment and its New Jersey coun-

terpart were designed to protect.").

Add after paragraph including footnotes 16-17:

The same approach has been taken where the statutory provision limits law enforcement power. That an Idaho statute limiting arrests for traffic offenses provides no significant remedy for improperly arrested defendants or repercussions for police making improper arrests is "concerning," the Idaho Supreme Court commented, but it nevertheless refused to find an implied suppression remedy.[17.50]

[17.50]State v. Green, 158 Idaho 884, 354 P.3d 446, 454 (2015) ("If the Legislature intends a violation . . . to result in suppression, it is the responsibility of that body to so provide.").

§ 171   Exclusion for nonconstitutional illegality: (c) Judicially developed requirements

n. 22.

The en banc Ninth Circuit in U.S. v. Dreyer, 804 F.3d 1266 (9th Cir. 2015) (en banc), considered at length the admissibility of evidence acquired in violation of the Posse Comitatus Act, 10 U.S.C.A. §§ 371-378. Without reference to congressional intention, the court assumed it had authority to require exclusion, particularly if "widespread and repeated violations" of the statute were shown. Although persuaded the violation in the case "was not an isolated incident," it held suppression inappropriate given that the military had acknowledged the systemic violation and had initiated stops to correct it. 804 F.3d at 1281.

Add new footnote to end of sentence following footnote 31:

Even if exclusion does not sufficiently serve to deter illegality of the sort involved, then, such exclusion is justified as a means of precluding judicial "justification" of the underlying illegality in a manner that would offend notions of what some courts and commentators regard as judicial integrity.[31.50]

[31.50]The West Virginia Supreme Court of Appeals in State v. Clark, 232 W. Va. 480, 52 S.E.2d 907 (2013), likewise announced it had inherent authority to protect the integrity of the judicial process by requiring the exclusion of evidence obtained in violation of state law. In considering whether such evidence should be suppressed, it added, it would consider "the societal interest in maintaining a prosecution," "the need of a court system to maintain public respect and integrity, "the need to deter similar misconduct in the future, "the overall procedural fairness for the criminal defendant and the animus of the State." 232 W. Va. at 499, 752 S.E.2d at 926. Other judicial discussions assume authority to recognize or develop an exclusionary penalty under limited circumstances. Pletcher v. State, 338 P.3d 953, 960-61 (Alaska Ct. App. 2014) ("[I]t is sometimes appropriate to apply the exclusionary rule to violations of a statute," and a court deciding whether to do so "must consider (1) whether the statutory requirement or restriction is clear and widely known; (2) whether the statute is primarily designed to protect individual rights, as opposed to being intended more 'for the benefit of the people as a whole'; (3) whether admission of evidence obtained in contravention of the statute would require the court to condone 'dirty business'; and (4) whether there is evidence that the police have engaged in widespread or repeated violations of the statute."); Copley v. Com., 361 S.W.3d 902, 907 (Ky. 2012) ("when a criminal procedure rule is violated but the defendant's constitutional rights are not affected, suppression may still be warranted if there is (1) prejudice to the defendant, in the sense that the search might not have occurred or been so abusive if the rule had been followed or (2) if there is evidence of deliberate disregard of the rule"); People v. Casillas, 2015 COA 15, ¶¶ 19-21, 2015 WL 795765 (Col. App. 2015) ("evidence obtained through 'willful and recurrent' statutory violations may be suppressed").

§ 172   Exclusion for nonconstitutional illegality: (d) Substance of exclusionary requirements

n. 10.
Accord State v. Sun, 82 So. 3d 866, 873-74 (Fla. 4th DCA 2011) (where detective failed to follow statutory procedure for obtaining access to medical records and did not make good faith effort to comply with statutes, evidence had to be suppressed).

§ 173   Use of illegally obtained evidence in noncriminal litigation

n. 5.
   Delete People v. $11,200.00 U.S. Currency cite.

§ 174   Use of illegally obtained evidence in criminal proceedings on matters other than guilt

n. 13.
U.S. v. Sanders, 743 F.3d 471, 472-75 (7th Cir. 2014) (announcing that "[t]he exclusionary rule does not apply at sentencing," and rejecting contentions that the exclusionary rule applies on proof of egregious violation of the defendant's rights or a violation for purposes of increasing the sentence);

n. 14.
   Delete U.S. v. Perez cite and parenthetical.

§ 179   Exceptions to exclusion: (a) Attenuation of taint

n. 12.
   One court, describing the lower courts as in disarray concerning application of attenuation of taint analysis to these situations, concluded attenuation can occur only if "a defendant's independent acts of free will" is interjected into the chain of events. It found this suggested by the similarity between attenuation of taint and proximate causation analysis and the need to preserve a clear line in exclusionary rule law between inevitable discovery and attenuation of taint. Since these cases involve no interjection into the events of defendants' acts of free will, attenuation of taint, it held, is simply inapplicable. State v. Strieff, 2015 UT 2, ¶¶ 41-56, 357 P.3d 532, 542-46, cert. granted, 136 S. Ct. 27, 192 L. Ed. 2d 997 (Oct. 1, 2015).

§ 180 Exceptions to exclusion: (b) Intervening illegal conduct

n. 1.
; Wilson v. U.S., 102 A.3d 751, 754 (D.C. 2014) ("[j]oining many other courts . . . we . . . hold that, absent unforeseen exceptional circumstances, where a defendant commits a separate and distinct crime while unlawfully in police custody, evidence uncovered by a search incident to the later, lawful arrest is not suppressible as the fruit of the poisonous tree")

n. 14.
Accord State v. Tapia, 2015-NMCA-055, 348 P.3d 1050, 1056-67 (N.M. Ct. App. 2015), cert. granted, 2015-NMCERT-005, 367 P.3d 441

(N.M. 2015) ("the policy reasons for recognizing a new crime exception to the exclusionary rule simply do not exist when a non-violent, identity-related offense is committed in response to un-constitutional police conduit"). *Tapia* reasoned in part that given the direct connection between the initial uncon-stitutional action and the new offense, applying the exclusionary rule serves to deter the initial unconstitutional conduct and the cost of excluding evi-dence of the non-violent offense is "minor."

Title 7 RELEVANCY AND ITS COUNTERWEIGHTS

Chapter 16

Relevance

> **KeyCite®:** Cases and other legal materials listed in KeyCite Scope can be researched through the KeyCite service on Westlaw®. Use KeyCite to check citations for form, parallel references, prior and later history, and comprehensive citator information, including citations to other decisions and secondary materials.

§ 185 The meaning of relevancy and the counterweights

n. 3.
Delete from second sentence to end of footnote.

Add after footnote 4:
In a prosecution for knowingly entering a military base for an unlawful purpose, defendant could not introduce prior statements showing that he "wished to pound the missile into scrap metal . . . to make an instrument of peace [as a result of] his concern about nuclear war and world starvation."[4.30] In a prosecution for driving while having a breath alcohol concentration above a statutorily established limit, expert testimony that the air that enters the measuring instrument does not come from deep within the lungs is inadmissible, since the statute rationally regards shallower samples as indicating impairment.[4.50] In such cases, the truth or falsity of the proposition that the evidence is offered to prove has no implications for an element of the claim or offense charged or to a recognized defense.[4.70]

[4.30]U.S. v. Dorrell, 758 F.2d 427, 17 Fed. R. Evid. Serv. 1293 (9th Cir. 1985).

[4.50]People v. Vangelder, 58 Cal. 4th 1, 164 Cal. Rptr. 3d 522, 312 P.3d 1045 (2013), cert. denied, 134 S. Ct. 2839, 189 L. Ed. 2d 806 (2014).

[4.70]For other applications of the materiality requirement, see U.S. v.

Cassidy, 616 F.2d 101 (4th Cir. 1979) (whether United States' possession and use of nuclear weapons violates international law is immaterial in prosecution for desecrating the walls of the Pentagon); People v. Grant, 45 Cal. 3d 829, 248 Cal. Rptr. 444, 755 P.2d 894 (1988), as modified on denial of reh'g, (Aug. 25, 1988) (the grisly nature of the executions of convicted offenders sentenced to death is immaterial in a capital case); Brady v. Urbas, 111 A.3d 1155, 1162 (Pa. 2015) (although discussion of risks with a patient is relevant to whether the physician exercised due care in obtaining informed consent, it is irrelevant to whether "the physician was negligent in either considering the patient an appropriate candidate for the operation or in performing it"); Reliance Steel & Aluminum Co. v. Sevcik, 267 S.W.3d 867, 868 (Tex. 2008) (in a highway accident case, it was reversible error to show that "the defendant's annual revenues were $1.9 billion" because "[n]either a plaintiff's poverty nor a defendant's wealth can help a jury decide whose negligence caused an accident").

Replace sentence ending in footnote 5 with:
However, some evidence that is merely ancillary to evidence that bears directly on the issues may be admissible. Leeway is allowed even on direct examination for proof of facts that merely fill in the background of the narrative and give it interest, color, and lifelikeness.[5]

Add at beginning of sentence ending in footnote 6:
Models, maps

n. 6.
Add in footnote, after "cf.":
; State v. Ehrlick, 158 Idaho 900, 354 P.3d 462 (2015) (plastic model of victim's head made using measurements and photographs to establish location and relative size of victim's head wound, and to establish state's theory that cause of the hole in defendant's apartment wall was defendant slamming the victim's head into the wall)

n. 7.
Delete U.S. v. Robinson cite.

n. 14.
Delete cite to Friedman following first sentence.
Delete Berger et al cite from end of footnote.

Add after footnote 14:
Indeed, information theory uses the logarithm of the ratio to express the weight of evidence.[14.50]

[14.50]MacKay, Information Theory, Inference and Learning Algorithms 264-65 (2003); Good, Weight of Evidence: A Brief Survey, in 2 Bayesian Statistics 249 (Bernardo et al. eds. 1985).

Add new footnote in sentence including footnotes 16-18, after " 'logical relevance,' ":
Probative evidence often is said to have "logical relevance,"[15.50]

[15.50]*E.g.*, Cox v. Kansas City Chiefs Football Club, Inc., 473 S.W.3d 107, 116 (Mo. 2015), reh'g overruled, (Nov. 24, 2015).

n. 18.
State v. Green, 232 Kan. 116, 652 P.2d 697 (1982) (disapproved of on other grounds by, State v. Gunby, 282 Kan. 39, 144 P.3d 647 (2006))

n. 25.

Replace contents of footnote with:
Some courts refer to the fact that evidence makes a material fact more probable than not in concluding that the evidence is relevant, *e.g.*, Special v. West Boca Medical Center, 160 So. 3d 1251, 1264 (Fla. 2014); People v. Watkins, 491 Mich. 450, 462, 818

N.W.2d 296, 302 (2012), but it is clear that less powerful evidence also can be relevant. McDougal v. McCammon, 193 W. Va. 229, 236, 455 S.E.2d 788, 795 (1995) ("the offered evidence does not have to make the existence of a fact to be proved more probable than not")

Add in sentence including footnotes 23-25, after footnote 25:
or more probable than any single alternative.[25.50]

[25.50]Bush v. Jackson, 191 Colo. 249, 251, 552 P.2d 509, 511 (1976) ("it does not matter that other inferences may be equally probable"); State v. Salas-Juarez, 349 Or. 419, 428, 245 P.3d 113, 118 (2010) ("the inference that the proponent of the evidence wishes to be drawn from the evidence need not be the necessary, or even the most probable, one."); State v. Russell, 189 Vt. 632, 2011 VT 36, 22 A.3d 455, 458 (2011) ("The test [is] thus not whether the evidence makes the proposition for which it is offered more probable than competing propositions . . . .").

n. 27.
; State v. Johnson, 290 Neb. 862, 879, 862 N.W.2d 757, 771 (2015) ("Relevancy requires only that the degree of probativeness be something more than nothing.")

n. 29.
Replace contents of footnote with:
See, *e.g.*, Douglass v. Eaton Corp., 956 F.2d 1339, 1344, 34 Fed. R. Evid. Serv. 1420 (6th Cir. 1992) (abrogated on other grounds by, Weisgram v. Marley Co., 528 U.S. 440, 120 S. Ct. 1011, 145 L. Ed. 2d 958, 53 Fed. R. Evid. Serv. 406, 45 Fed. R. Serv. 3d 735 (2000)) ("Even if a district court believes the evidence is insufficient to prove the ultimate point for which it is offered, it may not exclude the evidence if it has even the slightest probative value."); State v. Smith, 299 Kan. 962, 969, 327 P.3d 441, 449 (2014) ("any tendency in reason"); Russell, 22 A.3d at 458 (*"any* tendency to establish (or refute) the proposition").

n. 37.
U.S. v. Schipani, 289 F. Supp. 43 (E.D. N.Y. 1968) (disapproved of on other

grounds by, Lego v. Twomey, 404 U.S. 477, 92 S. Ct. 619, 30 L. Ed. 2d 618 (1972))
Add at end of footnote:
If direct evidence is believed, deductive reasoning suffices for it to be useful.

n. 38.
State v. Leitner, 272 Kan. 398, 415, 34 P.3d 42 (2001) (that a wife charged with shooting her ex-husband "was involved in witchcraft and attended at least one pagan ceremony . . . failed to show . . . bias or motivation . . . and was not relevant to the commission of the crime charged" and "had no probative value");
; Kia Motors Corp. v. Ruiz, 432 S.W.3d 865, 881 (Tex. 2014) (most other breach of warranty claims involving air bags that failed to open were irrelevant because they did not involve the specific product defect alleged by plaintiff)

n. 44.
Delete cite to Strong.

n. 49.
Add parenthetical to Dawson v. Delaware cite:
Dawson v. Delaware, 503 U.S. 159, 167, 112 S. Ct. 1093, 117 L. Ed. 2d 309 (1992) ("First Amendment rights were violated by the admission of the Aryan Brotherhood evidence in this case, because the evidence proved nothing more than Dawson's abstract beliefs.")

n. 51.
Add parenthetical to Borden, Inc. v. Florida East Coast Ry. Co. cite:
Borden, Inc. v. Florida East Coast Ry. Co., 772 F.2d 750, 756, 19 Fed. R.

Evid. Serv. 33, 3 Fed. R. Serv. 3d 1360 (11th Cir. 1985) ("[U]nfair prejudice as used in Rule 403 cannot be equated with evidence that is simply adverse to the opposing party.")

Delete "for one side" from sentence ending in footnote 53.

n. 65.
Coleman v. Home Depot, Inc., 306 F.3d 1333, 1346-47, 59 Fed. R. Evid. Serv. 431 (3d Cir. 2002) (The district court properly excluded an EEOC Letter of Determination finding systematic discrimination not because the letter was "unfairly prejudicial or confusing," as the district court thought, but because "in order to rebut these expansive allegations, Home Depot would have had to present . . . a great deal of testimony—a trial within a trial in fact—about the employment histories of a large number of former employees.");

n. 72.
Cox v. Kansas City Chiefs Football Club, Inc., 473 S.W.3d 107, 118 (Mo. 2015), reh'g overruled, (Nov. 24, 2015) (abuse of discretion to exclude evidence that other employees were terminated because of their ages even though no pattern or practice of age discrimination was pled);

n. 76.
; Johnson v. State, 406 S.W.3d 892, 902 (Mo. 2013), cert. denied, 134 S. Ct. 1495, 188 L. Ed. 2d 380 (2014)

Add after "See":
Glenn v. Union Pacific R. Co., 2011 WY 126, 262 P.3d 177, 184, (Wyo. 2011);

Chapter 17

Character and Habit

> **KeyCite®:** Cases and other legal materials listed in KeyCite Scope can be researched through the KeyCite service on Westlaw®. Use KeyCite to check citations for form, parallel references, prior and later history, and comprehensive citator information, including citations to other decisions and secondary materials.

§ 186   Character, in general

n. 2.

Imwinkelried, Uncharged Misconduct Evidence (1998);

; Park, Character at the Crossroads, 49 Hastings L.J. 717 (1998)

Delete from "On the history of development. . ." through end of footnote.

n. 3.

Replace contents of footnote with:
    See, e.g., Oakly Enterprises, LLC v. NPI, LLC, 354 P.3d 1073 (Alaska 2015); Kentucky Farm Bureau Mut. Ins. Co. v. Rodgers, 179 S.W.3d 815 (Ky. 2005); 1 Imwinkelried, Uncharged Misconduct Evidence § 2:4. For arguments against applying the usual rules to corporations and similar entitles, see Kim, Character Evidence of Soulless Persons: The Applicability of the Character Evidence Rule to Corporations, 2000 U. Ill. L. Rev. 763, 810; Wagner, Criminal Corporate Character, 65 Fla. L. Rev. 1293 (2013).

Add to end of sentence ending in footnote 5, after "evidence":

lest the "effect would be to generate heat instead of diffusing light, or . . . the minute peg of relevancy will be completely obscured by the dirty linen hung upon it."

n. 5.

Replace contents of footnote:
    State v. Goebel, 36 Wash. 2d 367, 218 P.2d 300, 306 (1950). See, e.g., U.S. v. Noah, 130 F.3d 490, 495-96, 48 Fed. R. Evid. Serv. 268 (1st Cir. 1997); State v. Rose, 206 N.J. 141, 19 A.3d 985, 997 (2011) (calling for "careful and prag-

matic evaluation of the evidence to determine whether [is] probative worth . . . is outweighed by its potential for undue prejudice"—a "more exacting [standard] than Rule 403 . . . .").

n. 8.

Replace contents of footnote:

On psychological theories and research on stability of character traits, see Lempert et al., A Modern Approach to Evidence 336-37 (4th ed. 2011); Imwinkelried, Reshaping the "Grotesque" Doctrine of Character Evidence: The Reform Implications of the Most Recent Psychological Research, 36 Sw. U. L. Rev. 741 (2008); Jonathan D. Kurland, Character as a Process in Judgment and Decision-making and Its Implications for the Character Evidence Prohibition in Anglo-American Law, 38 Law & Psychol. Rev. 135 (2013-14); Méndez, The Law of Evidence and the Search for a Stable Personality, 45 Emory L.J. 221 (1996); Jeffrey Waller, Federal Rules of Evidence 413-415: "Laws Are like Medicine; They Generally Cure an Evil by a Lesser . . . Evil," 30 Tex. Tech. L. Rev. 1503 (1999); Note, Recognizing Character: A New Perspective on Character Evidence, 121 Yale L.J. 1912, 1931-35 (2012).

§ 187   Character in issue

n. 1.
Daniels by Glass v. Wal-Mart Stores, Inc., 634 So. 2d 88 (Miss. 1993) (delinquency adjudication of shoplifting incident admissible to support defense of truth);

n. 4.
; Cleghorn v. New York Cent. & H.R.R. Co., 56 N.Y. 44, 1874 WL 11045 (1874) (evidence of "previous habits of intemperance known to the officers of the company")

n. 11.
Gibson v. Mayor and Council of City of Wilmington, 355 F.3d 215, 232-33, 63 Fed. R. Evid. Serv. 1285 (3d Cir. 2004);

§ 188   Character as circumstantial evidence: General rule of exclusion

n. 2.
Lard v. State, 2014 Ark. 1, 6, 431 S.W.3d 249, 258 (2014), cert. denied, 135 S. Ct. 76, 190 L. Ed. 2d 67 (2014) ("The test for admissibility under Rule 404(b) is whether the evidence is independently relevant");

n. 6.
; State v. Magers, 164 Wash. 2d 174, 182, 189 P.3d 126, 131 (2008) (accepting state's argument that victim's proof of "prior bad acts, including the fact that he had been in 'trouble' and in jail for fighting, was admissible to prove [an assault defendant's] state of mind: that she 'reasonably feared bodily injury' ")

n. 7.
U.S. v. Keiser, 57 F.3d 847, 853, 42 Fed. R. Evid. Serv. 40 (9th Cir. 1995).

Add after "See":

Chaiken et al., Predicting Violent Behavior and Classifying Violent Offenders, in Panel on the Understanding and Control of Violent Behavior, National Research Council, 4 Understanding and Preventing Violence: Consequences and Control 217, 280 (Reiss & Roth, eds. 1994) ("There is little doubt that criminal records (official or self-reported) are among the best predictors of violence, although there is some dispute about which aspects of criminal records have the greatest explanatory power. There is general agreement that violent offenders do not specialize in violence; nevertheless, past violence seems to be among the best predictors of future violence.");

Delete Klassen & O'Connor cite and parenthetical.

Replace sentence ending in footnote 9 with:
Used for this purpose, character evidence typically is of relatively slight value, but it still is laden with the dangerous baggage of prejudice, distraction, and time-consumption.[9]

n. 13.
U.S. v. Green, 617 F.3d 233, 244, 83 Fed. R. Evid. Serv. 537 (3d Cir. 2010); People v. VanderVliet, 444 Mich. 52,

508 N.W.2d 114, 121-22 (1993), opinion amended, 445 Mich. 1205, 520 N.W.2d 338 (1994).

§ 189   Character for care in civil cases

n. 1.
J & R Ice Cream Corp. v. California Smoothie Licensing Corp., 31 F.3d 1259, 40 Fed. R. Evid. Serv. 34 (3d Cir. 1994) (other alleged misrepresentations);

n. 6.
Thornburg v. Perleberg, 158 N.W.2d 188, 191 (N.D. 1968) (abrogated on

other grounds by, Ohio Cas. Ins. Co. v. Clark, 1998 ND 153, 583 N.W.2d 377 (N.D. 1998))

n. 8.
Comment, Help Me Doc! Theories of Admissibility of Other Act Evidence in Medical Malpractice Cases, 87 Marq. L. Rev. 981 (2004)

Add after footnote 8:
That a locomotive engineer suing his employer for injuries he suffered in a derailment had been disciplined for improperly driving trains four times in his career was not admissible to show that he was contributorily negligent in the derailment, but the "history of rule infractions and resulting interruptions of employment" should have been admitted "to support a lower lost earnings projection."[8.50]

[8.50]National R.R. Passenger Corp. v. McDavitt, 804 A.2d 275, 290-91   (D.C. 2002).

§ 190   Bad character as evidence of criminal conduct: Other crimes

n. 2.
Replace first sentence of footnote with:
Because the common law has long excluded proof of most other crimes and wrongs merely to show a criminal disposition, constitutional analysis of the need for a broad exclusionary rule has not been necessary.

n. 13.
Delete last sentence of footnote.

n. 20.
State v. Joy, 155 Idaho 1, 10, 304 P.3d

276, 285 (2013) (defendant's prior acts of abusing his wife were not part of a common plan); State v. McFarland, 228 W. Va. 492, 502, 721 S.E.2d 62, 72-73 (2011) ("there is no evidence that [the] crime in the instant case [of sexual assault in West Virginia] was part of a common scheme or plan that began several years earlier in California" where defendant was convicted of sexual assaults);

Add to end of permissible purpose (1), after paragraph including footnotes 17-20:

"This type of plan evidence is admissible because it is based on the permissible inference that, regardless of character, a person who has formulated a plan is more likely to carry out the elements of the plan."[20.50]

[20.50]State v. Verde, 2012 UT 60, 296 P.3d 673, 682 (Utah 2012) (separate acts of "entic[ing] teenage males to be his friends with the motive of exploiting their trust for his sexual gratification" is not a "plan").

n. 21.
People v. Lucas, 60 Cal. 4th 153, 177 Cal. Rptr. 3d 378, 333 P.3d 587, 642 (2014) (disapproved of on other grounds by, People v. Romero, 62 Cal. 4th 1, 191 Cal. Rptr. 3d 855, 354 P.3d 983 (2015)) ("[I]n addition to the targeted victims' gender, race, age, and appearance and the lack of apparent motive for the killings, all of the victims' wounds shared characteristics that were unlike anything the San Diego coroner had observed in the more than 20 years preceding defendant's trial. [T]he neck wounds here were unique . . . .");

Add new paragraph at end of permissible purpose (2):

In *Rex v. Smith*, an elaborate pattern of conduct characterized the different murders, but the "signature" quasi-exception also applies when the state proves that a specific implement, such as a particular gun known to have been used by the defendant in one crime, also was used in the separate crime with which the defendant is now charged. As in *Smith*, the crimes could be remarkably similar in many other idiosyncratic details, but even a single sufficiently individuating common aspect could mark the defendant as the likely perpetrator of both crimes.[27.50]

[27.50]See, e.g., St. Clair v. Commonwealth, 455 S.W.3d 869, 889 (Ky. 2015) ("The proof also touched directly on identity because the same gun and handcuffs were used in both kidnappings.").

n. 28.
State v. Tanner, 675 P.2d 539, 548 (Utah 1983) (abrogated on other grounds by, State v. Doporto, 935 P.2d 484 (Utah 1997))

n. 31.
Add after "But cf.":

U.S. v. Davis, 726 F.3d 434, 92 Fed. R. Evid. Serv. 123 (3d Cir. 2013) (previous convictions for possession of cocaine in unspecified forms not admissible to prove knowledge or intent of possession of cocaine with intent to distribute);

Start new paragraph with sentence ending in footnote 35, adding the following at beginning of sentence, after "these":

"no-accident"

n. 37.

Add after Imwinkelried cite:
, *and* Sullivan, Probative Inference from Phenomenal Coincidence: Demystifying the Doctrine of Chances 15 Law, Probability & Risk 27 (2014) Rothstein, The Doctrine of Chances, Brides of the Bath and a Reply to Sean Sullivan, 14 Law, Probability & Risk 51 (2015);

n. 40.

Delete State v. Gaines.

n. 41.
State v. Green, 232 Kan. 116, 652 P.2d 697, 701 (1982) (disapproved of on other grounds by, State v. Gunby, 282 Kan. 39, 144 P.3d 647 (2006)

Add after footnote 43:
evidence that a daughter was threatening to end an incestuous relationship was admissible to show the father's motivation to murder her;[43.30] and evidence of the need to silence a victim of a series of frauds to prevent the revelation of these crimes to her next defrauded paramour were admissible to show her reason for strangling the first man and leaving his body in a footlocker in the woods.[43.50]

[43.30]State v. Gaines, 144 Wash. 446, 258 P. 508, 512-13 (1927).

[43.50]U.S. v. Siegel, 536 F.3d 306, 77 Fed. R. Evid. Serv. 311 (4th Cir. 2008).

n. 44.
State v. Green, 232 Kan. 116, 652 P.2d 697, 701 (1982) (disapproved of on other grounds by, State v. Gunby, 282 Kan. 39, 144 P.3d 647 (2006); State v. Labrum, 2014 UT App 5, 318 P.3d 1151 (Utah Ct. App. 2014); State v. Lopez, 245 A.3d 1, 21 (R.I. 2012) (acts of aggression toward the deceased in

the same place and close in time considered "highly probative of, defendant's motive and intent to murder"); State v. McKinley, 234 W. Va. 143, 764 S.E.2d 303 (2014); Ortega v. State, 669 P.2d 935, 944 (Wyo. 1983) (overruled on other grounds by, Jones v. State, 902 P.2d 686 (Wyo. 1995))

Replace "a specific rule to allow" with:

by legislation a specific rule allowing

Replace sentence after footnote 45 with:
In other words, these statutes create a true exception to the propensity rule, and a defendant is not entitled to a limiting instruction.

Add to sentence ending in footnote 51, after footnote:
and prior sexual assaults are not admissble just to show the "motive" of "sexual gratification."[51.50]

[51.50]State v. McFarland, 228 W. Va.   492, 502, 721 S.E.2d 62, 72 (2011).

n. 58.
People v. Griffin, 33 Cal. 4th 536, 15
Cal. Rptr. 3d 743, 93 P.3d 344 (2004)
(disapproved of on other grounds by,
People v. Riccardi, 54 Cal. 4th 758, 144
Cal. Rptr. 3d 84, 281 P.3d 1 (2012))
; *and* Meece v. Com., 348 S.W.3d 627,
663 (Ky. 2011) (skill in shooting an

"upper-body spray" at human targets),

n. 64.
  Delete signal, Crossman cite and parenthetical.

Replace sentence ending in footnote 68 with:
Furthermore, courts in many of the jurisdictions that still do not
overtly admit evidence of sex crimes with other victims as revealing an incriminating propensity[67.50] achieve a similar result by
stretching to find a nonpropensity purpose.

[67.50]*E.g.*, Braunstein v. State, 118
Nev. 68, 74, 40 P.3d 413, 418 (2002)
(reliance on a "propensity for sexual
aberration" "represents a common law
approach that Nevada abandoned
when the Legislature enacted into law
the evidence code" in 1971).

n. 68.
  *Delete State v. T.W. and Findley v.
State cites and parentheticals.*

n. 71.
Orenstein, Propensity or Stereotype?
A Misguided Evidence in Indian
Country, 19 Cornell J. L. & Pub. Pol'y
173 (2009); Raeder, American Bar
Association Criminal Justice Section
Report to the House of Delegates,

reprinted in 22 Fordham Urban L.J.
343 (1995)

n. 74.
  *Add parenthetical following State v.
Reyes cite:*
(Rule 413-type statute, with the requirement of "clear proof" and balancing for prejudicial effect, satisfies due
process);

  Add at end of footnote:
Such cases are reviewed in Smith,
Prior Sexual Misconduct Evidence in
State Courts: Constitutional and
Common Law Challenges, 52 Am.
Crim. L. Rev. 321 (2015).

Add to end of first sentence of paragraph following footnote 74:
Unlike the quasi-exceptions for which other-crimes evidence is
admissible to support reasoning that differs in some meaningful
way from the ordinary propensity chain of inferences, the sex-
crime exception flouts the general prohibition of evidence whose
only purpose is to invite the inference that a defendant who committed a previous crime is disposed toward committing crimes,
and therefore is more likely to have committed the one at bar.[74.50]

[74.50]Inserting the exception into
Rule 404, as some states do, makes
this explicit. *See, e.g.,* Utah R. Evid.

404(c)(1) ("In a criminal case in which
a defendant is accused of child molestation, the court may admit evidence

that the defendant committed any other acts of child molestation to prove a propensity to commit the crime charged.").

n. 76.
Replace contents of footnote with:
Recidivism rates seem to vary according to the type of sex offense and other factors. *See* Rice & Orenstein, Empirical Fallacies of Evidence Law: A Critical Look at the Admission of Prior Sex Crimes, 81 U. Cin. L. Rev. 795 (2013); Rose, Caging the Beast: Formulating Effective Evidentiary Rules to Deal with Sexual Offenders, 34 Am. J. Crim. L. 1 (2006).

n. 77.
Delete Greenfield cite.
Rice & Orenstein, Empirical Fallacies of Evidence Law: A Critical Look at the Admission of Prior Sex Crimes, 81 U. Cin. L. Rev. 795 (2013);
Delete Rose cite.
Add at end of footnote:
But see Park, Character Evidence at the Crossroads, 49 Hastings L.J. 717 (1998) (explaining the limitations and nuances of recidivism statistics).

n. 78.
Add after "See":

Rice & Orenstein, Empirical Fallacies of Evidence Law: A Critical Look at the Admission of Prior Sex Crimes, 81 U. Cin. L. Rev. 795 (2013);

n. 85.
Delete U.S. v. Krezdorn cite and parenthetical and remainder of footnote beginning with State v. Gunby to end of footnote

n. 86.
U.S. v. Krezdorn, 639 F.2d 1327, 1332, 7 Fed. R. Evid. Serv. 1532 (5th Cir. 1981) ("an appellation that tends merely to obscure the analysis underlying the admissibility of the evidence."); State v. Gunby, 282 Kan. 39, 144 P.3d 647, 661 (2006) (endorsing Morgan's and Wigmore's view that the phrase "res gestae" is an impediment to clear thought); State v. Rose, 206 N.J. 141, 19 A.3d 985, 1011 (2011) ("invocations of res gestae as the basis for the admission of evidence do lack the analytic rigor, precision, and uniformity that evidential rulings were intended to have under the codified Evidence Rules."). For cogent summaries of such criticism, see Green, 617 F.3d 233;

Replace text of sentence including footnotes 88-89 with:
because the subject of the evidence is not *other* crimes,[88] these "integral acts"[88.50] can be proved as direct evidence of the offense at bar.

[88.50]State v. Scott, 184 So. 3d 2 (La. 2015).

n. 91.
Delete U.S. v. Green and signal.
Add after "For examples, see":
U.S. v. Siegel, 536 F.3d 306, 77 Fed. R. Evid. Serv. 311 (4th Cir. 2008) (preventing disclosure of financial frauds as a motive for murder);

n. 94.
Replace contents of footnote with:
See, e.g., State v. Altenberger, 139 So. 3d 510, 517 (La. 2014) (suggesting that "domestic violence, psychological

abuse, and coercive behavior . . . on three separate occasions [were] an integral part of the continuing nature and pattern of [a] 'cycle of violence' "); State v. Alvarado, 2008 ND 203, 757 N.W.2d 570, 571, 577 (N.D. 2008) (acts of domestic violence for a year-and-a-quarter before the alleged "felonious restraint . . . for knowingly restraining another under terrorizing circumstances by grabbing [the spouse] against her will, throwing her over his shoulder, and running toward their house" were admissible to provide " 'a more complete story of the crime by putting it in context of happenings near in time and place.' "); State v. McKinley, 234 W. Va. 143, 764 S.E.2d 303 (2014) (relying on the quasi-exceptions for motive and intent to justify admission of incidents of do-mestic violence in previous months, but only after holding that "the evidence [could be considered] necessary 'to complete the story of the crimes on trial' [homicide] or otherwise provide context to the crimes charged.").

n. 103.
State v. Putman, 848 N.W.2d 1 (Iowa 2014) ("clear proof");

n. 105.
U.S. v. Richards, 719 F.3d 746, 760 (7th Cir. 2013) (requiring a "specific and persuasive . . . link")
Delete U.S. v. Beasley cite and parenthetical.

n. 106.
Richards, 719 F.3d at 759 ("A defendant must 'meaningfully dispute' the nonpropensity issue justifying admission of the Rule 404(b) evidence.");
Delete State v. Gallegos cite and parenthetical.

n. 107.
Delete U.S. v. Figueroa cite and parenthetical.
Replace first sentence of second paragraph of footnote:
It has been said that Old Chief v. U.S., 519 U.S. 172, 117 S. Ct. 644, 136 L. Ed. 2d 574, 45 Fed. R. Evid. Serv. 835 (1997), undermined the general consensus of the federal courts that a defendant's stipulation as to intent bars the use of other-crimes evidence to prove intent.
Add at end of footnote:
For additional analysis of the effect of stipulations in this context, see Imwinkelried, Uncharged Misconduct Evidence § 8:11 [Factor no. 3].

n. 108.
Add at beginning of footnote:
Compare U.S. v. Figueroa, 618 F.2d 934, 941, 5 Fed. R. Evid. Serv. 811 (2d Cir. 1980) (where codefendants suggested that they were selling coffee "grinds" rather than heroin as a "rip-off," the government could not use defendant's prior involvement on issue of intent because "no one . . . claimed that the trio was unwittingly selling . . . heroin, thinking it was some other substance"), *with* U.S. v. Richards, 719 F.3d 746, 760-61 (7th Cir. 2013) (because "Richards placed his knowledge of the bag's contents directly at issue when he . . . testified that he believed the bag contained money, not drugs," evidence of conversations about drug trafficking by an individual with the same alias was admissible); *see also*

Add after footnote 109:
Thus, if opportunity[109.30] or motive[109.50] is manifest, that rationale cannot justify the evidence of other bad acts.

[109.30]State v. Gallegos, 152 P.3d at 838-39 (proof of a guard's sexual contact or indecent exposure with more than one prisoner was totally unnecessary to show opportunity, which was "wholly undisputed").

[109.50]State v. Putman, 848 N.W.2d 1 (Iowa 2014) ("Motive, like any other noncharacter purpose for which evidence might be offered, must have been at issue in the case.").

n. 110.
U.S. v. Richards, 719 F.3d 746, 762 (7th Cir. 2013) ("Rule 403 balancing applies with full force when consider-

ing the admission of prior bad acts   *Delete U.S. v. Beasley cite.*
evidence.")

Delete footnote 111.

n. 117.
*Delete remainder of footnote after
first sentence.*

Add after footnote 117:
A limiting instruction may be required,[118] but such instructions
arenot panaceas.[119]

Finally, "to reduce surprise and promote early resolution on
the issue of admissibility,"[120] case law[121] or rules[122] may require a
party to notify the opponent of the intention to introduce certain
types of evidence of other crimes or bad acts.[123]

---

[118]*E.g.*, U.S. v. Davis, 726 F.3d 434, 92 Fed. R. Evid. Serv. 123 (3d Cir. 2013); Kaufman v. People, 202 P.3d 542, 553 (Colo. 2009); Campbell v. State, 974 A.2d 156, 161 (Del. 2009); State v. Gunby, 282 Kan. 39, 144 P.3d 647 (2006); State v. Nelson, 221 W. Va. 327, 655 S.E.2d 73, 78 (2007); Leach, "Propensity" Evidence and FRE 404: A Proposed Amended Rule With Accompanying "Plain English" Jury Instructions, 68 Tenn. L. Rev. 825, 866-869 (2001) (arguing for a "looser" form of Rule 404 that provides more discretion for the trial court and a plain English jury instruction to ensure proper consideration of propensity evidence).

[119]Although it has been said that "properly administered limiting jury instructions cure the danger of unfair prejudice unless 'the jury could not follow the court's limiting instruction,'" U.S. v. Richards, 719 F.3d 746, 763 (7th Cir. 2013), the efficacy of such instructions is doubtful. U.S. v. Daniels, 770 F.2d 1111, 1118, 18 Fed. R. Evid. Serv. 1113 (D.C. Cir. 1985) ("To tell a jury to ignore the defendant's prior convictions in determining whether he or she committed the offense being tried is to ask human beings to act . . . well beyond mortal capacities."); Government of Virgin Islands v. Toto, 12 V.I. 620, 529 F.2d 278, 283, 1 Fed. R. Evid. Serv. 200 (3d Cir. 1976) ("A drop of ink cannot be removed from a glass of milk."); Dunn

v. U.S., 307 F.2d 883, 886 (5th Cir. 1962) ("one cannot unring a bell; after the thrust of the saber it is difficult to say forget the wound"); U.S. v. DeCastris, 798 F.2d 261, 264, 21 Fed. R. Evid. Serv. 504 (7th Cir. 1986) ("this is like telling someone not to think about a hippopotamus").

[120]Fed. R. Evid. 401(b) advisory committee note to 1991 amendment.

[121]Com. v. Adjutant, 443 Mass. 649, 665-66, 824 N.E.2d 1, 14 (2005) ("A defendant who intends to introduce evidence of the victim's specific acts of violence to support a claim that the victim was the first aggressor must provide notice to the court and the Commonwealth of such intent and of the specific evidence he intends to offer. This notice must come sufficiently prior to trial to permit the Commonwealth to investigate and prepare a rebuttal. The prosecutor, in turn, must provide notice to the court and the defendant of whatever rebuttal evidence he or she intends to offer at trial."); People v. VanderVliet, 444 Mich. 52, 508 N.W.2d 114 (1993), opinion amended, 445 Mich. 1205, 520 N.W.2d 338 (1994) (establishing disclosure obligations on both the prosecution and the defendant).

[122]A 1991 Amendment to Federal Rule 404(b) added the requirement that "[o]n request by a defendant in a criminal case, the prosecutor must . . . provide reasonable notice of the general nature of any such evidence

[falling within the quasi-exceptions of the rule] that the prosecutor intends to offer at trial . . . ." Some state laws sweep more broadly. For example, Michigan's rule 404(b)(2) requires notice from the prosecution of the nature of and rationale for admitting *all* evidence "of other crimes, wrongs, or acts" without reference to a demand from the defense, and it imposes a parallel duty on the defense.

[123]However, when the other bad-act evidence would have been admissible anyway, the absence of notice might not be seen as prejudicial. *E.g.*, State v. Reyes, 744 N.W.2d 95 (Iowa 2008); People v. Jackson, 498 Mich. 246, 279-80, 869 N.W.2d 253, 271 (2015).

§ 191 Good character as evidence of lawful conduct: Proof by the accused and rebuttal by the government

Replace "permit" in sentence ending in footnote 3 with:

provide a "mercy rule"[2.50] that permits

[2.50]Michaels, Character Evidence, 47 Ala. L. Rev. 203, 208 (1995-1996). As one commentator noted in 1883:

> The rule had its origin at that period in the history of our mother country when more than one hundred offenses were punishable with death, attended by corruption of blood and forfeiture of estate. We can not affect surprise at the grant of this indulgence to men whose lives were so frail, whose whole estate might be forfeited, and whose wives and children might be made penniless and homeless, and disgraced by the false testimony of even mistaken witnesses.

Greenhood, Admissibility of Evidence of Character in Civil Actions, 15 Central L.J 202, 206, 16 Cent. L.J. 202, 206 (1883).

n. 4.
Gaugh v. Commonwealth, 261 Ky. 91, 87 S.W.2d 94, 98 (1935) ("[I]n all criminal cases, . . . it is relevant for the defendant to offer affirmative evidence of reputation, with regard to the trait involved in the nature of the charge, to prove that it was unlikely that he would have committed the act charged against him.");

Replace "This argument overlooks the fact that" with:
However,
Add at end of footnote:
For some examples of traits and crimes lacking a sufficient nexus, see State v. Altamirano, 116 Ariz. 291, 569 P.2d 233 (1977) (brother's testimony as to defendant's part-time employment and fact that defendant was not a heroin addict not pertinent to traits involved in sale of heroin).

n. 5.
Add parenthetical to State v. Squire cite:
("Before the new rule [404(a)(1)], our law was clear that evidence of general good character was relevant to the issue of guilt or innocence of a criminal defendant. Under the present rule, an accused must tailor his character evidence to a "pertinent" trait, but the trait may be general in nature provided that it is relevant in the context of the crime charged.")

n. 6.
Replace parenthetical following Manna v. State:
(reputation for honesty and truthfulness in a trial for armed robbery)
Replace parenthetical following State v. Martinez:
(solicitation of burglary)
Replace parenthetical following State v. Kramp:
(stealing a compressor from a construction site)

Add new footnote in sentence including footnotes 6-7, after "peaceable,":

while someone accused of murder might show that he is peaceable,[6.50]

[6.50]State v. Roseboro, 351 N.C. 536, 553, 528 S.E.2d 1, 12 (2000) (murder defendant's reputation for "nonviolence or peacefulness").

n. 7.

Replace contents of footnote:

See cases cited, Admissibility of evidence of pertinent trait under Rule 404(a) of the Uniform Rules of Evidence, 56 A.L.R.4th 402; When is evidence of trait of accused's character "pertinent" for purposes of admissibility under Rule 404(a)(1) of the Federal Rules of Evidence, 49 A.L.R. Fed. 478. For cases holding defendant's good character for veracity inadmissible in defending against other charges, see U.S. v. Jackson, 588 F.2d 1046, 4 Fed. R. Evid. Serv. 245, 49 A.L.R. Fed. 461 (5th Cir. 1979) (not pertinent to narcotics charges); State v. Howland, 157 Kan. 11, 138 P.2d 424 (1943) (not pertinent to rape charge); State v. Hortman, 207 Neb. 393, 299 N.W.2d 187 (1980) (not pertinent to charges of assault and abuse of an incompetent); State v. Walston, 367 N.C. 721, 727, 766 S.E.2d 312, 317 (2014) ("Being respectful towards children does not bear a special relationship to the charges of child sexual abuse").

n. 11.

Rai v. State, 297 Ga. 472, 480-81, 775 S.E.2d 129, 138 (2015); State v. Hughes, 841 So. 2d 718, 722 (La. 2003) ("As to how a defendant may prove his good character, Louisiana law incorporates the traditional limit that the accused may do so by means of reputa-

tion only, as opposed to evidence of specific acts or of opinion.");

n. 15.

Replace cite to N.C. R. Evid. 405(a) and parenthetical after "See" with:

State v. Hughes, 841 So. 2d at 723 ("We therefore subscribe to the views of other appellate courts in states with evidentiary rules similar to those in Louisiana, that while a defendant may present evidence of his or her reputation in the community as a moral person and for safe and proper treatment of young children, he or she may not present the opinion of a mental health expert, based either on a "profile" of a child sex abuser or on the results of standardized psychological tests, that the defendant is a moral person without deviant sexual tendencies which might prompt pedophiliac behavior.") (citation omitted); State v. Heath, 316 N.C. 337, 341 S.E.2d 565 (1986) (applying N.C. R. Evid. 405(a) prohibiting "[e]xpert testimony on character or a trait of character . . . as circumstantial evidence of behavior"); Knospler v. State, 2016 WY 1, 366 P.3d 479 (Wyo. 2016) ("Expert opinion on the link between aggressive behavior and viewing child pornography or bestiality does not constitute proof of the victim's character by one of the methods permitted by Rule 405."); U.S. v. West, 670 F.2d 675, 682, 10 Fed. R. Evid. Serv. 725 (7th Cir. 1982) (overruled on other grounds by, U.S. v. Green, 258 F.3d 683, 56 Fed. R. Evid. Serv. 906 (7th Cir. 2001))

Replace "The" in sententence ending in footnote 29 with:
First, the

n. 29.

U.S. v. Lewis, 482 F.2d 632, 639 (D.C. Cir. 1973) (disapproved of on other

grounds by, U.S. v. Winter, 663 F.2d 1120 (1st Cir. 1981))

Replace sentence ending in footnote 30 with:
For instance, questions about the effect of the current charges on reputation or opinion usually are barred[29.30] on the grounds that they would require a reputation witness to speculate about the community as a whole,[29.50] and that it is unfairly prejudicial to ask any witness to indulge in a hypothetical assumption of the defendant's guilt;[30] however, some jurisdictions do not apply this per se rule to opinion witnesses.[30.50]

Replace "As" in sentence ending in footnote 31 with:
Second,

[29.30]U.S. v. Hough, 803 F.3d 1181, 1191 (11th Cir. 2015) (opinion witness); U.S. v. Shwayder, 312 F.3d 1109, 1121 (9th Cir. 2002), for additional opinion, see, 52 Fed. Appx. 886 (9th Cir. 2002) and opinion amended on denial of reh'g, 320 F.3d 889 (9th Cir. 2003) (unspecified character witness); U.S. v. Oshatz, 912 F.2d 534 (2d Cir. 1990) (opinion witness); U.S. v. Siers, 873 F.2d 747, 749, 28 Fed. R. Evid. Serv. 73 (4th Cir. 1989) (reputation witnesses) ("Such questions have been disapproved by, apparently, every court which has considered them, and we agree."); U.S. v. Barta, 888 F.2d 1220, 1224–25, 29 Fed. R. Evid. Serv. 110 (8th Cir. 1989) (reputation witness); U.S. v. Williams, 738 F.2d 172, 15 Fed. R. Evid. Serv. 1530 (7th Cir. 1984); U.S. v. Polsinelli, 649 F.2d 793, 797, 8 Fed. R. Evid. Serv. 412 (10th Cir. 1981) (reputation witness); U.S. v. Candelaria-Gonzalez, 547 F.2d 291 (5th Cir. 1977) (reputation witness).

[29.50]U.S. v. Hewitt, 663 F.2d 1381, 1391, 9 Fed. R. Evid. Serv. 835 (11th Cir. 1981) (Although the government could ask defendant's reputation witnesses whether they had heard of a pending indictment elsewhere, to ask whether hearing this fact would cause a witness to retract her testimony that defendant's reputation is good was "highly improper" because "the government had already shown that [she] knew little of [defendant's] reputation in the community by exposing her ignorance of his pending trial," and the witness was not an expert qualified to say how the community would react under hypothetical conditions.); U.S. v. Candelaria–Gonzalez, 547 F.2d at 294 ("Obviously the character witness . . . had heard nothing in the community about [the defendant's] post conviction reputation when he had been convicted of nothing whatsoever.").

[30]U.S. v. Mason, 993 F.2d 406, 410 (4th Cir. 1993); U.S. v. Oshatz, 912 F.2d 534 at 539 ("too great a risk of impairing the presumption of innocence [and] the jury might infer from the judge's permission to ask a guilt-based hypothetical question that the prosecutor has evidence of guilt beyond the evidence in the record"); Candelaria-Gonzalez, 547 F.2d at 294 ("These hypothetical questions struck at the very heart of the presumption of innocence which is fundamental to Anglo-Saxon concepts of fair trial. [T]he risk of prejudice to defendant's basic rights from such questions requires reversal.").

[30.50]U.S. v. Guerrero, 665 F.3d 1305, 1312, 87 Fed. R. Evid. Serv. 73 (D.C. Cir. 2011); U.S. v. Kellogg, 510 F.3d 188, 196, 75 Fed. R. Evid. Serv. 301 (3d Cir. 2007) ("no need to adopt a bright-line rule prohibiting a potentially probative type of inquiry [but] we are not suggesting, let alone holding, that guilt-assuming hypotheticals can properly be asked of opinion character witnesses in every case").

Replace "When" in sentence ending in footnote 33 with:
Finally, when

n. 36.
Aaron v. U.S., 397 F.2d 584, 585 (5th Cir. 1968) (illicit affair with a woman not pertinent to charges of willfully making false entries in bank records, embezzlement, and misapplication of bank funds);

§ 192   Character in civil cases where crime is in issue

n. 2.
; Torrance, Evidence of Character in Civil and Criminal Proceedings, 12 Yale L.J. 352, 356-57 (1902-1903)

Add new footnote at end of first sentence of paragraph beginning after footnote 2:
But this has never been the majority view.[2.50]

[2.50]Greenhood, Admissibility of Evidence of Character in Civil Actions, 16 Cent. L.J. 202, 206 (1883) (describing the few cases to the contrary as "repudiated and overruled").

n. 3.
Delete *Bosworth v. Bosworth, Northern Assur. Co. v. Griffin and Baker v. First Nat. Bank* cites and paretheticals.

Add after footnote 3:
Defendants in civil cases accused of assault and battery,[3.10] personal cruelty,[3.30] setting fires,[3.50] fraud,[3.70] and more[3.90] are barred from presenting evidence of their character.

[3.10]Givens v. Bradley, 6 Ky. 192, 3 Bibb 192, 1813 WL 644 (1813); Porter v. Seiler, 23 Pa. 424, 1854 WL 6374 (1854).

[3.30]Bosworth v. Bosworth, 131 Conn. 389, 40 A.2d 186 (1944) (divorce case).

[3.50]Northern Assur. Co. v. Griffin, 236 Ky. 296, 33 S.W.2d 7 (1930); Greenberg v. Aetna Ins. Co., 427 Pa. 494, 235 A.2d 582 (1967).

[3.70]Eisenberg v. Continental Cas. Co., 48 Wis. 2d 637, 180 N.W.2d 726 (1970).

[3.90]Baker v. First Nat. Bank, 1936 OK 10, 176 Okla. 70, 54 P.2d 355 (1936) (replevin); Torrance, Evidence of Character in Civil and Criminal Proceedings, 12 Yale L.J. 352, 357 (1902-1903) (adultery).

n. 4.
Torrance, Evidence of Character in Civil and Criminal Proceedings, 12 Yale L.J. 352, 357 (1902-1903)

n. 5.
Phillips v. State, 550 N.E.2d 1290 (Ind. 1990) (abrogated on other grounds by, Fry v. State, 990 N.E.2d 429 (Ind. 2013))

§ 193   Character of victim in cases of assault, murder, and rape

Add at beginning of sentence ending in footnote 3, after "The":

majority rule is that

n. 3.
U.S. v. Keiser, 57 F.3d 847, 855, 42 Fed. R. Evid. Serv. 40 (9th Cir. 1995);

Delete U.S. v. Piche cite and parenthetical

Delete from "Some opinions lose sight of this limitation" to the end of footnote.

Add after footnote 3:
However, some jurisdictions allow the victim's violent character to be proved by convictions,[3.30] and a minority position is that even specific acts without convictions can be proved as long as they shed sufficient light on the issue of who the first aggressor was.[3.50]

_____

[3.30]State v. Smith, 222 Conn. 1, 608 A.2d 63, 72-73 (1992) ("In this state, convictions of violent crimes constitute a narrow exception to the general prohibition on evidence of specific acts to prove the violent character of a homicide victim, because the dangers of injecting collateral issues confusing to a jury and prolonging the trial are minimal when only convictions may be admitted.").

[3.50]Com. v. Chambers, 465 Mass. 520, 527-530, 989 N.E.2d 483 (2013); Randolph v. Com., 190 Va. 256, 56 S.E.2d 226, 264-65 (1949).

n. 5.
U.S. v. Keiser, 57 F.3d at 855 ("a common understanding in the federal courts that 'personal knowledge' of the victim's propensity for violence is simply not a prerequisite for admission of victim character evidence under Rule 404(a)(2)");

Add new footnote to end of first sentence of fifth paragraph:
Federal Rule 404(a)(2) adopted the majority position by enumerating a true exception.[10.50]

_____

[10.50]*See, e.g.*, U.S. v. Keiser, 57 F.3d 847, 42 Fed. R. Evid. Serv. 40 (9th Cir. 1995).

n. 22.
Add at end of footnote:
The balancing may be more favorable to exclusion than is the usual rule that relevant evidence is admissible unless unfair prejudice *substantially* outweighs probative value. *E.g.*, Thacker v. State, 2015 Ark. 406, 474 S.W.3d 65 (2015) ("The rape-shield statute grants an exception where the circuit court, at an in camera hearing, makes a written determination that such evidence is relevant to a fact at issue and that its probative value outweighs its inflammatory or prejudicial nature."); State v. Shaw, 312 Conn. 85, 103, 90 A.3d 936, 499 (2014) (the defendant must show "that the probative value of the evidence outweighs its prejudicial effect on the victim"). Indeed, some statutes or opinions require that probative value substantially exceed the counterweights. McGarvey v. State, 2014 WY 66, ¶ 18, 325 P.3d 450, 456 (Wyo. 2014) ("this kind of evidence [must] substantially outweigh its highly probable prejudicial effect on the victim and the public policy underlying the statute's enactment"); N.J.S.A. 2C:14-7 ("the probative value of the evidence offered substantially outweighs its collateral nature or the probability that its admission will create undue prejudice, confusion of the issues, or unwarranted invasion of the privacy of the victim."). But whether this strict a standard respects constitutional rights is open to question. State v. J.D., 211 N.J. 344, 357, 48 A.3d 1031, 1038 (2012) ("requirements that the proffered evidence be 'highly material' and that its probative value must 'substantially' outweigh its prejudicial effect, could not be reconciled with a defendant's constitutional right of confrontation").

n. 30.
Johnston, How the Confrontation

Clause Defeated the Rape Shield Statute: Acquaintance Rape, the Consent Defense and the New Jersey Supreme Court's Ruling in *State v. Garron*, 14 S. Cal. Rev. L. & Women's Stud. 197 (2005); Orenstein, The Seductive Power of Patriarchal Stories, 58 How. L.J. 411 (2015); Constitutionality of "rape shield" statute restricting use of evidence of victim's sexual experi-ences, 1 A.L.R.4th 283

n. 32.

Add after State v. Robinson cite:
See also Tuerkheimer, Judging Sex, 97 Cornell L. Rev. 1461 (2012) (arguing that propensity-to-consent reasoning is untenable but that "[c]ourts should treat sexual history evidence consistently, by limiting its admissibility to a rebuttal function").

Add to sentence containing footnotes 36-42, after "alleged attack" preceding footnote 37:

or that defendant reasonably believed there was consent

n. 37.
State v. Montoya, 2014-NMSC-032, 333 P.3d 935, 944 (N.M. 2014) (exclusion of cross-examination on previous instances of sex following arguments ("make up sex") violated Confrontation Clause);

n. 40.
Replace contents of footnote with:
State v. Burns, 237 Ariz. 1, 16, 344 P.3d 303, 318 (2015), cert. denied, 136 S. Ct. 95, 193 L. Ed. 2d 80 (2015); People v. Mandel, 48 N.Y.2d 952, 425 N.Y.S.2d 63, 401 N.E.2d 185, 187 (1979).

n. 42.
Delete "See" from beginning of footnote.
State v. Burns, 237 Ariz. at 16, 344 P.3d at 318; State v. Shaw, 312 Conn. 85, 108, 90 A.3d 936, 950 (2014) ("These allegations [of sexual intercourse with a brother three days before the alleged assault], if proven, could have allowed the jury to conclude that A's injuries were caused by K and not by the defendant.");

Add after footnote 42:
Other exceptions also have been articulated in various states.[42.30]

[42.30]See Orenstein, The Seductive Power of Patriarchal Stories, 58 How. L.J. 411, 415 (2015); Tuerkheimer, Judging Sex, 97 Cornell L. Rev. 1461, 1462 (2012) (challenging the "pattern exception").

Replace second sentence of sixth paragraph and add new footnote:
The shield laws certainly apply to evidence of other acts of sexual intercourse or contact, for these laws are intended to protect victims from the embarrassment of having to disclose these acts.[42.50]

[42.50]Thacker v. State, 2015 Ark. 406, 474 S.W.3d 65 (2015).

n. 44.
State v. Carmichael, 240 Kan. 149, 727 P.2d 918, 925 (1986) (disapproved of on other grounds by, State v. Warrior, 294 Kan. 484, 277 P.3d 1111 (2012))

Replace "and" after "accusations of rape" in sentence ending in footnote 45 with:

sexual innuendos, banter, flirting,

n. 46.
Burns, 237 Ariz. at 16, 344 P.3d at 318 (shield law did not prevent victim from testifying that she was on her "first date");

Garron, 177 N.J. at 176, 827 A.2d at 261 (citing cases holding that "flirtatious speech and conduct" is not "sexual conduct");

Replace text of sentence including footnote 47 with (adding new footnote at end):
The rape shield laws have survived constitutional attacks,[47] albeit with occassional surgery.[47.50]

[47.50]State v. J.D., 211 N.J. 344, 357, 48 A.3d 1031, 1038 (2012) (describing cases changing the balancing test to be more favorable to a defendant's cross-examination).

A.2d 243, 254 (2003) ("The Shield Statute is intended to deter the unwarranted and unscrupulous foraging for character-assassination information about the victim.");

n. 48.
State v. Garron, 177 N.J. 147, 165, 827

§195 Habit and custom as evidence of conduct on a particular occasion

n. 4.
Oakly Enterprises, LLC v. NPI, LLC, 354 P.3d 1073, 1083-84 (Alaska 2015) (one later instance of a spill of diesel oil cannot establish a habit; it "can only reasonably be characterized as to show a propensity");

n. 24.
State v. Sigler, 210 Mont. 248, 688 P.2d 749, 753 (1984) (overruled on other grounds by, State v. Rothacher, 272 Mont. 303, 901 P.2d 82 (1995))

Chapter 18

Similar Happenings and Transactions

§ 196   Other claims, suits, or defenses of a party
§ 197   Other misrepresentations and frauds
§ 198   Other contracts and business transactions
§ 199   Other sales of similar property as evidence of value
§ 200   Other accidents and injuries

KeyCite®: Cases and other legal materials listed in KeyCite Scope can be researched through the KeyCite service on Westlaw®. Use KeyCite to check citations for form, parallel references, prior and later history, and comprehensive citator information, including citations to other decisions and secondary materials.

---

§ 196   Other claims, suits, or defenses of a party

n. 2.

Add at the end of footnote:
Another ground for admitting evidence of prior claims in accident cases is to show that the defendant did not cause the plaintiff's injuries. Cross-examination of plaintiff in personal injury action as to his previous injuries, physical condition, claims, or actions, 69 A.L.R.2d 593.

n. 9.

; Southwestern Energy Production Co. v. Berry-Helfand, 411 S.W.3d 581, 605 (Tex. App. Tyler 2013), review granted, (2 pets.)(Sept. 4, 2015) ("The insinua-

tion that one is litigious or claims-minded is inflammatory and unfairly prejudicial.")

n. 10.
Southwestern Energy Production Co. v. Berry-Helfand, 411 S.W.3d at 605.

n. 11.

Delete Daigle v. Coastal Marine, Inc. cite and parenthetical.

n. 15.

Delete State v. DeSantis cite and parenthetical.

§ 197   Other misrepresentations and frauds

n. 1.
Dorcal, Inc. v. Xerox Corp., 398 So. 2d 665 (Ala. 1981) ("In fraud cases, where intent, knowledge and scienter constitute essential elements of the offense, evidence of similar frauds and misrepresentations are commonly admissible.");

n. 3.

Add after second sentence of footnote:
For cases of fraud or similar prosecutions in which evidence of other frauds or deception has been offered, see, for

example, U.S. v. Oppon, 863 F.2d 141, 27 Fed. R. Evid. Serv. 491 (1st Cir. 1988) (previous acts of misrepresenting citizenship); U.S. v. Marine, 413 F.2d 214, 216 (7th Cir. 1969) (criminal fraud); U.S. v. Faust, 850 F.2d 575, 26 Fed. R. Evid. Serv. 571 (9th Cir. 1988) (forging a letter indicative of intent in forging checks); U.S. v. Fitterer, 710 F.2d 1328, 13 Fed. R. Evid. Serv. 1184 (8th Cir. 1983) (earlier insurance fraud indicative of intent in a mail fraud case); U.S. v. Hardrich, 707 F.2d 992, 12 Fed. R. Evid. Serv. 2036 (8th

144

Cir. 1983) (earlier utterance of a forged instrument indicative of intent in uttering forged treasury checks); U.S. v. Ramer, 2015 WL 1976436 (E.D. Ky. 2015) (mail fraud); Admissibility to establish fraudulent purpose or intent, in prosecution for obtaining or attempting to obtain money or property by false pretenses, of evidence of similar attempts on other occasions, 78 A.L.R.2d 1359; Admissibility, in forgery prosecution, of other acts of forgery, 34 A.L.R.2d 777.

n. 6.

Delete U.S. v. Oppon cite and parenthetical.

Add at the end of footnote:
Of course, if intent or knowledge are not prerequisites to liability and punitive damages are not sought, the other deceptions may not be admitted on this theory. Johnson v. Gulick, 46 Neb. 817, 65 N.W. 883, 884 (1896) (deceit); Karsun v. Kelley, 258 Or. 155, 482 P.2d 533 (1971) (action under state Blue Sky Law for false statements inducing stock purchases); Standard Mfg. Co. v. Slot, 121 Wis. 14, 98 N.W. 923, 924-25 (1904) (action on a contract).

Add after footnote 6:

In *Butler v. Watkins*,[6.30] for example, an inventor in New Orleans claimed that the Patent Nut and Bolt Company engaged in negotiations to make use of his patent, in bad faith, to keep him from marketing it while the company sold other such devices. He offered letters showing that this English manufacturing company had similar negotiations with a different inventor to keep a similar invention from entering the market that same year. The trial court excluded the letters as extrinsic because they involved a different patentee, and the company prevailed at trial. The Supreme Court reversed, stating that if "similar negotiations . . . conducted . . . deceitfully in order to keep [the other inventor's device] out of the market that year . . . tends to show that in their conduct towards the plaintiff, there was the same animus . . . ."[6.50]

[6.30]Butler v. Watkins, 80 U.S. 456, 13 Wall. 456, 20 L. Ed. 629, 1871 WL 14739 (1871).

[6.50]Butler v. Watkins, 180 U.S. at 865 (adding that "That the evidence offered was admissible for that purpose is abundantly proved by the authorities.").

n. 7.

Delete U.S. v. Faust, U.S. v. Fitterer and U.S. v. Hardrich cites and parentheticals.
Butler, 80 U.S. at 464 (because "intent may be shown by any evidence that has a tendency to persuade the mind of its existence . . . large latitude is always given"); Foremost Ins. Co. v. Parham, 693 So. 2d 409, 429 (Ala. 1997)

("great latitude must be extended so as to afford the admission of any relevant evidence bearing upon the ultimate issue of fraud").

Add to first sentence of second paragraph of footnote:
Although the usual view is that "[f]ormer and subsequent acts are admissible in evidence to show knowledge and intent as to like or similar acts," Jamestown Iron & Metal Co. v. Knofsky, 302 Pa. 483, 487, 154 A. 15, 17 (1930), some

Delete signal and Johnson v. State cite and parenthetical.

n. 8.

Delete Mudsill Min. Co. v. Watrous cite and parenthetical.

Add after footnote 8:

For example, evidence that defendants had "salted" ore samples that other intended buyers took from a mine is "competent and cogent evidence tending to establish their complicity in the like fraud now under consideration" since all the fraudulent acts were "in furtherance of same general design."[8.50]

[8.50]Mudsill Min. Co. v. Watrous, 61   F. 163, 179 (6th Cir. 1894).

Add to end of sentence ending in footnote 10, removing period:

or are content to describe the other acts as loosely defined "pattern-or-practice evidence."[11]

---

[11]Life Ins. Co. of Georgia v. Smith, 719 So. 2d 797, 808 (Ala. 1998) (forg- ing or deceptively obtaining signatures on insurance policies).

§ 198   Other contracts and business transactions

n. 2.
Simpson v. Pegram, 112 N.C. 541, 17   S.E. 430 (1893) (other letters of the parties regarding commissions);

Add in sentence ending in footnote 5, after "at bar,":
Finally, evidence of misconduct in other business dealings may be relevant to claims of bad faith or knowledge in the transaction at bar,[4.50]

[4.50]Butler v. Watkins, 80 U.S. 456, 13 Wall. 456, 20 L. Ed. 629, 1871 WL 14739 (1871) (discussed supra § 197); Kent v. White, 238 Ga. App. 792, 520 S.E.2d 481 (1999) (lawyer's failure to pay experts for their services).

§ 199   Other sales of similar property as evidence of value

n. 6.
Crow v. Cuyahoga County Bd. of   Revision, 50 Ohio St. 3d 55, 552 N.E.2d 892 (1990);

Add in sentence including footnotes 9-10, after "willing seller,":
Since the value sought is what, on average, a willing buyer would have paid a willing seller,[8.50]

[8.50]Missouri Baptist Children's Home v. State Tax Com'n, 867 S.W.2d 510, 512 (Mo. 1993).

n. 13.

Delete McAulton v. Goldstrin cite and parenthetical.

n. 14.

Delete McAulton v. Goldstrin cite and parenthetical.

§ 200   Other accidents and injuries

n. 11.

Delete signal and Glover v. BIC Corp. cite and parenthetical.

n. 24.

National R.R. Passenger Corp. v. McDavitt, 804 A.2d 275 (D.C. 2002) (two incidents during the previous year in which signals operated from a railroad control tower had reportedly malfunctioned);

Farley v. M M Cattle Co., 529 S.W.2d 751, 755 (Tex. 1975) (abrogated on other grounds by, Parker v. Highland Park, Inc., 565 S.W.2d 512 (Tex. 1978))

n. 29.

; Kia Motors Corp. v. Ruiz, 432 S.W.3d 865, 882 (Tex. 2014) (sufficient similarity not shown)

n. 31.

Birmingham Union Ry. Co. v. Alexander, 93 Ala. 133, 138, 9 So. 525, 527 (1891) ("The negative proof in the one case, equally with the affirmative proof in the other, serves to furnish the means of applying to the matter the practical test of common experience."). But cf. City of Birmingham v. Starr, 112 Ala. 98, 107, 20 So. 424, 427 (1896) (noting the importance of "evidence as to how long before the plaintiff was injured the facts occurred" and proof that "the sidewalk was in the same condition" with regard to the "affirmative proof" discussed in *Alexander*).

n. 38.

Add at end of footnote:
But see Forrest v. Beloit Corp., 424 F.3d 344, 363, 68 Fed. R. Evid. Serv. 288 (3d Cir. 2005) (discussing prejudicial aspects of "anecdotal" and overstated no-accident evidence).

n. 39.

Birmingham Union Ry. Co. v. Alexander, 93 Ala. 133, 9 So. 525, 527 (1891)

Chapter 19

Insurance Against Liability

§ 201   Insurance against liability as proof of negligence

Replace first two sentences in paragraph including footnotes 15-18 with:

Caselaw elaborates on these "other purposes." Varied opinions recognize that the fact that persons rarely purchase liability insurance to cover contingencies for which they are not responsible makes evidence that a party is insured relevant to questions of agency,[15] ownership,[16] and control[17] of vehicles and premises. More commonly, the fact of insurance can be relevant to the bias of a witness. This is most obvious when the witness is an investigator or other employee of the insurance company.[18]

---

[15]Hunziker v. Scheidemantle, 543 F.2d 489, 495 (3d Cir. 1976) (liability insurance may be admitted to show that pilot of light aircraft was acting as agent if adequate foundation is laid); McCoy v. Universal Carloading & Distributing Co., 82 F.2d 342, 344 (6th Cir. 1936) (whether driver of truck was agent or independent contractor); Eldridge v. McGeorge, 99 F.2d 835, 841 (8th Cir. 1938) (whether owner or driver of truck was an employee); Cook-O'Brien Const. Co. v. Crawford, 26 F.2d 574, 575 (9th Cir. 1928) (whether worker injured by explosion was employee); Cherry v. Stockton, 75 N.M. 488, 406 P.2d 358, 360 (1965) (whether owner or driver of truck was employee); Biggins v. Wagner, 60 S.D. 581, 245 N.W. 385, 386–87 (1932) (same).

[16]Newell v. Harold Shaffer Leasing Co., Inc., 489 F.2d 103, 110 (5th Cir. 1974) (check for repair bill from insurance company naming defendant as the insured properly received under Mississippi law "on the issue of ownership and agency"); Layton v. Cregan & Mallory Co., 263 Mich. 30, 248 N.W. 539 (1933) (ownership of automobile); Anderson v. Ohm, 258 N.W.2d 114, 118 (Minn. 1977) (same); cf. Leavitt v. Glick Realty Corp., 362 Mass. 370, 285 N.E.2d 786, 787 (1972) (evidence of liability insurance to show ownership or control of building is not admissible when these matters are not disputed).

[17]Pinckard v. Dunnavant, 281 Ala. 533, 206 So. 2d 340, 342–43 (1968) (management and maintenance of premises); Appelhans v. Kirkwood, 148 Colo. 92, 365 P.2d 233, 239 (1961) (proof that father insured vehicle driven by son); Perkins v. Rice, 187 Mass. 28, 72 N.E. 323, 324 (1904) (defendant admitted ownership of

premises but denied control of elevator).

[18]Ingalls Shipbuilding Corp. v. Trehern, 155 F.2d 202, 203–04 (5th Cir. 1946) (cross-examination to show that defendant's witness was insurance adjuster); Vindicator Consol. Gold Mining Co. v. Firstbrook, 36 Colo. 498, 86 P. 313, 314 (1906) (cross-examination to show witness acting as agent for insurance company); Pickett v. Kolb, 250 Ind. 449, 237 N.E.2d 105, 106 (1968) (error to sustain objection to question "who paid you to do this inspection?"); Baker v. Kammerer, 187 S.W.3d 292, 296 (Ky. 2006) ("abuse of discretion to prevent disclosure of the fact that a witness presented as an "investigator" of an "incident [that] had been investigated by police" worked for an insurance company); Mac Tyres, Inc. v. Vigil, 92 N.M. 446, 589 P.2d 1037, 1039 (1979) (abuse of discretion to exclude deposition of witness admitting to having lied to insurance representative); Rigelman v. Gilligan, 265 Or. 109, 506 P.2d 710, 714 (1973).

When plaintiff's witness is impeached by a prior inconsistent written statement prepared by an insurance adjuster and plaintiff disputes the correctness of the statement, the majority of courts allow the plaintiff to show the insurance company's employee prepared the statement for plaintiff's signature. Complete Auto Transit, Inc. v. Wayne Broyles Engineering Corp., 351 F.2d 478, 481–82 (5th Cir. 1965); Roland v. Beckham, 408 S.W.2d 628, 633 (Ky. 1966); Brave v. Blakely, 250 S.C. 353, 157 S.E.2d 726, 730 (1967). *Contra* Texas Co. v. Betterton, 126 Tex. 359, 88 S.W.2d 1039 (Comm'n App. 1936).

Create new paragraph after footnote 18, replacing sentences in remainder of paragraph, including footnotes 19-22, with:

Cross-examination affords the usual means of revealing bias, and, at the very least, the fact that the witness is being compensated (even if the insurer is not identified) is fair game.[19] Moreover, it is well established that the trial court has discretion to allow more candid and complete disclosure that this employer is actually the defendant's insurer.[20] But bias also is an issue with experts who are not employees of the insurer. These witnesses can face pressures or incentives comparable to those arising from the employment relationship. Consequently, the cross-examiner is usually allowed to exposure a "substantial connection" to the insurance carrier.[21] However, the phrase "substantial connection" is hardly self-defining.[22] In imbuing it with meaning, most courts have concluded, on the one hand, that evidence that an expert witness merely has the same insurance carrier as the defendant is normally not admissible.[22.10] Likewise, being paid to appear in the single case at bar does not require the insurance carrier to be named as the source of the compensation.[22.20] On the other hand, when the expert has a clear and substantial financial interest in the insurer's not having to pay its insured for a judgment, the need to disclose this influence dominates. Deriving a significant fraction of income from insurers,[22.30] working for companies that rely on insurers for a major part of their revenue,[22.40] or having other close ties to insurance carriers[22.50] can constitute the substantial connection.

_____

[19]Jones v. Munn, 140 Ariz. 216, 681 P.2d 368 (1984) (witness may be

cross-examined to establish that he is an investigator for defendant's "representative"); Matthews v. Jean's Pastry Shop, Inc., 113 N.H. 546, 548, 311 A.2d 127, 129 (1973) ("Here the witness' potential bias was disclosed to the jury when it was shown that he had been acting for the defendant. The implied finding that prejudice to the defendant from disclosure of the witness' employment by the insurer would outweigh additional benefit to the plaintiffs was not error as a matter of law.").

[20]Mideastern Contracting Corporation v. O'Toole, 55 F.2d 909, 912 (C.C.A. 2d Cir. 1932) (L. Hand, Cir. J., "The defendant need not have put in the statement [that the plaintiff allegedly made] at all; when it chooses to do so, it laid open to inquiry its authenticity, and that inevitably involved the relation of the person who took it"); Eppinger & Russell Co. v. Sheely, 24 F.2d 153, 155 (C.C.A. 5th Cir. 1928) (proper to ask physician testifying for defendant whether he was retained by employer's insurer); Charter v. Chleborad, 551 F.2d 246, 248, 1 Fed. R. Evid. Serv. 878 (8th Cir. 1977) (error to prohibit plaintiff in medical malpractice action from establishing on cross-examination that defendant's witness (an attorney who testified that plaintiff's expert witness had a bad reputation for truth and veracity) represents defendant's liability carrier from time to time); Dempsey v. Goldstein Bros. Amusement Co., 231 Mass. 461, 121 N.E. 429 (1919) (to show bias of physician who testified that plaintiff had no permanent injuries); Gibson v. Grey Motor Co., 147 Minn. 134, 179 N.W. 729, 730 (1920) (insurance investigator); O'Donnell v. Bachelor, 429 Pa. 498, 240 A.2d 484, 486, 489 (1968) (Error to limit cross-examination to show that defendant's insurer employed investigator-witness, for "[o]nce a witness commits himself to the ocean of legal controversy, he must, under cross-examination, disclose the flag under which he sails." To which a dissent replied that disclosing the presence of the insurance company reveals "not only the flag, but the seamstress who sewed it").

[21]Ray v. Draeger, 353 P.3d 806,

812 (Alaska 2015); Yoho v. Thompson, 345 S.C. 361, 548 S.E.2d 584, 586 (2001).

[22]Woolum v. Hillman, 329 S.W.3d 283, 288 (Ky. 2010) ("The only brightline solution to this problem has been developed by the Supreme Court of Ohio, which . . . has conclusively held that 'in a medical malpractice action, evidence of a commonality of insurance interests between a defendant and an expert witness is sufficiently probative of the expert's bias as to clearly outweigh any potential prejudice evidence of insurance might cause.' ").

[22.10]Kansas Medical Mut. Ins. Co. v. Svaty, 291 Kan. 597, 244 P.3d 642 (2010) (discovery requests for medical malpractice insurance company's records are not reasonably calculated to lead to discovery of admissible evidence of bias of expert witness simply because defendant and expert practice in same state and purchase insurance in same market); Wells v. Tucker, 997 So. 2d 908 (Miss. 2008); Reimer v. Surgical Services of Great Plains, P.C., 258 Neb. 671, 605 N.W.2d 777, 780-81 (2000); Hoffart v. Hodge, 9 Neb. App. 161, 609 N.W.2d 397, 407-08 (2000); Daniels v. Gamma West Brachytherapy, LLC, 2009 UT 66, 221 P.3d 256, 268 (Utah 2009). *But see* Woolum v. Hillman, 329 S.W.3d 283 at 288 (Ky. 2010) (admissible when defendant's expert physician deposition showed such concern about his malpractice premiums that "Dr. Butcher is no average, passive policyholder, but instead a practitioner very concerned with the affairs of his insurer"); Ede v. Atrium S. OB-GYN, Inc., 71 Ohio St. 3d 124, 1994-Ohio-424, 642 N.E.2d 365 (1994) (abuse of discretion to prevent medical-malpractice plaintiff from showing that testifying physicians were all insured by a physicians' mutual insurance company, so that fewer successful malpractice claims means lower premiums). For a case rejecting the last view, see Hensley v. Methodist Healthcare Hospitals, 2015 WL 5076982 (W.D. Tenn. 2015).

[22.20]McDaniel v. Pickens, 45 Mass. App. Ct. 63, 66, 695 N.E.2d 215, 218 (1998) ("where an expert has had no relation to any liability insurer apart from the fact that the defendant's insurer in the end footed his bill, a judge might decide to limit the cross-examination to exclude reference to the insurance altogether, and so avoid any collateral entanglements.").

[22.30]Ray v. Draeger, 353 P.3d at 815 ("receives between $300,000 to $350,000 a year for his insurance reviews [which] represents a large percentage of his total yearly income of up to $800,000"); Oliveira v. Jacobson, 846 A.2d 822, 828 (R.I. 2004) (paid $35,000-$40,000 a year for services as a board member of a medical malpractice insurance company and omitted this information on his curriculum vitae); Yoho v. Thompson, 345 S.C. 361, 366, 548 S.E.2d 584, 586 (2001) ("consulted for Nationwide in other cases and gave lectures to Nationwide's agents and adjusters," and "[t]en to twenty percent of Dr. Brannon's practice consisted of reviewing records for insurance companies"); Lombard v. Rohrbaugh, 262 Va. 484, 495, 551 S.E.2d 349, 355 (2001) ("a substantial connection with Allstate, including receipt of over $100,000 per year in payments for the years 1998 and 1999").

[22.40]See Draeger, 353 P.3d at 815; Mitchell v. Glimm, 819 So. 2d 548 (Miss. Ct. App. 2002); Henning v. Thomas, 235 Va. 181, 366 S.E.2d 109, 112 (1988).

[22.50]Bonser v. Shainholtz, 3 P.3d 422, 425-27 (Colo. 2000) (expert's role as co-founder of insurance trust).

Replace first sentence of paragraph including footnotes 23-24 with:

Plainly, the purposes enumerated in Rule 411 do not exhaust the possibilities.

n. 23.

Add at beginning of footnote:
Miller v. Szelenyi, 546 A.2d 1013 (Me. 1988) (a doctor's alleged statement to nurses that a woman in cardiac arrest should not be defibrillated because his malpractice insurance would not cover the procedure was admissible to show that punitive damages were warranted).

Add after footnote 23:

That a defendant is insured can be important to rebut a suggestion that the defendant is too poor to pay a large judgment;[23.30] conversely, that a defendant in not insured can be relevant to plaintiff's demand for punitive damages.[23.50]

[23.30]Schaefer v. Ready, 134 Idaho 378, 381, 3 P.3d 56, 59 (Ct. App. 2000); Wheeler v. Murphy, 192 W. Va. 325, 333, 452 S.E.2d 416, 424 (1994); *cf.* Humana Health Ins. Co. of Florida, Inc. v. Chipps, 802 So. 2d 492, 497-98 (Fla. 4th DCA 2001) (evidence of indemnity agreement admissible to rebut defendant's assertions that a large punitive damages award would place the company in grave financial distress).

[23.50]Valdes v. Miami-Dade County, 2015 WL 7253045 (S.D. Fla. 2015); Fleegel v. Estate of Boyles, 61 P.3d 1267, 1271 (Alaska 2002); Ayers v. Christiansen, 222 Kan. 225, 229-30, 564 P.2d 458, 461 (1977).

n. 24.
Jentz v. ConAgra Foods, Inc., 767 F.3d 688, 95 Fed. R. Evid. Serv. 393 (7th Cir. 2014), cert. denied, 135 S. Ct. 1472, 191 L. Ed. 2d 371 (2015) and cert. denied, 135 S. Ct. 1476, 191 L. Ed. 2d 371 (2015) (to show that the owner of a flour mill delayed remedying a dangerous condition because it took too long negotiating over matters such as insurance coverage with companies that specialized in remediation);

Delete Fleegel v. Estate of Boyles cite and parenthetical.

; Oliveira v. Jacobson, 846 A.2d 822, 828 (R.I. 2004) (expert's concealing his ties to insurance company was a proper subject for impeachment)

n. 27.

Delete Hazeltine v. Johnson cite.

n. 28.

Delete Ballinger v. Gascosage Elec. Co-op. cite.

n. 29.

Ray v. Draeger, 353 P.3d 806, 814 (Alaska 2015) ("Though a jury may infer from this evidence that a party is insured, this inference presents a low risk of unfair prejudice because jurors will be aware that Alaska law requires drivers to carry automobile insurance.");

Ede v. Atrium S. OB-GYN, Inc., 71 Ohio St. 3d 124, 1994-Ohio-424, 642 N.E.2d 365, 368 (1994) ("It is naive to believe that today's jurors, bombarded for years with information about health care insurance, do not already assume in a malpractice case that the defendant doctor is covered by insurance. The legal charade protecting juries from information they already know keeps hidden from them relevant information that could assist them in making their determinations."); Oden v. Schwartz, 71 A.3d 438, 455 (R.I. 2013) ("The concept of liability insurance is a wholly familiar concept—from mandatory motor vehicle insurance coverage to the vigorous nationwide debate concerning medical insurance and medical liability, it can hardly be said that jurors are not thinking about liability coverage in one sense or another.");

Chapter 20

Experimental and Scientific Evidence

I. SCIENTIFIC TESTS IN GENERAL

§ 202   Pretrial experiments
§ 203   Scientific evidence: Admissibility and weight *[Retitled]*

II. PARTICULAR TESTS

§ 204   Physics and electronics: Speed detection and recording
§ 205   Biology and medicine: Drunkenness and blood, tissue, and DNA typing
§ 206   Psychology: Lie detection; drugs and hypnosis; eyewitness testimony; profiles and syndromes
§ 207   Criminalistics: Identifying persons and things

III. STATISTICAL STUDIES

§ 208   Surveys and opinion polls
§ 209   Correlations and causes: Statistical evidence of discrimination

IV. PROBABILITIES AS EVIDENCE

§ 210   Identification evidence and probabilities *[Retitled]*
§ 211   Paternity testing

KeyCite®: Cases and other legal materials listed in KeyCite Scope can be researched through the KeyCite service on Westlaw®. Use KeyCite to check citations for form, parallel references, prior and later history, and comprehensive citator information, including citations to other decisions and secondary materials.

I. SCIENTIFIC TESTS IN GENERAL

§ 202   Pretrial experiments

n. 1.

  Delete Faigman cite.

n. 3.

U.S. v. Law, 528 F.3d 888, 912-13 (D.C. Cir. 2008) (chemist testified about ion mobility spectrometry, infrared spectroscopy, and gas chromatography-mass spectrometry tests that established that evidence recovered from trash cans and from apartments contained residue of controlled substances); 5 Faigman, et al., Modern Scientific Evidence: The Law and Science of Expert Testimony §§ 40:1 et seq. (2015-2016 ed.)

n. 4.
Adams v. Toyota Motor Corp., 2015 WL 3742898 (D. Minn. 2015) (engineer's tests indicated that the throttle control mechanism will stick at temperatures above 160°F);

Delete Patricia R. v. Sullivan and

Dritt v. Morris cites and parentheticals.

n. 5.
Delete Stumbaugh v. State cite and parenthetical.

Delete Faigman cite.

Add in sentence including footnotes 3-9, preceding "effects of drugs":

presence[5.50] or

[5.50]Missouri v. McNeely, 133 S. Ct. 1552, 185 L. Ed. 2d 696 (2013) (blood alcohol test).

n. 6.
Vermont Food Industries, Inc. v. Ralston Purina Co., 514 F.2d 456 (2d Cir. 1975) (experiment on plaintiff's farm indicating that a new formulation of chicken feed caused excessive obesity and lower egg production in hens); 3 Faigman, et al., Modern Scientific Evidence: The Law and Science of Expert Testimony §§ 22:1 et seq. (2015-

2016 ed.)

n. 7.
4 Faigman, et al., Modern Scientific Evidence: The Law and Science of Expert Testimony §§ 34:1 et seq. (2015-2016 ed.)

n. 9.
Admissibility in evidence, in automobile negligence action, of charts showing braking distance, reaction times, etc., 9 A.L.R.3d 976

Add to end of sentence following footnote 9, after "visible":
Some of these experiments can be simple affairs, such as driving an automobile along a stretch of road to determine where a particular object on the road first becomes visible, or driving from one place to another to estimate how long the trip might take.[9.50]

[9.50]U.S. v. Jackson, 479 F.3d 485, 72 Fed. R. Evid. Serv. 742 (7th Cir. 2007); Branion v. Gramly, 855 F.2d 1256, 11 Fed. R. Serv. 3d 1178 (7th Cir. 1988).

n. 10.
Delete remainder of footnote following cross-reference.

Replace "it" in last clause of sentence including footnotes 11-12 with:

the experiments

Replace "Pretrial experiments" in sentence ending in footnote 14 with:
Pretrial experiments that do not demand scientific expertise for their intepretation are the main subject of this section.[13.50] These experiments

---

13.50These experiments may be designed by scientists or engineers, but if they are readily understood and are not presented as scientific truths or used as the basis for scientific opinions, the special rules for scientific or other expert evidence may not need to be applied. *See* Aleo v. SLB Toys USA, Inc., 466 Mass. 398, 405, 995 N.E.2d 740, 749 (2013) (testimony about sliding a mannequin down a Banzai Falls In-Ground Pool Slide and dropping it onto the bottom of the slide was admissible "for its 'limited utility' in demonstrating . . . the physical properties of the slide"; the expert who conducted the experiment was not permitted to give an opinion on whether the slide would be more likely to collapse when a user was sliding or diving).

n. 14.

Delete signal and Hasson v. Ford Motor Co. cite and parenthetical.

Replace the two sentences following footnote 14 with:
The only form of prejudice that might operate in this context is that of giving experimental results more weight than they deserve, and that can depend on how they are presented. If the interpretation of the experiment does not entail expert scientific testimony, the danger of misusing the findings is not likely to be excessive.

n. 15.
Delete Spurlin v. Nardo cite and parenthetical.

Replace sentence ending in footnote 18 with:
The requirement is at its strictest when the experiment seeks to replicate the event in question to show that things happened (or did not happen) as alleged.

n. 18.
Dunn v. Nexgrill Industries, Inc., 636 F.3d 1049, 1056, 84 Fed. R. Evid. Serv. 1014 (8th Cir. 2011) (although plaintiffs maintained that their experiment was not subject to the substantial-similarity requirement because it was "just testing scientific principles," the trial judge properly found that it "instead was trying to recreate the cause and origin of the fire");

n. 20.
Lapsley v. Xtek, Inc., 689 F.3d 802, 815 (7th Cir. 2012);

n. 26.
Add at beginning of footnote and

move State v. Don cite to follow Osborne v. United States cite.
For example, cases in which police drive from one place to another to demonstrate that even if evidence in support of alibi defense were believed, defendant still would have had opportunity to commit the crime need not (and cannot) duplicate the conditions precisely. *See* U.S. v. Jackson, 479 F.3d 485, 490, 72 Fed. R. Evid. Serv. 742 (7th Cir. 2007); Osborne v. U.S., 542 F.2d 1015, 1019-20, 1 Fed. R. Evid. Serv. 362, 36 A.L.R. Fed. 555 (8th Cir. 1976); State v. Don, 318 N.W.2d 801, 805 (Iowa 1982). *See also*

Replace last sentence of paragraph that includes footnotes 29-33 with:
In addition, tests for composition or properties often are highly scientific, thus triggering an inquiry into their scientific validity and reliability as described in the next section.

Add after footnote 34:

As we have seen, that rule is applicable to efforts to re-create or simulate an accident or other event that is the subject of the litigation.

Start new paragraph and replace "Nevertheless, these cases rarely provide an analysis of" in sentence following footnote 34 with:

To confine the substantial-similarity rule to re-creations and simulations, however, one needs some principle that explains

Add new footnote to end of sentence following sentence including footnote 35:

Of course, the question for the jury was whether 2,4-D was more destructive on appellant's farm, and an experiment could have been designed to control for possible differences in soil conditions, humidity, and other variables.[36]

---

[36]*Cf.* Vermont Food Industries, Inc. v. Ralston Purina Co., 514 F.2d 456, 459 (2d Cir. 1975) (when "the conditions and environmental factors of [flocks of hens on plaintiff's farm] were identical for all practical purposes"—except for a known difference in the feed—a jury could attribute excessive obesity and lower egg production in the flocks that were fed defendant's new product to that difference).

Delete paragraph including footnotes 36-40 and accompanying footnotes.

Replace last paragraph in section, renumbering footnotes:

In view of the widespread use of experiments to re-create or simulate accidents, explosions, product failures, and some crimes, it is appropriate to consider procedures to improve the design and implementation of case-specific experiments before they are conducted. Consideration might be given to excluding experiments unless the adversary has had reasonable notice, an opportunity to make suggestions, and to be present during the experiment.[37] Also worthy of consideration is appointment by the court of an impartial person to conduct or supervise an experiment.[38] Such prophylactic procedures could lead to findings that would invite much less in the way of time-consuming or distracting attack and defense at trial.

---

[37]*See* Fortunato v. Ford Motor Co., 464 F.2d 962, 966 (2d Cir. 1972) (dictum that "[t]est results should not even be admissible as evidence, unless made by a qualified, independent expert or unless the opposing party has the opportunity to participate in the test"); *cf.* People v. Griffin, 46 Cal. 3d 1011, 1021 n.2, 251 Cal. Rptr. 643, 648 n.2, 761 P.2d 103, 108 n.2, (1988) ("[I]n those cases where the amount of material available for testing is small, or

when the state's duty to preserve evidence would otherwise be enhanced, it may be incumbent on the state to contact the defendant to determine whether he wishes his expert to be present during the tests."). Under present practice, lack of notice and opportunity to be present are not grounds for rejection, but they may be argued on weight. U.S. v. Love, 482 F.2d 213, 218-19 (5th Cir. 1973) (no Sixth Amendment right to have defense expert present for chemical tests); Burg v. Chicago, R.I. & Pac. Ry. Co., 90 Iowa 106, 57 N.W. 680, 683 (1894) (visibility test). The recommendation offered here would allow rejection of experimental evidence on these grounds in appropriate circumstances to encourage better designed experiments and to obviate objections that could have been raised in advance. The proposal would not apply to routine laboratory tests, but would cover experiments initiated *post litem mo-* *tam* for the purpose of litigation.

[38]A notable example appeared in the course of the grand jury investigation of the White House's involvement in the Watergate break-in in 1974. A panel of six court-appointed experts agreeable to the Watergate Special Prosecutor and the White House conducted extensive tests to determine the cause of a notorious 18.5-minute gap on a subpoenaed tape recording of a conversation between President Nixon and an aide that took place shortly after the break-in. The experts' report made it plain that the gap consisted of intentional erasures made after the tape had been subpoenaed. The grand jury concluded that only a handful of people could have been responsible for these erasures, but it never secured sufficient evidence to prosecute any of these individuals. Watergate Special Prosecution Force, U.S. Dep't of Justice, Report 53 (1975).

§ 203 Scientific evidence: Admissibility and weight [Retitled]

Add at end of first paragraph:

In one product liability case, counsel's complaint that an expert's calculations of energy and pressure—using formulas in existence for centuries—should have been excluded as "scientific 'Sanskrit' " provoked this lecture from the Court of Appeals:

Law must apply itself to the life of a society driven more and more by technology and technological improvements. Judges and lawyers do not have the luxury of functional illiteracy in either of these two cultures [the sciences and humanities]. Sometimes, as in this case, effective presentation, cross-examination, and evaluation of expert testimony require lawyers and judges to fill in gaps in their scientific, engineering, or mathematics educations or refresh their memories about them.[0.50]

[0.50]Lapsley v. Xtek, Inc., 689 F.3d 802, 811 (7th Cir. 2012).

n. 1.
Giannelli et al., Scientific Evidence (5th ed. 2012)

n. 3.
Delete content of footnote following cross-reference.

n. 6.
Add at end of footnote:

For more on the history of the case and the colorful defense expert, see Tal Golan, Laws of Men and Laws of Nature: The History of Scientific Expert Testimony in England and America (2007); Jill Lepore, The Secret History of Wonder Woman (2015); Jill Lepore, On Evidence: Proving Frye as a Matter of Law, Science, and History, 124 Yale L.J. 1092 (2015).

n. 29.
In re Detention of New, 2014 IL 116306,

386 Ill. Dec. 643, 21 N.E.3d 406 (Ill. 2014) (diagnosis of hebephilia);

Replace parenthetical following People v. McKown:
(horizontal gaze nystagmus test for alcohol intoxication)

n. 30.

Replace "In the past three decades or so" with:
Since the 1970s,

n. 36.

State v. Hodges, 239 Kan. 63, 716 P.2d 563, 569 (1986) (disapproved of on other grounds by, State v. Stewart, 243 Kan. 639, 763 P.2d 572 (1988))

n. 38.

State v. Hurd, 86 N.J. 525, 432 A.2d 86 (1981) (abrogated on other grounds by, State v. Moore, 188 N.J. 182, 902 A.2d 1212 (2006))

Add new paragraph after footnote 48:

Following this 1993 opinion, an untold number of lower court opinions have elaborated on such factors. The Supreme Court soon discussed their application in another toxic tort case, *General Electric Company v. Joiner*,[48.30] and then again in *Kumho Tire Co. v. Carmichael*,[48.50] a fatal automobile accident case that turned on an engineer's opinion that a tire failed because of a manufacturing defect. In 2000, an amendment to Rule 702 codified the major themes of these opinions. The current rule, which governs all expert testimony, demands that: "(a) the expert's . . . specialized knowledge will help the trier of fact to understand the evidence or to determine a fact in issue; (b) the testimony is based on sufficient facts or data; (c) the testimony is the product of reliable principles and methods; and (d) the expert has reliably applied the principles and methods to the facts of the case."[48.70]

[48.30]General Elec. Co. v. Joiner, 522 U.S. 136, 118 S. Ct. 512, 139 L. Ed. 2d 508, 48 Fed. R. Evid. Serv. 1, 177 A.L.R. Fed. 667 (1997).

[48.50]Kumho Tire Co., Ltd. v. Carmichael, 526 U.S. 137, 119 S. Ct. 1167, 143 L. Ed. 2d 238, 50 Fed. R. Evid. Serv. 1373 (1999).

[48.70]For the view that the amended rule is not a simple codification, but a selection of ideas from the more stringent line of post-*Daubert* cases, see Bernstein & Lasker, Defending Daubert: It's Time to Amend Federal Rule of Evidence 702, 57 William & Mary L. Rev. 1 (2015); Bernstein, The Misbegotten Judicial Resistance to the Daubert Revolution, 89 Notre Dame L. Rev. 27 (2014).

Replace "bitemark identification" in third sentence of paragraph including footnotes 59-61 with:

handwriting identification

n. 59.

Replace parenthetical following Ex Parte Dolvin cite:
(bitemark comparison admitted as "physical comparisons" that do not require general scientific acceptance); People v. Lucas, 60 Cal. 4th 153, 177 Cal. Rptr. 3d 378, 333 P.3d 587 (2014) (disapproved of on other grounds by,

People v. Romero, 62 Cal. 4th 1, 191 Cal. Rptr. 3d 855, 354 P.3d 983 (2015)) (handwriting comparison properly admitted without regard to general scientific acceptance); State v. Reid, 254 Conn. 540, 757 A.2d 482 (2000) (microscopic hair comparison, later shown to be erroneous, admitted);

Add at end of footnote:
However, greater receptivity to some types and presentations of forensic-science evidence cannot be a blank check for admissibility. A sufficient scientific foundation for the testimony still needs to be established, and a history of general acceptance among criminalists notwithstanding, it is doubtful that all the "physical comparison" evidence that some jurisdictions have exempted from serious scrutiny would satisfy a careful relevancy-plus analysis.

Replace sentence ending in footnote 60 and the footnote with:
On the other hand, when the nature of the technique is more esoteric, as with some types of statistical analyses and chemical tests,[59.30] when subjective judgments are misleadingly presented as hard science,[59.50] or when the inferences from the scientific evidence sweep broadly or cut deeply into sensitive areas, a stronger showing of probative value should be required.[60]

[59.30]*See, e.g.,* People v. Collins, 68 Cal. 2d 319, 66 Cal. Rptr. 497, 438 P.2d 33, 36 A.L.R.3d 1176 (1968) (probability calculations); State v. Catanese, 368 So. 2d 975, 981 (La. 1979) (polygraph); Kaye, The NRC Bullet-Lead Report: Should Science Committees Make Legal Findings?, 46 Jurimetrics J. 91, 101-02 (2005) ("testimony of an analytical chemist or forensic scientist as to the results of Optical Emission Spectroscopy of bullet lead and Hotelling's T^2 test" should not be readily admissible in light of a National Academy of Sciences study of such methods).

[59.50]*See* State v. Lusareta, 270 Or. App. 102, 108, 346 P.3d 514, 518 (2015) ("When an expert couches her testimony in the 'vocabulary of scientific research' she 'effectively announce[s] to the jury that the basis of her testimony [is] "scientific."'") (quoting State v. Whitmore, 257 Or. App. 664, 672, 307 P.3d 552 (2013)); Kaye, Ultracrepidarianism in Forensic Science: The Hair Evidence Debacle, 72 Wash. & Lee L. Rev. Online 227 (2015).

[60]McGrew v. State, 682 N.E.2d 1289, 1292 (Ind. 1997) ("Inherent in any reliability analysis is the understanding that, as the scientific principles become more advanced and complex, the foundation required to establish reliability will necessarily become more advanced and complex as well.").

Add in sentence ending in footnote 61, after "context":

and manner

n. 69.
1 Faigman, et al., Modern Scientific Evidence § 1:6 (2015-2016 ed.)

n. 70.
1 Modern Scientific Evidence § 1:6

Delete footnote 73.

n. 74.
   Delete Faigman cite.

n. 75.
; Weinstein, Improving Expert Testimony, 20 U. Richmond L. Rev. 473, 478 (1986).

(2015-2016 ed.) ("Different fields have widely varying standards.")

Replace to end of footnote, starting with "There is some empirical evidence . . ."

The empirical evidence is mixed. *See* Kaye et al., The New Wigmore: A

Treatise on Evidence § 7.6.4(b)(1)   ing Scientific Evidence (5th ed. 2014)
(Cum. Supp. 2016).

n. 77.
Imwinkelried, The Methods of Attack-

Add in sentence ending in footnote 79, after "If so,":

are standards to guide the process of reaching conclusions in place, and

Replace sentence ending in footnote 82 with:
In particular, requiring adequate pretrial disclosure of the witness's scientific reasoning in written form and adequate detail for review by other scientists would be valuable.[82]

---

[82]*See, e.g.,* NIST Expert Working Group on Human Factors in Latent Print Analysis, Latent Print Examination and Human Factors: Improving the Practice through a Systems Approach (Kaye ed. 2012); Nat'l Research Council Comm. on Identifying the Needs of the Forensic Sci. Cmty., Strengthening Forensic Science in the United States: A Path Forward 186 (2009); Giannelli, Wrongful Convic- tions and Forensic Science: The Need to Regulate Crime Labs, 86 N.C. L. Rev. 163 (2007); Kaye & Freedman, Reference Guide on Statistics, in Reference Manual on Scientific Evidence 83 (Fed. Judicial Ctr. ed., 2d ed. 2000); Nesson & Demers, Gatekeeping: An Enhanced Foundational Approach to Determining the Admissibility of Scientific Evidence, 49 Hastings L.J. 335 (1998).

II. PARTICULAR TESTS

§ 204   Physics and electronics: Speed detection and recording

Replace "Acceleration" in fifth sentence of paragraph following heading "(A) Mechanical Timing Devices" with:
Average acceleration

n. 2.
; State v. Helke, 2015-Ohio-4402, 46 N.E.3d 188 (Ohio Ct. App. 2d Dist. Montgomery County 2015) (recognizing admissibility of a visual estimate of speed, but applying Ohio Rev. Code § 4511.091 (C)(1), which makes "unaided visual estimation" of speed insufficient for an arrest or conviction)

n. 7.
Moenssens et al., Scientific Evidence in Civil and Criminal Cases (6th ed. 2012)

n. 10.
State v. Finkle, 66 N.J. 139, 329 A.2d 65 (1974);

n. 11.
  Add at the end of footnote:
See infra § 204(C)&(D) (discussing evidence of proper calibration of RADAR and LIDAR instruments).

n. 13.
Villegas v. Bryson, 16 Ariz. App. 456, 494 P.2d 61 (1972) (accuracy of tachograph chart properly established);

Start new paragraph with sentence ending in footnote 16.

Add after footnote 16:
Some devices record specific data on sudden deceleration and air bag deployment.[16.30] Others reveal when a train's bell and horn are activated.[16.50]

Replace sentence ending in footnote 17 with:
To date, no serious doubts have been raised about the general acceptance or validity of Event Data Recorders for recording information immediately before crashes.

[16.30]Bachman v. General Motors Corp., 332 Ill. App. 3d 760, 267 Ill. Dec. 125, 776 N.E.2d 262 (4th Dist. 2002) (SDM technology is generally accepted).

[16.50]The records of sounds generally are not treated as conclusive when they conflict with the testimony of percipient witnesses. Illinois Cent. R. Co. v. Young, 120 So. 3d 992 (Miss. Ct. App. 2012).

n. 17.
Com. v. Safka, 2014 PA Super 131, 95 A.3d 304, 308 (2014), appeal granted in part, 104 A.3d 525 (Pa. 2014) ("the technology has existed for almost 40 years, has been adopted by the major automobile manufacturers, and has been recognized as an acceptable tool used by accident reconstruction experts to determine a vehicle's speed prior to an impact");

Add after footnote 17:
Naturally, foundational evidence that the instruments are performing as expected and recording the events in question is necessary.

n. 19.
Replace "rely" in first sentence of footnote with:
relied

n. 20.
Replace sentence preceding Landsberg & Evans cite with:
All electromagnetic radiation and other forms of energy transmission exhibit the Doppler effect.

n. 23.
Delete signal and People v. Persons cite and parenthetical.

n. 24.
State v. Tailo, 70 Haw. 580, 779 P.2d 11, 13 (1989) ("Because of the strength of the scientific principles on which the radar gun is based, every recent court which has dealt with the question has taken judicial notice of the scientific reliability of radar speedmeters as recorders of speed.")

n. 26.
State v. Tailo, 70 Haw. 580, 779 P.2d 11, 14 (1989) ("once the State puts in evidence that the police conducted a tuning fork test indicating the K-15 gun was properly calibrated, this evidence creates a prima facie presumption that the tuning fork itself was accurately calibrated");

n. 31.
Moenssens et al., Scientific Evidence in Civil and Criminal Cases (6th ed. 2012)

Replace sentence ending in footnote 38 with:
Yet another device uses a laser to generate many pulses of infrared radiation per second.

n. 38.

Ryan V. Cox & Carl Fors, Admitting Light Detection and Ranging (Lidar) Evidence in Texas: a Call for Statewide Judicial Notice, 42 St. Mary's L.J. 837 (2011);

Add at end of footnote:

More generally, such laser pulses are the basis for LiDAR (Light Ranging and Detection) measurements of distances, with applications in forestry and vegetation mapping, geosciences, natural hazards mapping, and archaeological surveys. Dong, LiDAR Remote Sensing and Applications (2016).

n. 39.

Hall v. State, 264 S.W.3d 346, 350 (Tex. App. Waco 2008), petition for discretionary review granted, (Jan. 14, 2009) and aff'd but criticized on other grounds, 297 S.W.3d 294 (Tex. Crim. App. 2009)

n. 40.

State v. Williamson, 144 Idaho 597, 166 P.3d 387 (Ct. App. 2007) (LiDAR is "generally reliable");

n. 41.

Goldstein, 664 A.2d at 380

Add after footnote 45:

As with radar and other instruments that measure speed, once the general acceptance and validity of both the theory and the measuring instrument have been established, the case-specific issues of the accuracy and authenticity of particular measurments may be subject to further rules.[46]

---

[46]State v. Assaye, 121 Haw. 204, 216 P.3d 1227, 1235 (2009) (although the officer "conducted four tests prior to his shift in order to determine whether the laser gun" was function-ing accurately and was "certified" to use it, the results were inadmissible without evidence that these tests and his training were approved by the manufacturer).

§ 205 Biology and medicine: Drunkenness and blood, tissue, and DNA typing

n. 1.

Replace contents of footnote:

Garriott's Medical-Legal Aspects of Alcohol (Caplan & Goldberger eds., 6th ed. 2014); Taylor & Oberman, Drunk Driving Defense § 6.02 (7th ed. 2010); Valentine & Valentine, Alcohol Testing: Scientific Status, in 5 Faigman, et al., Modern Scientific Evidence: The Law and Science of

Expert Testimony § 39:32 (2015-2016 ed.).

n. 2.

Valentine & Valentine, Alcohol Testing: Scientific Status, in 5 Faigman et al., Modern Scientific Evidence: The Law and Science of Expert Testimony §§ 39:63 to 39:67 (2015-2016 ed.)

Delete footnotes 4-5.

Replace sentence ending in footnote 6 with:

Good scientific practice requires that the probable range of errors that arise even when chemical or other tests are performed properly be quantified and described along with the more familiar "point estimates" of alcohol concentration long encountered in court.[6]

---

[6]On some statistical procedures for doing so, see Gullberg, Estimating the Measurement Uncertainty in Forensic Blood Alcohol Analysis, 36 J. Analytical Toxicology 153 (2012); Vosk et al., The Measurand Problem in Breath Alcohol Testing, 59 J. Forensic Sci. 811 (2014). *But see* Elias-Cruz v. Idaho Dept. of Transp., 153 Idaho 200, 280 P.3d 703 (2012) (due process permits finding blood alcohol concentration just above statutory limit without considering statistical error of measurement); State v. King County Dist. Court West Div., 175 Wash. App. 630, 307 P.3d 765 (Div. 1 2013) (state not required to estimate uncertainty in the point estimate in its case-in-chief).

n. 7.
Replace signal at beginning of footnote with:
State v. Dist. Ct. (Armstrong), 267 P.3d 777, 780, 127 Nev. Adv. Op. No. 84 (Nev. 2011) ("The calculation requires information regarding the rates at which alcohol is absorbed and excreted. Those rates can vary based on a number of factors, including: the amount of time between a person's last drink and the blood test, the amount and type of alcohol consumed, the time period over which alcohol was consumed, and personal characteristics such as age, weight, alcohol tolerance, and food intake.");

n. 8.
People v. Floyd, 2014 IL App (2d) 120507, 381 Ill. Dec. 704, 11 N.E.3d 335, 341-42 (App. Ct. 2d Dist. 2014), appeal denied, 388 Ill. Dec. 5, 23 N.E.3d 1203 (Ill. 2015) ("calculation was premised on the assumption that defendant was in the elimination phase, without consideration of other relevant factors");
Delete Stewart v. State cite and parenthetical.

n. 9.
State v. Downey, 195 P.3d at 1252
Stewart v. State, 129 S.W.3d 93 (Tex. Crim. App. 2004)
Ganert & Bowthorpe, Evaluation of Breath Alcohol Profiles Following a Period of Social Drinking, 33 Canadian Soc'y Forensic Sci. J. 137-43 (2000);

n. 10.
Burns v. State, 298 S.W.3d 697, 702

(Tex. App. San Antonio 2009), petition for discretionary review refused, (Dec. 9, 2009) ("Because the State's witness conceded and admitted he knew none of the [pertinent] factors . . . when only a single test is available, the trial court abused its discretion in admitting the testimony");

n. 12.
2 Giannelli et al., Scientific Evidence § 22.04 (5th ed. 2012)

n. 13.
Add after "E.g.,":
State v. Chun, 194 N.J. 54, 64 & 148, 943 A.2d 114, 120 & 170 (2008), subsequent determination, 215 N.J. 489, 73 A.3d 1241 (2013) ("For decades, this Court has recognized that certain breath testing devices, commonly known as breathalyzers, are scientifically reliable and accurate instruments for determining blood alcohol concentration (BAC)"; likewise, the newer Alcotest 7110 machine "with the safeguards we have required, is sufficiently scientifically reliable");
Delete Faigman cite.
Add at end of footnote:
But see Com. v. Camblin, 471 Mass. 639, 31 N.E.3d 1102 (2015) (hearing on reliability of results from Alcotest 7110 required).

n. 15.
Valentine & Valentine, Alcohol Testing: Scientific Status, in 5 Faigman, et al., Modern Scientific Evidence: The Law and Science of Expert Testimony § 39:43 (2015-2016 ed.)

n. 16.
Valentine & Valentine, Alcohol Testing: Scientific Status, in 5 Faigman, et al., Modern Scientific Evidence: The Law and Science of Expert Testimony § § 39:43 (2015-2016 ed.) ("[R]atio of 2300:1 has been shown to be more accurate in post-absorption subjects," but citing only one 1979 study);
Delete Giannelli & Imwinkelried cite.
Gainsford, et al., A Large-Scale Study of the Relationship Between Blood and Breath Alcohol Concentrations in New Zealand Drinking Drivers, 51 J. Forensic Sci. 173 (2006)

n. 17.
Delete Faigman and Giannelli & Imwinkelried cites.

163

Add new footnote to sentence including footnotes 18-19, after "intoxication," and move footnote 18 to follow "ideal conditions":
Since the links from breath-alcohol concentration to blood-alcohol level to intoxication,[17.50]

[17.50]State v. Chun, 194 N.J. 54, 74, 943 A.2d 114, 126 (2008), subsequent determination, 215 N.J. 489, 73 A.3d 1241 (2013) ("the basic physiological mechanisms on which all breath testing devices rely are not themselves controversial").

n. 19.
Add after Ballou v. Henri Studios parenthetical:
. On the adequacy of case-specific showings of proper use of the machinery, see Volk v. U.S., 57 F. Supp. 2d 888, 897 (N.D. Cal. 1999) (testimony of accuracy sufficient);
People v. Vangelder, 58 Cal. 4th 1, 11, 164 Cal. Rptr. 3d 522, 529, 312 P.3d 1045, 1051, (2013), cert. denied, 134 S. Ct. 2839, 189 L. Ed. 2d 806 (2014) ("defendant remained free to argue, and present evidence, that the particular machines used in this case malfunctioned, or that they were improperly calibrated or employed");
Delete Faigman cite.

n. 20.
Com. v. Colturi, 448 Mass. 809, 818, 864 N.E.2d 498 (2007);
Delete U.s. v. DuBois, State v. Dist. Ct. (Armstrong) and Stewart v. State cites and parenthetical from second paragraph of footnote.

n. 21.
Replace State v. Dist. Ct. (Armstrong) cite annd parenthetical with:
U.S. v. DuBois, 645 F.2d 642 (8th Cir. 1981); People v. Floyd, 2014 IL App (2d) 120507, 381 Ill. Dec. 704, 11

N.E.3d 335 (App. Ct. 2d Dist. 2014), appeal denied, 388 Ill. Dec. 5, 23 N.E.3d 1203 (Ill. 2015); State v. Dist. Ct. (Armstrong), 267 P.3d 777, 127 Nev. Adv. Op. No. 84 (Nev. 2011); Veliz v. State, 474 S.W.3d 354 (Tex. App. Houston 14th Dist. 2015), petition for discretionary review filed, (Aug. 20, 2015); Stewart v. State, 129 S.W.3d 93 (Tex. Crim. App. 2004);

n. 22.
State v. Turbyfill, 776 S.E.2d 249 (N.C. Ct. App. 2015), review denied, 780 S.E.2d 560 (N.C. 2015) (retrograde extrapolation based on average elimination rate admissible under *Daubert*);
Delete State v. Teate cite.
State v. Trujillo, 271 Or. App. 785, 353 P.3d 609 (2015);
State v. Giese, 2014 WI App 92, 356 Wis. 2d 796, 854 N.W.2d 687 (Ct. App. 2014), review denied, 2015 WI 24, 862 N.W.2d 602 (Wis. 2015);
Delete Faigman cite.

n. 24.
Add at beginning of footnote:
E.g., Vuong v. Florida Dept. of Law Enforcement, 149 So. 3d 174 (Fla. 4th DCA 2014) (rules not shown to be invalid).

n. 25.
Add at beginning of footnote:
Compare
Add at end of footnote:
, *with* Vuong v. Florida Dept. of Law Enforcement, 149 So. 3d 174 (Fla. 4th DCA 2014) (using a much less demanding standard for reviewing validity of administrative regulations)

Replace portion of sentence betewen footnote 25 and footnote 26 with:
then, under the first wave of statutes, the results of this testing would trigger two rebuttable presumptions:

Replace sentences following sentence including footnotes 25-27 and ending with footnote 28 with:
An intermediate reading usually was deemed "competent evi-

dence" for consideration along with the other evidence in the case. In most jurisdictions, a party offering test results pursuant to such a statute had to lay a foundation by producing witnesses to explain how the test was conducted, to identify it as duly approved under the statutory scheme, and to vouch for its correct administration in the particular case.[28]

---

[28]Schirado v. North Dakota State Highway Com'r, 382 N.W.2d 391 (N.D. 1986) (conviction reversed for failure to establish compliance with regulations defining fair administration of breath alcohol test); State v. Bobo, 909 S.W.2d 788 (Tenn. 1995) (failure to lay foundation of compliance with statute for breath alcohol test requires exclusion even if the deviation worked to the benefit of the defendant); City of West Allis v. Rainey, 36 Wis. 2d 489, 153 N.W.2d 514 (1967) (expert testimony not required for admissibility and presumptions); 2 Giannelli et al., Scientific Evidence § 22.06 (5th ed. 2012); Necessity and sufficiency of proof that tests of blood alcohol concentration were conducted in conformance with prescribed methods, 96 A.L.R.3d 745. This evidence must show that the instrument was in proper working order and the chemicals were of a kind and mixed in the proper proportions. People v. Freeland, 68 N.Y.2d 699, 506 N.Y.S.2d 306, 497 N.E.2d 673 (1986); People v. Campbell, 73 N.Y.2d 481, 541 N.Y.S.2d 756, 539 N.E.2d 584 (1989) (blood alcohol tests conducted by hospital technician); People v. Mertz, 68 N.Y.2d 136, 506 N.Y.S.2d 290, 497 N.E.2d 657 (1986) (breathalyzer).

n. 29.
2 Giannelli et al., Scientific Evidence § 22.01 (5th ed. 2012)

n. 31.
State v. Chun, 194 N.J. 54, 71-74, 943 A.2d 114, 124-26 (2008), subsequent determination, 215 N.J. 489, 73 A.3d 1241 (2013) (tracing the evolution of New Jersey statutes);

Add in sentence ending in footnote 32, after "these statutes":

create a presumption that BAC is equal to or greater than BrAC,[31.50] simplifying the prosecution's case; others

---

[31.50]Conrad v. State, 54 P.3d 313 (Alaska Ct. App. 2002), opinion adhered to on denial of reh'g, 60 P.3d 701 (Alaska Ct. App. 2002). The statute was later amended to criminalize driving followed by a high test result. Valentine v. State, 215 P.3d 319, 326 (Alaska 2009).

n. 32.
2 Giannelli et al., § 22.01, at 477, & § 22.08[c] (5th ed. 2012)

Replace sentence including footnotes 33-34 with:
Furthermore, to avoid the need to present testimony extrapolating from later to earlier measurements, some statutes create a presumption as to what the BAC or BrAC was at the time of driving,[33] or leave it to a jury to infer that the concentration exceeded the allowed amount,[33.30] at least when the test was administered with "a reasonable time."[33.50] Finally, not content with a permissive inference or presumption, some legislatures even redefined the offense to consist of having a given BAC or BrAC within sev-

eral hours after operating a motor vehicle.[33.70] By and large, these laws have weathered constitutional challenges.[34]

Delete "typical" from beginning of sentence ending with footnote 35.

---

[33]*E.g.*, Coffey v. Shiomoto, 60 Cal. 4th 1198, 185 Cal. Rptr. 3d 538, 345 P.3d 896 (2015); State v. Korhn, 41 Conn. App. 874, 678 A.2d 492 (1996) (presumption equating measured BAC with BAC at the time of operation of motor vehicle did not impermissibly shift burden of proof); State v. Sutliff, 97 Idaho 523, 525, 547 P.2d 1128, 1130 (1976) ("this statute does not require extrapolation back but establishes that the percentage of blood alcohol as shown by chemical analysis relates back to the time of the alleged offense for purposes of applying the statutory presumption"). The law was repealed and replaced in 1984 and further stiffened in 1987. *See* Elias-Cruz v. Idaho Dept. of Transp., 153 Idaho 200, 280 P.3d 703 (2012).

[33.30]State v. Robinett, 141 Idaho 110, 106 P.3d 436 (2005) (expert extrapolation required under impairment theory but not for per se violation, under which time lapse affects only the weight of the measured value); State v. Parker, 317 Or. 225, 232 n.9, 855 P.2d 636, 640 n.6 (1993) (dictum that "[t]he state did not need to call an expert on the dissipation of alcohol [because the] common knowledge that the level of alcohol in the blood and alcohol's effect . . . dissipate over time" would have enabled a jury to infer that a defendant had the requisite BAC while driving given that the BAC five hours later was still .07%).

[33.50]Com. v. Colturi, 448 Mass. 809, 816, 864 N.E.2d 498, 503 (2007) (dictum that a three-hour delay would be reasonable).

[33.70]*See, e.g.*, Valentine v. State, 215 P.3d 319, 326 (Alaska 2009).

[34]*Compare* State v. Baker, 720 A.2d 1139 (Del. 1998) (striking down as vague and overbroad a statute making it a crime to have an "alcohol concentration" of .10 or more "within four hours after the time of driving"),

and Com. v. Barud, 545 Pa. 297, 681 A.2d 162 (1996) (same result as to statute making it a crime to have a BAC above .10 within three hours after operating a motor vehicle), *with* U.S. v. Skinner, 973 F. Supp. 975 (W.D. Wash. 1997) (two-hour rule constitutional); Valentine v. State, 215 P.3d 319, 326 (Alaska 2009) (4-hour rule constitutional for per se violation); State v. Poshka, 210 Ariz. 218, 109 P.3d 113 (Ct. App. Div. 2 2005) (two hours, not unconstitutionally vague); Bohannon v. State, 269 Ga. 130, 497 S.E.2d 552 (1998) (statute making it "a crime to have a blood-alcohol concentration of .10 or greater, as measured within three hours of driving" is not vague or overbroad); State v. Pollman, 41 Kan. App. 2d 20, 204 P.3d 630 (2008) (two-hour rule not overbroad or vague); Sereika v. State, 114 Nev. 142, 955 P.2d 175 (1998) (statute making it a crime to be "found by measurement within 2 hours after driving . . . to have 0.10" BAC is not vague or overbroad); Com. v. Finchio, 592 Pa. 577, 926 A.2d 968 (2007) (within-two-hours per se law does not create an irrebuttable presumption and complies with due process); Com. v. Duda, 592 Pa. 164, 923 A.2d 1138 (2007) (same); *and* State v. Robbins, 138 Wash. 2d 486, 980 P.2d 725 (1999) (two hours, within police power); *cf.* Valentine v. State, 215 P.3d 319 (Alaska 2009) (within-four-hours per se statute satisfies due process, but the addition to a traditional DUI statute of a provision barring scientifically valid "delayed absorption" evidence violates due process).

n. 35.
   Add at end of footnote:
And a test requirement in a criminal case may not preclude admission in a civil action. Henkel v. Heri, 274 N.W.2d 317 (Iowa 1979).

n. 54.
   Delete last sentence in footnote.

n. 56.
Beach v. Beach, 114 F.2d 479, 480–81 (D.C. Cir. 1940)

n. 65.
Ellman & Kaye, 54 NYU L. Rev. at 1132 n.7

Replace "for which the gene codes" in sixth sentence of paragraph after paragraph including footnote 67 and add new footnotes at end of sentence and at end of following sentence:

that the gene encodes.[67.30] However, most of the DNA in human beings (and many other organisms) is noncoding. Indeed, much of it has no known function, and even within functional regions, the variants in many sequences from one person to another are of little or no consequence to health or bodily function.[67.50]

[67.30]For a more complete exposition of the process by which genes express proteins, see Greely & Kaye, A Brief of Genetics, Genomics and Forensic Science Researchers in *Maryland v. King*, 53 Jurimetrics J. 43 (2013).
[67.50]Greely & Kaye, 53 Jurimetrics J. 43.

Replace first sentence in paragraph including footnotes 68-69:
Examining cell surface antigens (such as the ABO and HLA systems) or blood serum enzymes or proteins gives some information about the underlying DNA sequences—if the markers differ, then the DNA must differ.

n. 68.
Greely & Kaye, 53 Jurimetrics J. 43;

Replace sentence ending in footnote 72 with:
However, it has discrete alleles that can be detected with sequencing procedures that determine the order of the base pairs one after the other.[72]

n. 83.
Delete from Thompson & Ford cite through end of footnote.

Replace sentence ending in footnote 89 with:
Such matters are better handled as aspects of the balancing of probative value and prejudice (that also may be addressed at a pretrial hearing) rather than as an inherent part of the special screening test for scientific evidence.

n. 89.
Delete cross-reference at beginning of footnote.
Kaye et al., The New Wigmore on Evidence: Expert Evidence § 6.3.3 (a)(2) (2d ed. 2011).

Replace "new analytical procedures" in sentence including footnotes 99-100 with:

instrumentation

n. 100.
Attorney General of Oklahoma v. Tyson Foods, Inc., 565 F.3d 769 (10th Cir. 2009) (proper to accord "scant weight" to a new test for "poultry-litter-specific DNA fragments");
Nat'l Research Council Comm. on Review of the Sci. Approaches Used During the FBI's Inv. of the 2001 Bacillus Anthracis Mailings, Review of the Scientific Approaches Used During the FBI's Investigation of the 2001 Anthrax Letters (2011);

n. 101.
Replace contents of footnote with:
    Compare U.S. v. Morgan, 53 F. Supp. 3d 732, 95 Fed. R. Evid. Serv. 770 (S.D. N.Y. 2014) (low-template

"DNA test results and analysis at issue in this case are admissible under the standards set forth in *Daubert* and Federal Rule of Evidence 702."); People v. Lopez, 50 Misc. 3d 632, 23 N.Y.S.3d 820 (Sup 2015) (LT-DNA testing and statistical analysis generally accepted) *and* R. v Dlugosz (Kuba), [2013] (CA Crim Div.) EWCA Crim 2, [2013] 1 Cr. App. R. 32, [2013] Crim. L.R. 684 (LT-DNA analysis admissible), *with* People v. Collins, 49 Misc. 3d 595, 15 N.Y.S.3d 564 (Sup 2015) (LT-DNA testing not generally accepted). For further discussion of the developing caselaw, see Kaye et al., The New Wigmore on Evidence: Expert Evidence § 9.5.1 (Cum. Supp. 2016).

Replace sentence ending in footnote 102 with:
So have the procedures that analysts follow in interpreting complex mixed stains,[101.50] including particular software designed to automate or assist in the interpretive process.

[101.50]U.S. v. McCluskey, 954 F. Supp. 2d 1224, 1265 (D.N.M. 2013) ("mixtures are routinely found and analyzed in forensic science; . . . the laboratory had protocols in place to control for flaws and guidelines for interpretation when analyzing mixed samples," but the inferences based solely on experience for mixtures in samples that are in the size range in which the laboratory has found stochastic effects are not admissible); Com. v. DiCicco, 470 Mass. 720, 25 N.E.3d 859 (2015)

(proper to exclude testimony of expert using personal experience and self-professed skill to exclude an individual as a source of DNA based on a single peak well below the laboratory's normal threshold).

n. 102.
State v. Wakefield, 47 Misc. 3d 850, 9 N.Y.S.3d 540 (Sup 2015) (finding an automated system for computing Bayes' factors for profiles in DNA mixtures to be generally accepted);

Add in sentence ending in footnote 103, after "biological":

and statistical

§ 206   Psychology: Lie detection; drugs and hypnosis; eyewitness testimony; profiles and syndromes

Replace first paragraph of section with:

The law and its procedures have long attracted the interest of psychologists and psychiatrists. Their preeminent contributions as expert witnesses have come in presenting clinical diagnoses or evaluations in criminal and other cases.[1] Traditionally, such diagnoses were seen as the contributions of skilled witnesses rather than the products of scientific tests and procedures.

However, less conventional forensic applications received more searching analyses, and modern courts typically apply the special tests for scientific evidence discussed in Section 203 to evidence derived from psychological and psychiatric theories and tests. In this section, we survey issues arising from expert testimony about physiological indicators of deception, "truth" drugs and hypnosis, eyewitness identifications, and "profiles" of certain types of offenders or victims.

---

[1]Barefoot v. Estelle, 463 U.S. 880, 103 S. Ct. 3383, 77 L. Ed. 2d 1090, 13 Fed. R. Evid. Serv. 449 (1983) (psychiatrist's predictions of future violence constitutionally admissible in capital sentencing hearing despite professional skepticism over the ability of mental health experts to make such predictions); 2 Faigman, et al., Modern Scientific Evidence: The Law and Science of Expert Testimony, chs. 8, 10, 11 (2015-2016 ed.) (insanity and diminished capacity; predictions of violence; projective techniques); Appelbaum, Reference Guide on Mental Health Evidence, in Reference Manual on Scientific Evidence 813 (3d ed. 2011).

n. 4.
Honts et al., The Case for Polygraph Tests, in 5 Faigman, et al., Modern Scientific Evidence: The Law and Science of Expert Testimony § 38:22

(2015-2016 ed.); Iacono & Lykken, The Case Against Polygraph Tests, in 5 Faigman, et. al., Modern Scientific Evidence: The Law and Science of Expert Testimony § 38:47 (2015-2016 ed.)

Honts et al., The Case for Polygraph Tests, in 5 Faigman, et. al., Modern Scientific Evidence: The Law and Science of Expert Testimony § 38:21 (2015-2016 ed.)

n. 5.
Honts et al., The Case for Polygraph Tests, in 5 Faigman, et. al., Modern Scientific Evidence: The Law and Science of Expert Testimony §§ 38:23 (2015-2016 ed.); Iacono & Lykken, The Case Against Polygraph Tests, in 5 Modern Scientific Evidence: The Law and Science of Expert Testimony §§ 38:45 to 38:119 (Faigman et al. eds. 2015-2016)

Replace sentence ending in footnote 8 with:
In making this judgment, most practitioners employ some type of numerical scoring system, and this process may be performed by a computer.

n. 8.
Iacono & Lykken, The Case Against Polygraph Tests, in 5 Faigman, et. al., Modern Scientific Evidence: The Law and Science of Expert Testimony § 38:49 (2015-2016 ed.)

n. 9.
Iacono & Lykken, The Case Against Polygraph Tests, in 5 Faigman, et. al., Modern Scientific Evidence: The Law

and Science of Expert Testimony § 38:49 (2015-2016 ed.) ("a 'global' procedure");

n. 12.
Iacono & Lykken, The Case Against Polygraph Tests, in 5 Faigman, et. al., Modern Scientific Evidence: The Law and Science of Expert Testimony § 38:45 (2015-2016 ed.)

In sentence ending in footnote 13, replace 92% with:

95%

n. 13.
Gosciminski v. State, 132 So. 3d 678, 703 (Fla. 2013) ("eighty to ninety percent accuracy"); In re Luke E., 2012 WL 2053540 (Cal. App. 2d Dist. 2012), unpublished/noncitable, (June 7, 2012) and as modified, (July 3, 2012) ("95 to 96 percent accurate"); State v. Underhill, 269 Or. App. 647, 649, 346 P.3d 1214, 1217 (2015), review denied, 357 Or. 743, 361 P.3d 608 (2015) ("97.3 percent accurate");

Replace URL for American Polygraph Ass'n:
https://apoa.memberclicks.net/assets/d ocs/validated techniques faq 1-9-2012.pdf

Replace parenthetical for Moenssens, et al. article:

("a known error percentage of less than one percent . . . based on the examinations of over 100,000 persons suspected or accused of criminal offenses or involved in personnel investigations initiated by their employers")

n. 14.
Honts et al., The Case for Polygraph Tests, in 5 Faigman, et al., Modern Scientific Evidence: The Law and Science of Expert Testimony § 38:26 (2015-2016 ed.)

n. 23.
Honts et al., The Case for Polygraph Tests, in 5 Modern Scientific Evidence: The Law and Science of Expert Testimony § 38:33 (Faigman et al. eds. 2015-2016)

Replace two sentences, the second of which ends with footnote 24 with:

They analyze the frequency spectrum of a speaker's voice to detect subaudible, involuntary tremors said to result from emotional stress (microtremors). The scientific literature on these lie detection devices indicates that they do not actually measure microtremors and have no validity.[24] Another technique, known as layered voice anaylsis, which relies on unspecified vocal characteristics, also performs no better than chance in laboratory tests.[24.50]

---

[24]Comm. to Review the Sci. Evidence on the Polygraph, Nat'l Research Council, The Polygraph and Lie Detection 167–68 (2003); Hollien, The Acoustics of Crime: The New Science of Forensic Phonetics 288 (1990) ("very difficult, if not impossible, to defend the validity of this approach"); Lykken, A Tremor in the Blood: Uses and Abuses of the Lie Detector 173 (2d ed. 1998) ("the voice stress 'lie test' has roughly zero validity"); Saks & Hastie, Social Psychology in Court 202 (1978) ("no scientific evidence to support the claim that they are accurate beyond chance levels"); Vrij, Detecting Lies and Deceit: Pitfalls and Opportunities 338–39 (2d ed. 2008); Hollien et al., Voice Stress Evaluators and Lie Detection, 32 J. Forensic Sci. 405, 415 (1987) ("a device that will permit the detection of lying from the voice analysis alone presently does not exist"); Horvath, Detecting

Deception: The Promise and the Reality of Voice Stress Analysis, 27 J. Forensic Sci. 340 (1982) ("none of these devices has yet been shown to yield detection rates above chance levels in controlled situations"); Fitzpatrick et al., Automatic Detection of Verbal Deception 10 (2015) ("tests . . . have failed to show that VSA devices perform at a level above chance").

[24.50]Fitzpatrick et al., Automatic Detection of Verbal Deception 10 (2015); Horvath et al., The Accuracy of Auditors' and Layered Voice Analysis (LVA) Operators' Judgments of Truth and Deception During Police Questioning, 58 J. Forensic Sci. 385 (2013).

n. 25.
Farah et al., Functional MRI-based Lie Detection: Scientific and Societal Challenges, 15 Nature Rev. Neurosci. 123 (2014);

Delete Simpson and Spence cites.

n. 26.
Meixner & Rosenfeld, A Mock Terrorism Application of the P300-Based Concealed Information Test, 48 Psychophysiology 149 (2010);

n. 27.
Rissman et al., Detecting Individual Memories Through the Neural Decoding of Memory States and Past Experience, 107 Proc. Nat'l Acad. Sci. 9849 (2010);

n. 28.
Farah et al., Functional MRI-based Lie Detection: Scientific and Societal Challenges, 15 Nature Rev. Neurosci. 123 (2014);

Delete Wagner, Adelsheim and Keckler cites.
Law, Cherry-picking Memories: Why Neuroimaging-based Lie Detection Requires a New Framework for the Admissibility of Scientific Evidence under FRE 702 and Daubert, 14 Yale J. L. & Tech. 1 (2011)

Replace Langleben cite with:
Langleben & Moriarty, Using Brain Imaging for Lie Detection: Where Science, Law and Research Policy Collide, 19 Psychol., Public Pol'y & L. 222-34 (2013);

Delete New cite.
Rusconi & Mitchener-Nissen, Prospects of Functional Magnetic Resonance Imaging as Lie Detector, 7 Frontiers Human Neurosci. 594 (2013);

n. 29.
1 Giannelli et al., Scientific Evidence § 8.04 (5th ed. 2012)

n. 34.
Delete remainder of footnote following second sentence.

n. 38.
People v. Muniz, 190 P.3d 774, 785 (Colo. App. 2008), as modified on denial of reh'g, (Apr. 3, 2008)

n. 42.
State v. Alexander, 364 P.3d 458 (Alaska Ct. App. 2015);

n. 44.
Honts et al., The Case for Polygraph

Tests, in 5 Modern Scientific Evidence: The Law and Science of Expert Testimony § 38:39 (Faigman et al. eds. 2015-2016)

n. 46.
Iacono & Lykken, The Case Against Polygraph Tests, in 5 Faigman, et al., Modern Scientific Evidence: The Law and Science of Expert Testimony § 38 (2015-2016 ed.)

n. 47.
1 Giannelli et al., Scientific Evidence § 8.03, at 451 (5th ed. 2012)
Honts et al., The Case for Polygraph Tests, in 5 Faigman, et al., Modern Scientific Evidence: The Law and Science of Expert Testimony § 38:38 (2015-2016 ed.)
; Kaye et al. The New Wigmore, A Treatise on Evidence: Expert Evidence § 6.3.3(d)(4)(iii) (2d ed. 2011)

n. 48.
Add to cases collected concluding that modern polygraphy does not satisfy Daubert:
; Leonard v. State, 385 S.W.3d 570 (Tex. Crim. App. 2012).

Add preceding "Contra":
But see State v. Alexander, 2015 WL 9257270 (Alaska Ct. App. 2015) (not an abuse of discretion to find Daubert standard satisfied).

n. 55.
; Rathe Salvage, Inc. v. R. Brown & Sons, Inc., 191 Vt. 284, 2012 VT 18, 46 A.3d 891, 900, 77 U.C.C. Rep. Serv. 2d 140 (2012)

n. 57.
Honts et al., The Case for Polygraph Tests, in 5 Modern Scientific Evidence: The Law and Science of Expert Testimony § 38:43 (Faigman et al. eds. 2015-2016)

n. 64.
State v. A.O., 198 N.J. 69, 965 A.2d 152 (2009);

n. 69.
1 Giannelli et al., Scientific Evidence § 8.05 (5th ed. 2012)

Start new paragraph after footnote 69.

n. 70.

Add at beginning of footnote:
For a typical assessment of the research, see Greely, Neuroscience, Mindreading, and the Courts: The Example of Pain, 18 J. Health Care L. & Pol'y 171, 192 (2015) ("This kind of method to detect a brain signal of deceptive intent might turn out to work at some point, but much more work needs to be done before it can reliably be used."); *see also* Woodruff, Evidence of Lies and Rules of Evidence: The Admissibility of fMRI-based Expert Opinion of Witness Truthfulness, 16 N.C. J.L. & Tech. 105 (2014) (more comprehensive analysis of legal issues).

Add after footnote 70:
And voice stress analysis, having less scientific support than polygraphy, is almost universally inadmissible.[70.50]

[70.50]Dixon v. Conway, 613 F. Supp. 2d 330, 378-80 (W.D. N.Y. 2009); Barrel of Fun, Inc. v. State Farm Fire & Cas. Co., 739 F.2d 1028, 1030, 1032, 16 Fed. R. Evid. Serv. 187 (5th Cir. 1984); People v. Lippert, 125 Ill. App. 3d 489, 80 Ill. Dec. 824, 466 N.E.2d 276, 47 A.L.R.4th 1183 (5th Dist. 1984); Neises v. Solomon State Bank, 236 Kan. 767, 696 P.2d 372, 377-78 (1985); State v. Davis, 2008 WI 71, 310 Wis. 2d 583, 597, 751 N.W.2d 332, 339 (2008); Admissibility of voice stress evaluation test results or of statements made during test, 47 A.L.R.4th 1202.

Add in sentence ending in footnote 71 after "treatment of", deleting "hysterical" that follows:

pain,

n. 71.
Hilgard & Hilgard, Hypnosis in the Relief of Pain (2013); Kroger, Clinical and Experimental Hypnosis In Medicine, Dentistry, and Psychology (rev. ed. 2008); Spiegel & Spiegel, Trance and Treatment: Clinical Uses of Hypnosis (2d ed. 2008);

Delete Erickson cite.

n. 72.
Laurence & Perry, Hypnosis, Will, and Memory: A Psycho-legal history. (1988);

n. 73.
Kroger, Clinical and Experimental Hypnosis In Medicine, Dentistry, and Psychology 28 (rev. ed. 2008) ("has always been an enigma . . . one of the seven wonders of psychology");

n. 74.
1 Giannelli et al., Scientific Evidence § 12.06 (5th ed. 2012)

n. 76.
1 Giannelli et al., Scientific Evidence § 12.04 (5th ed. 2012)

n. 78.
2 Faigman, et al., Modern Scientific Evidence: The Law and Science of Expert Testimony §§ 19:3 to 18:7 (2015-2016 ed.); 1 Giannelli et al., Scientific Evidence § 12.05 (5th ed. 2012)

n. 99.
Replace contents of footnote:
See generally State v. Henderson, 208 N.J. 208, 27 A.3d 872 (2011) (holding modified by, State v. Chen, 208 N.J. 307, 27 A.3d 930 (2011)) (making recommendations and describing the state of psychological knowledge as described in a hearing ordered by the New Jersey Supreme Court); Expert Testimony on the Psychology of Eyewitness Identification (Cutler, ed. 2009); Cutler & Kovera, Evaluating Eyewitness Identification (2010); Elizabeth Loftus, Eyewitness Testimony (1979); Nat'l Research Council, Comm. on Sci. Approaches to Understanding and Maximizing the Validity and Reliability of Eyewitness Identification in Law Enforcement and the

Courts, Identifying the Culprit: Assessing Eyewitness Identification (2014); Wells, Scientific Status, in 2 Faigman, et al., Modern Scientific Evidence § 15:11 to 15-43 (2015-2016 ed.).

n. 100.
2 Faigman, et al., Modern Scientific Evidence § 15:2 to 15-6 (2015-2016 ed.); 1 Giannelli et al., Scientific Evidence § 9.02[d] (5th ed. 2012)

n. 113.
In parenthetical to second cross-reference, replace "biological" with:
genetic

n. 115.
Perry v. New Hampshire, 132 S. Ct.

716, 728, 181 L. Ed. 2d 694, 711 (2012) (recognizing "the fallibility of eyewitness identifications");

n. 117.
Wells, Scientific Status, 2 Faigman et al., Modern Scientific Evidence § 15:40 (2015-2016 ed.);

n. 118.
Add at the end of footnote:
; Wells, Scientific Status, 2 Faigman et al., Modern Scientific Evidence § 15:40 (2015-2016 ed.) (acknowledging that "[i]t is possible that such testimony makes jurors too skeptical of eyewitnesses").

Replace sentence following footnote 119, adding a new footnote at end:

Nevertheless, it is clear that the researchers have something to offer and that when a case turns on uncorroborated eyewitness recognition, the courts should be receptive to expert testimony about the knowledge, gleaned from methodologically sound experimentation, of the factors that may have produced a faulty identification and that are present in the case at bar.[119.50]

[119.50]Nat'l Research Council, Comm. on Sci. Approaches to Understanding and Maximizing the Validity and Reliability of Eyewitness Identification in Law Enforcement and the Courts, Identifying the Culprit: Assessing Eyewitness Identification 111 (2014) ("Contrary to the suggestion of some courts, the committee recommends that judges have the discretion to allow expert testimony on relevant precepts of eyewitness memory and identifications. Expert witnesses can explain scientific research in detail, capture the nuances of the research, and focus their testimony on the most relevant research. Expert witnesses can convey current information based on the state of the research at the time of a trial. Expert witnesses can also be cross-examined, and limitations of the research can be expressed to the jury.").

n. 120.
; Nat'l Research Council, Committee on Scientific Approaches to Understanding and Maximizing the Validity and Reliability of Eyewitness

Identification in Law Enforcement and the Courts, Identifying the Culprit: Assessing Eyewitness Identification 112 (2014) ("[T]he committee has seen no evidence that the scientific research has reached the point that would properly permit an expert to opine, directly or through an equivalent hypothetical question, on the accuracy of an identification by an eyewitness in a specific case.").

n. 123.
Nat'l Research Council, Committee on Scientific Approaches to Understanding and Maximizing the Validity and Reliability of Eyewitness Identification in Law Enforcement and the Courts, Identifying the Culprit: Assessing Eyewitness Identification 112 (2014) ("The committee recommends the use of clear and concise jury instructions as an alternative means of conveying information regarding the factors that the jury should consider. [T]he instructions should allow judges to focus on factors relevant to the specific case, since not all cases implicate the same factors. . . . Appropri-

ate legal organizations, together with law enforcement, prosecutors, defense counsel, and judges, should convene a body to establish model jury instructions regarding eyewitness identifications.").
Com. v. Gomes, 470 Mass. 352, 354, 22 N.E.3d 897, 900 (2015) (requiring, "where appropriate," "a provisional jury instruction regarding eyewitness identification evidence");

n. 128.
; State v. Copeland, 226 S.W.3d 287 (Tenn. 2007) (overturning rule that expert testimony is always inadmissible)
Commonwealth v. Walker, 625 Pa. 450, 92 A.3d 766 (2014) (overturning rule that expert testimony is always inadmissible);

n. 129.
Turvey, Criminal Profiling: An Introduction to Behavioral Evidence Analysis (4th ed. 2011);

n. 131.
Add at the end of footnote:
Other terms are used to differentiate situations falling within the broad "syndrome." Reid. Battered-Child Syndrome, in Encyclopedia of Victimology and Crime Prevention (Fisher & Lab eds. 2010).

n. 132.
Replace the last sentence of footnote and cite with:
There also is a psychological version of the battered child syndrome analogous to the "battered woman syndrome" discussed later in this section. *See* State v. Smullen, 380 Md. 233, 844 A.2d 429 (2004); 2 Faigman, et al., Modern Scientific Evidence: The Law and Science of Expert Testimony §§ 13:1 et seq. (2015-2016 ed.).

n. 135.
State v. Lee, 191 Ariz. 542, 959 P.2d 799, 69 A.L.R.5th 749 (1998) ("a significant majority of jurisdictions have condemned the use of drug courier profile evidence as substantive proof of guilt");
Giannelli et al., Scientific Evidence § 9.07[c] (5th ed. 2012)

n. 138.
Hamilton, Adventures in Risk: Predict-

ing Violent and Sexual Recidivism in Sentencing Law, 47 Ariz. St. L.J. 1, 14 (2015) ("actuarial risk models fail to meet the high standards of validity and reliability for admissibility in the law as expert evidence")
Delete Monahan cite.
Starr, Evidence-based Sentencing and the Scientific Rationalization of Discrimination, 66 Stan. L. Rev. 803 (2014); Woodworth & Kadane, Expert Testimony Supporting Post-sentence Civil Incarceration of Violent Sexual Offenders, 3 L., Probability & Risk 221 (2004)

n. 139.
Delete Jackson v. State cite.
In re Girard, 296 Kan. 372, 294 P.3d 236 (2013) (*Frye* must be and is satisfied by the tests in question); In re Detention of Thorell, 149 Wash. 2d 724, 756, 72 P.3d 708, 725 (2003) ("the *Frye* standard has been satisfied by both clinical and actuarial determinations of future dangerousness"); In re Detention of McGary, 175 Wash. App. 328, 306 P.3d 1005 (Div. 2 2013) (upholding exclusion of an opinion based in part on a mental test that had not achieved widespread acceptance); 2 Faigman, et al., Modern Scientific Evidence chs. 9 & 10 (2015-2016 ed.); 1 Giannelli et al., Scientific Evidence § 9.10 (5th ed. 2012);

n. 140.
Hanson et al., The Accuracy of Recidivism Risk Assessments for Sexual Offenders: A Meta-analysis of 118 Prediction Studies, 21 Psychol. Assessment 1 (2009);

n. 141.
State v. Guthrie, 2001 SD 61, 627 N.W.2d 401, 419 (S.D. 2001) ("[I]n the present state of psychological knowledge, a suicide profile alone cannot be used to declare with scientific certainty that a person did or did not commit suicide. Berman's opinion in that respect was inadmissible under the *Daubert* standards.");

n. 143.
Delete from "But see" to the end of footnote.

n. 144.
State v. Smullen, 380 Md. 233, 844 A.2d 429, 440-45 (2004) (discussing

this development);
1 Giannelli et al., Scientific Evidence § 9.03[a] (5th ed. 2012)

n. 146.
1 Giannelli et al., Scientific Evidence § 9.03[b] (5th ed. 2012)

n. 148.
2 Faigman, et al., Modern Scientific Evidence: The Law and Science of Expert Testimony §§ 12:1 et seq. (2015-2016 ed.); Russell, Battered Woman Syndrome as a Legal Defense: History,

Effectiveness and Implications (2010);

n. 149.
2 Faigman, et al., Modern Scientific Evidence: The Law and Science of Expert Testimony § 12:17 (2015-2016 ed.)

n. 150.
; Note, The Admissibility of Expert Testimony on Battering and Its Effects After Kumho Tire, 79 Wash. U. L.Q. 367 (2001)

Add after footnote 150:
Yet, criticism of its scientific underpinnings has been intense.[150.50]

[150.50]Angel, The Myth of the Battered Woman Syndrome, 24 Temp. Pol. & Civ. Rts. L. Rev. 301, 302-03 (2015) ("numerous problems"); Faigman & Wright, 39 Ariz. L. Rev. at 109-10 ("remains little more than an unsubstantiated hypothesis"); Mosteller, Syndromes and Politics in Criminal Trials and Evidence Law, 46 Duke L.J. 461, 482 (1996); Schuller & Erentzen, Scientific Status, in 2 Faigman, et al., Modern Scientific Evidence: The Law and Science of Expert Testimony §§ 12:23 to 12:29 (2015-2016 ed.); Note, The Battered Woman Syndrome and Self-Defense: A Legal and Empirical Dissent, 72 Va. L. Rev. 619, 647 (1986) ("the leading research suffers from significant methodological and interpretive flaws"). *But see* Vidmar & Schul-

ler, Juries and Expert Evidence: Social Framework Testimony, 52 Law & Contemp. Probs. 133, 148-55 (1989).

n. 151.
Delete first sentence of footnote.
Smith, Diagnosing Liability: The Legal History of Posttraumatic Stress Disorder, 84 Temp. L. Rev. 1 (2011).

n. 152.
Add after "Compare":
State v. Kinney, 171 Vt. 239, 762 A.2d 833 (2000) (admissible, except for testimony on rate of false reporting), 1 Giannelli et al., Scientific Evidence § 9.04 (5th ed. 2012); 2 Faigman, et al., Modern Scientific Evidence: The Law and Science of Expert Testimony §§ 14:1 et seq. (2015-2016 ed.)

In first bullet of list following footnote 150, replace portion of sentence ending in footnote 154 with:
to prove sexual assault

n. 154.
State v. Chauvin, 846 So. 2d 697, 705 (La. 2003) (holding PTSD inadmissible for this purpose, but noting that "courts are divided");

n. 156.
Commentary on the evidentiary use or scientific foundations of this "syndrome" includes Giannelli et al., Scientific Evidence § 9.05 (5th ed. 2012)
Delete Myers, Evidence in Child, Domestic and Elder Abuse Cases cite.
Delete Roe, Younts and Note cites from footnote

; Admissibility of Expert Testimony on Child Sexual Abuse Accommodation Syndrome (CSAAS) in Criminal Case, 85 A.L.R.5th 595

n. 157.
State v. Dudley, 856 N.W.2d 668 (Iowa 2014) (admissible to prove sexual abuse but direct or indirect vouching for the witness is not);

n. 158.
State v. Salazar-Mercado, 234 Ariz. 590, 595, 325 P.3d 996, 1001 (2014) (admissible to explain delay in reporting and changes in story, but "on a

more complete record, a trial court may exercise its gatekeeping role to conclude that proffered expert testimony does not satisfy Rule 702 or that such testimony should be excluded under Rule 403");
King v. Commonwealth, 472 S.W.3d 523, 529 (Ky. 2015) (inadmissible because "we are unable to find any conscientious effort by any party to establish the validity of the CSAAS theory" in Kentucky);

n. 160.
People v. Williams, 20 N.Y.3d 579, 584, 964 N.Y.S.2d 483, 486, 987 N.E.2d 260, 263 (2013) (hypothetical questions that mirrored the facts "had the prejudicial effect of implying that the expert found the testimony of this particular complainant to be credible");

n. 162.
1 Giannelli et al. § 9.07[a] (4th ed. 2012)

n. 169.
Brewington v. State, 98 So. 3d 628,

630-31 (Fla. 2d DCA 2012) (trial court properly found that the defendant had not "shown that the scientific or psychological community generally accepted battered woman syndrome to negate the mens rea element for a woman charged with failing to protect a child from abuse");
State v. Chauvin, 846 So. 2d 697, 708 (La. 2003) ("Although PTSD is widely accepted among professionals as an anxiety disorder attributable to some type of trauma, it has not been proven to be a reliable indicator that sexual abuse is the trauma underlying the disorder or that sexual abuse has even occurred.");
Schuller & Erentzen, Scientific Status, in 2 Faigman, et al., Modern Scientific Evidence: The Law and Science of Expert Testimony §§ 12:28 & 13:12 (2015-2016 ed.)

n. 175.
State v. Chauvin, 846 So. 2d 697 (La. 2003) (rape trauma);

Add in sentence ending in footnote 178, preceding "clear":

entirely

n. 184.
State v. Dudley, 856 N.W.2d 668, 677 (Iowa 2014) ("an expert witness [may not] testify [that] a child's physical manifestations or symptoms are consistent with sexual abuse trauma or CSAAS");

People v. Williams, 20 N.Y.3d 579, 584, 964 N.Y.S.2d 483, 486, 987 N.E.2d 260, 263 (2013) (CSAAS expert went beyond permissible generalizations by answering hypothetical questions that mirrored the facts of the case);

Replace sentence ending in footnote 185 with:
It also is similar to still-controversial expert testimony on the variables associated with false confessions.[185]

---

[185]Opinions allowing such testimony in the discretion of the trial court include Miller v. State, 770 N.E.2d 763, 770-74 (Ind. 2002) (testimony erroneously excluded); People v. Kowalski, 492 Mich. 106, 821 N.W.2d 14 (2012) ("because the claim of a false confession is beyond the common knowledge of the ordinary person, expert testimony about this phenomenon is [potentially] admissible" but "[a]n expert explaining the situational or psychological factors that might lead to a false confession may not comment on the truthfulness of a defen-

dant's confession, vouch for the veracity of a defendant recanting a confession, or give an opinion as to whether defendant was telling the truth when he made the statements to the police.") (footnotes and internal quotation marks omitted); People v. Bedessie, 19 N.Y.3d 147, 947 N.Y.S.2d 357, 970 N.E.2d 380 (2012) (but exclusion was proper); State v. Perea, 2013 UT 68, 322 P.3d 624 (Utah 2013) (error to exclude expert testimony). Opinions requiring the exclusion of expert testimony on the variables that are thought to increase the risk of false confessions include U.S. v. Benally, 541 F.3d 990, 996 (10th Cir. 2008); State v. Lamonica, 44 So. 3d 895 (La. Ct. App. 1st Cir. 2010), writ denied, 57 So. 3d 331 (La. 2011) (excluding psychologist's testimony as unnecessary given juror's ordinary knowledge and under *Daubert*); Com. v. Robinson, 449 Mass. 1, 864 N.E.2d 1186, 1190 (2007) (abrogated on other grounds by, Com. v. Smith, 471 Mass. 161, 28 N.E.3d 385 (2015)) (excluded as lacking general acceptance and scientific validity) (but see Com. v. Hoose, 467 Mass. 395, 5 N.E.3d 843, 863 (2014) ("[W]e do not foreclose the possibility that under appropriate circumstances this sort of expert testimony could be relevant to a defendant's case and helpful to a jury."); Com. v. Alicia, 625 Pa. 429, 92 A.3d 753, 764 (2014) ("[W]ere the defense permitted to offer Dr. Leo's testimony concerning interrogation techniques that might lead to false confessions, it is highly likely that the Commonwealth would seek to present rebuttal expert testimony that the same techniques elicit true confessions—and elicit true confessions in substantially greater numbers than false confessions. We cannot conclude that expert testimony as to such generalities would help the jury."); State v. Free, 351 N.J. Super. 203, 798 A.2d 83 (App. Div. 2002) (inadmissible without proof of general acceptance); State v. Rafay, 168 Wash. App. 734, 285 P.3d 83 (Div. 1 2012). This developing caselaw is discussed in Kaye et al., The New Wigmore: A Treatise on Evidence: Expert Evidence § 8.9.6 (Cum. Supp. 2016).

n. 186.
Faigman et al., Group to Individual (G2i) Inference in Scientific Expert Testimony, 81 U. Chi. L. Rev. 417 (2014);

n. 189.
1 Giannelli et al., Scientific Evidence § 9.03, at 548 (5th ed. 2012)

§ 207   Criminalistics: Identifying persons and things

n. 1.
Add after Dillon et al. cite:
"It includes areas such as drugs, firearms and toolmarks, fingerprints, blood and body fluids, footwear, and trace evidence." Houck & Siegel, Fundamentals of Forensic Science 4 (3d ed. 2015).

Faigman, et al., Modern Scientific Evidence: The Law and Science of Expert Testimony (2015-2016 ed.) (with chapters by forensic scientists); Giannelli et al., Scientific Evidence (5th ed. 2012) (two volumes)

Add in last sentence of first paragraph, after "hair,":

fibers,

n. 8.
Faigman, et al., Modern Scientific Evidence: The Law and Science of Expert Testimony (2015-2016 ed.); Giannelli & Imwinkelried, Scientific Evidence (5th ed. 2012).
Delete cross-reference at end of footnote.

n. 16.
4 Faigman, et al., Modern Scientific Evidence: The Law and Science of Expert Testimony §§ 32:1 to 32:17 (2015-2016 ed.)

Add in sentence ending in footnote 17, after "courts":

that have been willing to apply, nominally at least, the strict scrutiny normally accorded scientific evidence[16.50]

[16.50]See supra § 203. A few courts in *Frye* jurisdictions have ruled that fingerprint analysis is not the type of evidence that requires general scientific acceptance. Barber v. State, 952 So. 2d 393, 417 (Ala. Crim. App. 2005); In re O.D., 221 Cal. App. 4th 1001, 164 Cal. Rptr. 3d 578 (1st Dist. 2013),

review filed, (Jan. 7, 2014).

n. 22.
Kaye, Beyond Uniqueness: The Birthday Paradox, Source Attribution and Individualization in Forensic Science Testimony, 12 Law, Probability & Risk 3 (2013)

Replace sentence ending in footnote 26 with:

Even though only two or three opinions have disapproved of the traditional description of a match as *necessarily* excluding everyone else in the world as a possible source of the latent print,[26] this claim of global individualization exceeds the bounds of what is scientifically demonstrable and what is recommended in the field.[26.50]

---

[26]U.S. v. Llera Plaza, 179 F. Supp. 2d 492, 57 Fed. R. Evid. Serv. 983 (E.D. Pa. 2002), withdrawn from bound volume and opinion vacated and superseded on reconsideration, 188 F. Supp. 2d 549, 58 Fed. R. Evid. Serv. 1 (E.D. Pa. 2002); U.S. v. Zajac, 2010 WL 3546782 (D. Utah 2010); State v. Rose, No. K06-0545 (Md. Cir. Ct. Oct. 19, 2007).
[26.50]NIST Expert Working Group on Human Factors in Latent Print Analysis, Latent Print Examination and Human Factors: Improving the Practice Through a Systems Approach (Kaye ed. 2012); Page et al., Uniqueness in the Forensic Identification Sciences—Fact or Fiction?, 206 Forensic Sci. Int'l 12 (2011).

n. 28.
Delete NIST Expert Working Group on Human Factors in Latent Print Analysis paper from beginning of

footnote.
Egli et al., Evidence Evaluation in Fingerprint Comparison and Automated Fingerprint Identification Systems: Modeling Between Finger Variability, 235 Forensic Sci. Int'l 86 (2014); Neumann et al. Quantifying the Weight of Fingerprint Evidence Through the Spatial Relationship, Directions and Types of Minutiae Observed on Fingermarks, 248 Forensic Sci. Int'l 154 (2015);

Delete "more or less" in second sentence of footnote.

n. 34.
1 Giannelli et al., Scientific Evidence ch. 10 (5th ed. 2012)
Faigman et al., Modern Scientific Evidence: The Law and Science of Expert Testimony §§ 36:1 to 36:3 (2015-2016 ed.)

III. STATISTICAL STUDIES

§ 208   Surveys and opinion polls

n. 7.
Kaye et al., The New Wigmore, A Treatise on Evidence: Expert Evidence § 12.6 (2d ed. 2011) & § 12.10.3 (Cum. Supp. 2016)

n. 10.
Diamond & Franklyn, Trademark Surveys: An Undulating Path, 92 Tex. L. Rev. 2029 (2014);

n. 13.
; In re NJOY, Inc. Consumer Class Action Litigation, 120 F. Supp. 3d 1050, 98 Fed. R. Evid. Serv. 214 (C.D. Cal. 2015) (economist can rely on existing "economic studies involving tobacco smokers, each of which found that consumers were willing to pay a price premium for purported health and safety improvements").

n. 16.
Medisim Ltd. v. BestMed LLC, 861 F. Supp. 2d 158 (S.D. N.Y. 2012), on reconsideration in part, 2012 WL 1450420 (S.D. N.Y. 2012) (same);

n. 18.
Weisberg, The Total Survey Error

Approach: A Guide to the New Science of Survey Research 22 (2005);

Delete signal and Barnett cite.

Add in next to last sentence of eighth paragraph that begins with "This means that if the same method for drawing samples. . .", preceding "90%":

proportion, close to

Replace last sentence of eighth paragraph that begins with "This many would include" with:
The intervals obtained from these hypothetically repeated samples would vary, but about 90% of them would include the population proportion, whatever that number happens to be.

n. 29.
Replace second sentence up to "Bright" with:
The Bayesian statistical procedure that does produce this probability is presented in a legal context in

n. 31.
E.g., Larry Wasserman, All of

Statistics: A Concise Course in Statistical Inference 92-93 (2004).
Hall v. Florida, 134 S. Ct. 1986, 188 L. Ed. 2d 1007 (2014) (examining implications of the standard error of measurement for IQ scores);

§ 209   Correlations and causes: Statistical evidence of discrimination

n. 2.
Kaye & Freedman, Statistical Proof, in 1 Faigman, et al., Modern Scientific Evidence: The Law and Science of Expert Testimony § 5.9 (2015-2016 ed.)

n. 4.
; Kheifets et al., Pooled Analysis of Recent Studies on Magnetic Fields and Childhood Leukaemia, 103 British J. Cancer 1128 (2010)

n. 5.
Soldo v. Sandoz Pharmaceuticals Corp., 244 F. Supp. 2d 434, 542 (W.D. Pa. 2003) ("[P]laintiff's experts' reliance on anecdotal case reports to support their causation opinions is contrary to both good scientific practice and the *Daubert* case law. Such testimony is not 'scientific knowledge' and will not assist the trier of fact, and the data are not of a type reasonably relied on by experts in the field.");

Delete Dixon v. Ford Motor Co. cite and parenthetical.

n. 7.
Berghuis v. Smith, 559 U.S. 314, 130 S. Ct. 1382, 176 L. Ed. 2d 249 (2010) (petit jury);

n. 9.
Replace first sentence of footnote with:
Initially, courts measured the disparity by the arithmetic difference between the population proportion (as deduced from census data) and the sample proportion (the actual rate of representation of jury venires).

Add after "See":
U.S. v. Hernandez-Estrada, 749 F.3d 1154, 1164-65 (9th Cir. 2014) (en banc) (abandoning "the absolute disparity approach" in favor of "a more robust set of analytical tools" that "largely

depend on the particular circumstances of each case");

*Replace the two sentences following footnote 12 and sentence
ending in footnote 13 with:*

The statistical analyst compares the proportion of the protected
class actually were chosen for jury service to the proportion
expected if each selection were made by the random process
described above. This probability of a disparity as large or larger
than this amount is called a "*p*-value." It states the chance that
so large a disparity would come about purely as a matter of bad
luck or coincidence. The *p*-value thus expresses how improbable
or surprising such extreme outcomes are when null hypothesis is
true. If the *p*-value is very small, it is taken to indicate that the
null hypothesis is implausible.[13]

n. 14.
Delete *Brown v. Nucor Corp., In re
Ephedra Products Liability Litigation
and In re Phenylpropanolamine (PPA)
Products Liaiblity Litigation* cites and
parentheticals.
Smith v. City of Boston, 128 Fair
Empl. Prac. Cas. (BNA) 497, 2015 WL
7194554 (D. Mass. 2015) ("In other
words, if one utilized a two-tailed test
and found that the mean test scores of
minority candidates were located 1.96
standard deviations away from the
overall mean, there would be only a
5% probability that such difference
was due to chance.");

n. 16.
Delete *Killeen* and *Natrella* articles.

n. 17.
; U.S. v. Starks, 99 F. Supp. 3d 227,
231 (D. Mass. 2015)

n. 18.
Delete third through fifth sentences

of footnote, from *Braun* cite to cross-
reference.

n. 19.
Jones v. City of Boston, 752 F.3d 38
(1st Cir. 2014) (recognizing the distinction between statistical and practical
significance, but holding that practical
significance is not required to establish a prima facie case of a racially
disparate impact of an employers practice);
U.S. v. Hernandez-Estrada, 749 F.3d
1154, 1165 (9th Cir. 2014) (en banc)
("[I]f a statistical analysis shows un-
derrepresentation, but the under-
representation does not substantially
affect the representation of the group
in the actual jury pool, then the under-
representation does not have legal significance in the fair cross-section
context.");

Delete footnote 28 at end of sentence including footnote 27-28.

Replace sentence following footnote 28 with:

For example, just as one cannot accept a small *p*-value at face
value when it has been obtained by subdividing the data and
performing many significance tests,[28] given enough latitude in
the number of variables and the form of a statistical model, a
statistician eventually can construct a particular model that will
fit the data remarkably well and have low *p*-values for the quanti-
ties of interest.[28.50] This same model easily can be worthless in the
sense that it probably would not work well with any other data.

[28]Karlo v. Pittsburgh Glass Works, LLC, 97 Fed. R. Evid. Serv. 1484 (W.D. Pa. 2015) ("This sort of sub-grouping 'analysis' is data-snooping, plain and simple.").

[28.50]Yet, models with as many as 128 variables have been relied on, The Evolving Role of Statistical Assessments as Evidence in the Courts (Fienberg ed., 1988), and as many as 73 regression models have been presented in a single case. In re Polyurethane Foam Antitrust Litigation, 2014 WL 6461355 (N.D. Ohio 2014). Another problem is the tendency of some courts to misuse the descriptive statistic R-squared when, as is almost always the case, there are statistics or *p*-values that are much more to the point. *See, e.g.,* Valentino v. U.S. Postal Service, 511 F. Supp. 917, 944 (D.D.C. 1981), judgment aff'd, 674 F.2d 56 (D.C. Cir. 1982) (defendant's model said to give a better estimate of a regression coefficient merely because it "measured many more variables" and yielded a larger R-squared).

n. 32.

Replace "despite" in parenthetical following DeLuca v. Merrell Dow Pharmaceuticals cite with:

using

IV. PROBABILITIES AS EVIDENCE

§ 210 Identification evidence and probabilities *[Retitled]*

Add in sentence including footnotes 4-5, after "philosophers":

, economists,

n. 6.

Add at the end of footnote:
; Posner, An Economic Approach to the Law of Evidence, 51 Stan. L. Rev. 1477, 1508-10 (1999). *See also* Enoch & Fisher, Sense and "Sensitivity": Epistemic and Instrumental Approaches to Statistical Evidence, 67 Stan. L. Rev. 557 (2015) (positing a need for resilient probabilities).

Add new footnote at end of first sentence of paragraph following footnote 6:

Second, it should be clear that any global objection to using group statistics to draw inferences on individual instances is untenable.[6.50]

_____

[6.50]*Cf.* Faigman et al., Group to Individual (G2i) Inference in Scientific Expert Testimony, 81 U. Chi. L. Rev. 417 (2014) (seeking a framework for ascertaining when individual-specific statements should be admissible).

Add after sixth sentence of fifth paragraph:
A defendant claiming intellectual disability may even be sentenced to die if his IQ score lies within a range for measurement error derived from data on other people.[12.50]

_____

[12.50]Hall v. Florida, 134 S. Ct. 1986, 188 L. Ed. 2d 1007 (2014).

n. 17.
; Tribe, 84 Harv. L. Rev. 1329

n. 25.
U.S. v. Hicks, 103 F.3d 837, 846, 46 Fed. R. Evid. Serv. 15 (9th Cir. 1996) (overruled on other grounds by, U.S. v. W.R. Grace, 526 F.3d 499 (9th Cir. 2008))

Delete State v. Washington cite and parenthetical.

n. 26.
State v. Lantz, 21 Neb. App. 679, 842 N.W.2d 216, 226 (2014), review denied, (Mar. 12, 2014) (1 in 12 septillion (1 divided by 12,000,000,000,000,000,000,000,000))

Delete Com. v. Jones cite and parenthetical.

n. 27.
Add parenthetical to State v. Garrison cite.
(bitemark)

n. 30.
Add at end of first paragraph of footnote:
But see Kaye, Ultracrepidarianism in Forensic Science: The Hair Evidence Debacle, 72 Wash. & Lee L. Rev. Online 227 (2015).

n. 39.
Replace "dozens" in second sentence of footnote with:
scores
Replace from "The prosecutor and criminalist. . ." through to the end of the footnote with:
The prosecutor and the criminalist in the trial that was the subject of protracted postconviction hearings in

McDaniel v. Brown, 558 U.S. 120, 130 S. Ct. 665, 175 L. Ed. 2d 582 (2010), also misconstrued the probability that DNA would match by coincidence as the probability of that the match was nothing more than coincidence. Although transposition is not generally correct, when there are only two possibilities—that the trace evidence comes from defendant or that the match is coincidental—and when the probability of the latter event is exceedingly small, the transposition may be approximately correct. See Kaye, "False, But Highly Persuasive": How Wrong Were the Probability Estimates in *McDaniel v. Brown?*, 108 Mich. L. Rev. First Impressions 1 (2009); Meier & Zabell, Benjamin Pierce and the Howland Will, 75 J. Am. Stat. Ass'n 497, 502 (1980).

n. 42.
Add at end of footnote:
A related but less easily implemented approach is described in Ayres & Nalebuff, The Rule of Probabilities: A Practical Approach for Applying Bayes' Rule to the Analysis of DNA Evidence, 67 Stan. L. Rev. 1447 (2015).

n. 48.
European Network of Forensic Science Institutes, ENFSI Guideline for the Formulation of Evaluative Reports in Forensic Science (2015).

§ 211   Paternity testing

n. 10.
Gordon v. Hedrick, 159 Idaho 604, 364 P.3d 951 (2015) (citing Idaho Code § 7-1116(1)) ("A genetic test result with a probability of paternity of at least ninety-eight percent (98%) shall create a rebuttable presumption of paternity."); Kerry S. v. Avelda B., 122 A.D.3d 429, 430, 995 N.Y.S.2d 574, 575 (1st Dep't 2014) ("under Family Court Act § 532, DNA test results which indicate at least a 95% probability of paternity were not only admissible, but create a rebuttable presumption of paternity");
42 U.S.C.A § 666(a)(5)(G)
4 Faigman, et al., Modern Scientific Evidence: The Law and Science of

Delete footnote 20.

Expert Testimony § 31:8 (2015-2016 ed.)

n. 11.
Morris & Gjertson, Scientific Status, in 4 Faigman, et al., Modern Scientific Evidence: The Law and Science of Expert Testimony §§ 31:10 to 31:21 (2015-2016 ed.)

n. 16.
Balding & Steele, Weight-of-evidence for Forensic DNA Profiles 109 (2d ed. 2015) ("there is a shamefully high prevalence of an unjustified assumption that both [the alleged father] and an unrelated "random man" have a prior probability 1/2 of being the father");

Add new footnote to end of first sentence of paragraph following footnote 23:

Nonetheless, to serve up any single number computed in this fashion as "the" probability of paternity connotes more than the mathematical logic can deliver.[23.50]

[23.50]Evett & Weir, Interpreting DNA Evidence: Statistical Genetics for Forensic Scientists 164 (1998) ("We do not advocate the use of the probability of paternity because of the implicit assumption of a prior probability of 0.5, irrespective of the nongenetic evidence.").

n. 26.

Kaye, The Probability of an Ultimate Issue: The Strange Cases of Paternity Testing, 75 Iowa L. Rev. 75, 95 n.96 (1989); Balding, Weight-of-evidence for Forensic DNA Profiles 112 (2005); ; Evett & Weir, Interpreting DNA Evidence: Statistical Genetics for Forensic Scientists 164 (1998).

n. 32.

Snyder v. State, 2015 WY 91, 353 P.3d 693, 695 (Wyo. 2015) (likelihood ratio of 7,343,000,000)